SOCIAL PROBLEMS AND SOCIAL JUSTICE

SOCIAL PROBLEMS AND SOCIAL JUSTICE

NEIL THOMPSON

 macmillan education palgrave

First published 2017 by
PALGRAVE

Palgrave in the UK is an imprint of Macmillan Publishers Limited, registered in England, company number 785998, of 4 Crinan Street, London, N1 9XW.

Palgrave® and Macmillan® are registered trademarks in the United States, the United Kingdom, Europe and other countries.

ISBN 978–1–13–760361–6 paperback

This book is printed on paper suitable for recycling and made from fully managed and sustained forest sources. Logging, pulping and manufacturing processes are expected to conform to the environmental regulations of the country of origin.

A catalogue record for this book is available from the British Library.

A catalog record for this book is available from the Library of Congress.

Printed and bound by CPI Group (UK) Ltd, Croydon, CR0 4YY

For John and Jan

CONTENTS

ACKNOWLEDGEMENTS

Once again I am indebted to a number of people in the development of this book. I am grateful to Peter Hooper and his colleagues at the publishers for their efforts to make the project a reality. I am also grateful to those friends and colleagues who were kind enough to offer helpful comments on the initial draft and endorse its value as a text. Dr John Bates, formerly of Liverpool Hope University, Dr Hefin Gwilym of Bangor University, Professor Bernard Moss of Staffordshire University, Dr Iolo Madoc-Jones and Dr Wulf Livingston of Glyndŵr University, Dr Jan Pascal of Bishop Grosseteste University, John Sawtell, formerly of La Trobe University, Dr Paul Stepney of Tampere University, Finland, Graham Thompson, formerly of Bangor University, plus Jan Cartmell and Nigel Hinks from my online learning community (the Avenue Professional Development Programme). In addition, Dr Sue Thompson has been immensely supportive in so many different ways.

Anna Thompson and Sioned Phillips deserve mention for their practical support and eagerness to help.

Finally, it would be remiss of me not to acknowledge my debt of gratitude to two groups of people. One would be the range of professionals I have worked alongside 'at the coal face' in tackling a wide range of social problems while also seeking to promote social justice. The other would be the large number of people I have worked with in trying to help them overcome, resist and learn from the detrimental consequences of a society that pays more attention to profit than to people I have learned so much from both groups, especially the latter.

ABOUT THE AUTHOR

Dr Neil Thompson is an independent writer and online tutor. He has held full or honorary professorships at four UK universities. He is currently visiting professor at Wrexham Glyndŵr University where he is involved in the MSc Advanced Practice in the Human Services which is based around his published work. He has almost forty years' experience in the people professions as a practitioner, manager, educator and consultant. He has thirty-seven books to his name. These include:

Power and Empowerment (Russell House Publishing, 2007)
The Critically Reflective Practitioner (with Sue Thompson, Palgrave Macmillan, 2008)
Promoting Equality: Working with Diversity and Difference (Palgrave Macmillan, 3rd edn, 2011)
Effective Communication (Palgrave Macmillan, 2nd edn, 2011)
The People Solutions Sourcebook (Palgrave Macmillan, 2nd edn, 2012)
People Management (Palgrave Macmillan, 2013)
People Skills (Palgrave Macmillan, 4th edn, 2015)
The Authentic Leader (Palgrave Macmillan, 2016)

In addition, he has produced a growing number of e-books, including *Stress Matters, Effective Teamwork* and *Effective Writing*. He has been involved in developing a range of other learning resources, training manuals, DVDs, e-learning courses (www.avenuelearningcentre.co.uk) and the innovative online learning community, the Avenue Professional Development Programme, geared towards promoting continuous professional development, based on supported self-directed learning principles (www.apdp.org.uk).

He has qualifications in: social work; management (MBA); training and development; mediation and dispute resolution; as well as a first-class honours degree in social sciences, a doctorate (PhD) and a higher doctorate (DLitt). His PhD and DLitt focused on existentialism. Neil is a Fellow of the Chartered Institute of Personnel and Development, the Royal Society of Arts and the Higher Education Academy and a Life Fellow of the Institute of Welsh Affairs. He was the founding editor of the *British Journal of Occupational Learning* and was also previously the editor of the US-based international journal, *Illness, Crisis & Loss*. He currently edits the free e-zines, **THE** *humansolutions* **BULLETIN** and *Learning* IMPACT (www.neilthompson.info/connect). His personal website and blog are at www.neilthompson.info.

FOREWORD

Two of the most important concepts upon which the helping or people professions are based are those of social problems and social justice. Social work and social care, youth and community work, probation services, and other areas of social helping were established to deal with social problems within a moral framework of social justice. However, the great paradox is that these two important concepts are not well understood and receive only cursory and ambiguous treatment in the literature, in programmes of study, and in the workplace. Lip service may be paid to them, but this overlooks the fact that these two concepts are complex and contested and contain multiple layers of meaning. If you asked most people working within the helping professions if they understood what social problems are, the answer would likely be in the affirmative, but there would almost certainly be disagreement on the origins, causes, dynamics, and remedy for them. Similarly, most people would agree with the idea of social justice and see it as somehow related to a notion of fairness, but have little understanding of the complex nature of this concept and how one carries out a practice where social justice is an integral part and not just an empty slogan attached to practice. Instead of a full understanding of the complexities, contested nature, and multiple layers of meaning, these two concepts seem to be taken-for-granted givens that are just there and that must be dealt with by persons working in the helping professions.

The work of the social services sector is to address, ameliorate, and/ or to eliminate the causes and consequences of social problems, such as homelessness, crime, poverty, child abuse or neglect, unemployment and so on. However, although there is a long and voluminous social science literature on social problems, there is no agreed-upon definition or explanation of what a social problem is or why it occurs. Evidence of the contentious and pluralistic nature of social problems lies in the frequently cited book, *The Study of Social Problems*, by Rubington and Weinberg (2010) where seven competing sociological perspectives on social problems are presented. In spite of the multiplicity of views, there is still a number of questions left unanswered. Is the condition that gave rise to the problem real or imagined? Does it affect a significant number of people or a number of significant people? Who considers the condition undesirable or problematic? What can be done to rectify the problem and who decides? Should a social problem imply the primacy of human agency, or should it focus on values and social structures? Should the magnitude of an event or condition be the criterion for calling it a social problem? There are, of course, no standard answers to these questions or similar questions. Like all social phenomena, social problems are, in whole or in part, social constructs based on subjective, objective, and ideological factors. As such, social problems will have different definitions, interpretations, and proposed remedies.

Unlike the sociological literature, there is a dearth of discussion or explanation of the nature and causes of social problems in the social services literature. The eminent American social policy writer, David Gil (2004) makes the point that many writers in the social services area seem to view social problems as a normal feature of society to be dealt with by social policy measures and/or social services work. He contends that social problems are not normal features of any society, but are consequences of societies characterized by hierarchy, inequality, and oppression. It is an unfortunate paradox that the helping professions, which deal with the victims of social problems on a daily basis, tend to accept social ills as an inherently problematic given. Consequently, they fail to provide a general definition or explanation for social problems. For example, a colleague and I carried out a content analysis study of 14 introductory North American social work textbooks published between 1988 and 1997 (Wachholz and Mullaly, 2000). We chose introductory textbooks, since they are often the first exposure that students will have to social services work, and experience tells us that knowledge or impressions gained in the first instance are often lasting. In those introductory texts, we found no discussion of the concept, nature, or explanation of social problems, although most of the books contained entire chapters on working with people experiencing problems of housing, domestic violence, unemployment, poor health, poverty, racism, and so on. In the absence of any theories or discussions on the nature and causes of social problems, social service workers in general, and beginning social services students in particular, will tend to adopt the prevailing lay or agency-based definitions of social problems, which traditionally have been victim blaming. This is not to say that the social services area is totally devoid of any literature or theoretical work that discusses the nature, causes, and effects of social problems. Explanatory accounts of social problems may be found in the social services literature, but only in an exceptional and inconsistent way. How, then, do students make sense of social problems when there are so many competing perspectives, but so little discussion or analysis or definition of the nature of social problems in the classroom or in the literature? Since so many writers of social services textbooks seem to take societal ills as a given, the only question addressed in the books is how to tackle them. And, since there are so many competing answers to this question, the student or worker is continuously confronted by what Canadian Professor Ben Carniol (2005) calls a 'jumble of confusion'.

Like social problems, social justice is also a complex and contested concept, which has been described in a recent text as the foundation of social work (Morgaine and Capous-Desyllas, 2015). These authors cite an article by Michael Reisch (2002) that presents an overview of the historical trajectory of the meanings and uses of the term social justice. He notes that it dates back to the Old Testament and was the focus of such philosophers as Plato (circa 428–328) who theorized in *The Republic* about socially just arrangements that were necessary for human well-being (although he maintained a belief in the necessity for class distinctions). Secular theories of social justice have their origins during the Enlightenment period between the mid 1600s and mid 1700s. This time period was characterized by the growth of rationalism, scientific reasoning, and calls for the separation of church and state. Marked by the French Revolution and the American Revolution, questions of freedom and equality were at the forefront of this period. Social and political philosophers, such as Thomas Hobbes, John Locke, Jean-Jacques Rousseau, Immanuel Kant, and David Hume, wrote on this topic. It is important to note that, while these white men wrote about the tenets of freedom and justice, such principles of rights and freedom were reserved for white, male property owners and were not accessible to women, people of colour, or persons without property among others (Morgaine and Capous-Desyllas, 2015).

In spite of its long history, agreement on a definition and a shared understanding of the meaning of social justice remain elusive. It seems that almost everyone in the helping professions agrees with the concept of social justice and that professional associations and councils of social work and social care rely on the term in their descriptions of social work as a profession, but there is little agreement on the meaning of the term. This is not surprising, given that Morgaine and Capous-Desyllas (2015) identified six different major definitions and views of social justice. In a study carried out on workers in a variety of areas – mental health, child welfare, domestic violence, ageing, and community organization – it was found that the contributing workers believed that helping should be predicated on the concept of social justice, but many struggled with defining the term and identifying how to actually engage in social justice practice (Morgaine, 2014). A few believed that the term was 'too political', while others saw it as only a macro issue unrelated to micro practice. All this begs the question: if professional associations and councils of education identify the promotion of social justice as a primary role for professionals and there is a requirement or expectation that educational programmes teach students about the promotion of social justice, and the term is conceptually obscure, how can practitioners and educators best embrace this foundational aspect of helping?

In his book *Social Problems and Social Justice* Neil Thompson addresses the above-mentioned issues among many others associated with social problems and social justice. He is well qualified to write a book about these two complex and contested concepts and the relationship between the two. He has been working with social problems and social justice issues for almost forty years within the people professions as a practitioner, manager, educator, and consultant. He is the author of 37 books – tackling a wide range of social problems and promoting social justice. His writings have influenced literally thousands of students and practitioners with respect to learning and practising progressive forms of social services work and dealing with the detrimental consequences of a society that values profit more than people. His cutting-edge scholarship has also influenced many progressive educators and writers of social justice based books and articles – and I include myself among them. *Social Problems and Social Justice* challenges us to look beyond common and simplistic views of social problems and to go beyond paying mere lip service to social justice as our moral practice compass. It is a book that is well overdue and one that will play a significant role in furthering the practical and intellectual work necessary in the struggle to develop emancipatory and just forms of practice. I am pleased and honoured to commend it to you.

Bob Mullaly, PhD
Senior Scholar
Faculty of Social Work
University of Manitoba
Winnipeg, Manitoba
Canada

References

Carniol, B. (2005) *Case Critical: The Dilemma of Social Work in Canada*. 5th edn, Toronto, Between the Lines.

Gil, D. (2004) 'Foreword', in van Wormer, K. (2004) *Confronting Oppression, Restoring Justice: From Policy Analysis to Social Action*. Alexandria, VA. Council on Social Work Education.

Morgaine, K. and Capous-Desyllas, M. (2015) *Anti-Oppressive Social Work Practice*. Thousand Oaks, CA, Sage.

Morgaine, K. (2014) 'Conceptualizing Social Justice in Social Work: Are Social Workers "Too Bogged Down in the Trees?"', *Journal of Social Justice*, 4, 1–18.

Reisch, M. (2002) 'Defining Social Justice in a Socially Unjust World', *Families in Society*, 83(4).

Rubington, E. and Weinberg, S. M. (2010) *The Study of Social Problems*, 7th edn. New York, Oxford University Press.

Wachholz, S. and Mullaly, B. (2000) 'The Politics of the Textbook: A Content Analysis of Feminist, Radical, and Anti-racist Scholarship in American Introductory Social Work Textbooks Published between 1988 and 1997', *Journal of Progressive Human Services* 11(2).

PREFACE

In developing this book my aim was to provide a sound foundation of understanding of a range of complex issues relating to social problems and social justice and the relationship between them. My hope is that this will enable students and practitioners from a range of disciplines to approach the subject matter from a more informed basis.

My specific intentions were:

> To provide a clear introduction to the relationship between social problems and social justice;

> To clarify the value of understanding the relevance of social justice to social problems;

> To analyse a range of social problems from a social justice perspective; and

> To review efforts to address social problems and promote social justice.

This book will be of value primarily to students and practitioners from a range of social science disciplines, whether in the applied professional fields of: social work; social care; youth and community work; probation studies; police studies; and so on; or students in the academic fields of social policy; sociology; social studies; criminology and related areas. It should offer a solid foundation of understanding and encourage further reading and study of these complex, but vitally important issues.

There is a wealth of material available around both social problems and social justice, but what makes this book distinctive is that it systematically relates social problems to social justice, showing clearly how social problems both reflect and perpetuate social injustice, inequality and discrimination.

Here you will not find a comprehensive review of social problems, as that would be far too ambitious a task. More realistically, what you can expect is a discussion of the nature and significance of social problems, a consideration of the two-way relationship between social problems and social justice, an overview of some of what I see as key social problems that currently challenge us in various ways, a review of how social policy initiatives to tackle social problems have fared to date and my own reflections on how social problems can be more effectively addressed in ways that are supportive of social justice.

No easy answers are offered, as such an oversimplification would not do justice to the complexities and major challenges involved. But, if the book does its job effectively, you should have a good basis of understanding to build on and an awareness of why we need to develop our understanding further.

1
Introduction

This book reflects a set of interests that I have had for over forty years. It is rooted in not only extensive study of the phenomena involved, but also vast experience in responding to social problems in a professional capacity (as a practitioner, manager and educator). Throughout all that time I have had a strong interest in, and commitment to, social justice (as is reflected in my publications to date). So, this book provides me with the opportunity to combine my interests in social problems on the one hand, and social justice on the other. However, it is not simply a matter of my personal interests. Both social problems and social justice are areas of major challenge in the contemporary world. They deserve our close and considered attention.

Why social problems?

The vast range of social problems that currently exist bring about immense suffering for a significant number of people, with many lives being ruined by the consequences of one or more of these problems. Although much of the literature on the subject of social problems, with its emphasis on facts and figures, does not reflect or capture the human costs of this suffering and the wasting of human potential, this (often unnecessary) human degradation is clearly in evidence if we know where to look.

In terms of one of the problems covered in this book (destruction of habitat), the human problems are already of significant proportions, but if appropriate robust steps are not taken to address the problem, the longer-terms consequences are likely to be disastrous for everyone on the planet.

All in all, then, the study of social problems is not just a fascinating intellectual inquiry into significant aspects of social life, but also a pragmatic challenge to take steps to do whatever we reasonably can to eliminate social problems where we can or at least reduce their impact as far as possible.

Another important reason for focusing on social problems is the recognition that some efforts to address social problems, historically and

1

> **Practice focus 1.1**
>
> Irene was delighted to get the job when she applied for a post as a support worker in a neighbourhood support project. She approached the job with considerable enthusiasm, but what she found difficult at first was just the sheer range and depth of difficulties faced by the families she was being paid to support. In her first week, she saw terrible poverty, drugs problems, the consequences of crime, poor-quality housing, various conflicts and a strong sense of insecurity. She had expected to meet people facing difficulties and challenges – she knew that was what the job was all about – but she had not anticipated just how many difficulties there were and how deeply ingrained they were. It took quite a while for her to get used to the circumstances she was dealing with on a daily basis.

culturally, have actually made those problems worse; they have had a knock-on effect on other problems or created new ones. There is therefore much to be gained, in both intellectual and pragmatic terms, by studying social problems, their causes and consequences.

Why these social problems?

It would take a very large book indeed even to begin to approach a comprehensive account of social problems, so I have had to be selective. My choice of problems to explore is partly as a result of my own preferences and interests, but also partly because of what I see as the most important, those that I see as worthy of attention. Inevitably, other people will have their own views of what should or should not have been included, but that is not my concern, as I make no claim to be providing a definitive textbook or final word on the subject.

The specific social problems I have selected all inter-relate in some way, some more so than others. In that way, my selection reflects both similarities and differences across the areas covered. This should help to illustrate the common themes I outline below, while also indicating the diversity and range of issues involved.

Why social justice?

It is fair to say that the social problems literature has relatively little to say about social justice and the social justice literature has relatively little to say about social problems. This is a great pity, as the two sets of issues have much in common and influence each other in powerful and significant ways.

Justice is, by definition, about fairness. Social justice is about the social context of fairness and the fairness of the social context. That is, it is not just about individual issues in specific contexts, but, rather, how those individual issues reflect wider patterns of injustice, discrimination and oppression. As Jansen puts it: 'Our emphasis on the qualifier *social* in social justice is intended to signal solidarity with primary struggles for the creation of *social institutions* that promote human equality, dignity and fairness' (2012, p. 8).

We will explore these issues in more detail in Chapter 2, but for now I want to emphasize that social injustices are strongly implicated in social problems. As we shall see, there are various ways in which social problems both reflect and contribute to wider inequalities.

Consequently, a fundamental argument of this book is that, if we are to develop an adequate understanding of social problems (for intellectual and/or pragmatic reasons), we need to have at least a basic understanding of the role of social injustices as a set of key factors that intertwine in various ways with aspects of social problems.

There are important links between the two areas of study and practice, not least that they both involve the extensive suffering, waste of potential and human degradation I mentioned earlier. Of course, in just one book there will not be scope to explore all those connections, but what we do examine should be sufficient to clarify why we need to consider social justice issues in our efforts to tackle and understand social problems and to consider social problems in any efforts to promote equality and social justice.

Voice of experience 1.1

Some people at university moaned a lot about the course, but I felt it prepared me well for my role. One thing the tutors talked about a lot was how social problems are interconnected, but the significance of that didn't really strike me until I was out here in the field. I see it every day, just how so many different social problems link together. It's like a web really. It makes you realize just how daunting a task it can be to help young people from deprived backgrounds when you realise how many challenges they face.

Kim, a youth and community worker

Why now?

Social problems have been with us since time immemorial, as have social injustices. So, why produce this book now? What is new and different about the subject area? Primarily, the key change factor is the growing inequality associated with the dominance of neoliberalism as a political ideology. We shall explore what this means in Chapter 2, but for present purposes I simply want to highlight that the wider sociopolitical sphere is characterized by increasing inequality (Dorling, 2014; Stiglitz, 2016; Wilkinson and Pickett, 2009). This places social problems and social justice in even sharper focus.

A key part of neoliberalism is the belief that market forces should be allowed free reign and that government restrictions and involvement should be kept to a minimum. We shall explore later how this is a deeply flawed political ideology and a dangerous approach to social policy. The pursuit of maximum profit becomes the prime, if not sole, consideration. As Witcher comments:

> No longer is the litmus test for policy what the voters will think of it, but how the markets will respond. Evidence suggests that they [the markets] respond well to privatisation, cuts to welfare benefits and services, the removal of protection for employees / consumers / citizens / the environment, and anything else that enables the rich to get richer.
>
> (2015, p. ix)

The significance of this ideology, and its impact, will be one of seven recurring themes that will run throughout the book.

The seven themes

These seven themes are captured in the acronym of CHOICES. I am presenting them in this way to emphasize the significance of choice – that is, to make the point that the current situation in terms of social problems and social injustices does not have to be the way it is. As Dorling puts it:

> What is certain is that there is no shortage of evidence, ideas and choices for us to consider if we wish to. There are many policies we could adopt if we really want to be collectively happier and healthier. We *could* have a government that makes our lives happier, if we win the argument for it.
>
> (2016, p. xvi)

The current circumstances have arisen largely as a result of choices made, individually and collectively, particularly at a political level. We shall return to this idea in Chapter 13. But first, let us be clear about what the seven themes are and how they can cast light on our areas of interest.

Practice focus 1.2

Mark was the manager of an advice bureau. One day he was involved in interviews for potential new volunteers. He was pleased that the overall calibre was very high and he felt they would strengthen the team nicely. However, there was one applicant they had to turn down. This was because she had a strongly judgemental attitude. She saw the role of an adviser as one of providing guidance on how people could 'better themselves'. What came across strongly was her assumption that people brought their problems on themselves. As another interview panel member put it, she seemed to see herself as some sort of Lady Bountiful committed to rescuing people from their own inadequacies. To her social problems were just a matter of individual failing.

Constructing pathology

A common, but not universal, characteristic of the way social problems are conceived is for people who are on the receiving end of social problems to be portrayed as being responsible for their own difficulties. For example, poverty is often presented as the fault of poor people who are assumed to be lazy and not willing to work hard. It is as if the problem is not a social problem at all, but just the consequences of certain individuals having 'something wrong with them' (hence the idea of 'constructing pathology').

The work of Ryan (1973) discusses this approach and captures it in the phrase 'blaming the victim'. Much of this comes from media (mis) representations, but it is not simply a case of how such matters are presented. There are also structural power issues to consider (see the discussion below of PCS analysis). That is, presenting the problem in individual terms distracts attention from wider sources of problems (inequality, for example).

This ideological tendency to 'blame the victim' by presenting social phenomena as individual failings is known, in technical terms as 'atomism'. This is a philosophical term that refers to the tendency to focus narrowly on individual aspects of situations and neglect wider contextual factors that can often be critical. We shall see at various points how significant atomism is in distorting our understanding of social problems.

Owen Jones, in his study of class prejudice, also highlights the tendency to individualize social issues and, in so doing, to 'pathologize' the people so affected – to hold them responsible for situations that are complex, multilevel and containing many elements beyond their control:

Social problems like poverty and unemployment were once understood as injustices that sprang from flaws within capitalism which, at the very least, had to be addressed. Yet today they have become understood as the consequences of personal behaviour, individual defects and even choice.

(2012, p. 10)

This is an ideological 'sleight of hand' – that is, it is a subtle way that dominant ideas distract attention from wider social and political issues. This leads us nicely into a discussion of hegemony.

Hegemony and universalized interests

Hegemony means dominance, particularly dominance through ideas and beliefs (in the form of ideologies). For example, in a sexist society male dominance is maintained not so much by physical force (although that can be held in reserve), but by the dominance of ideas that justify ('legitimize', to use the technical term) specific roles for men and women respectively – roles that reflect a power imbalance of domination and subordination.

This is a significant sociological concept in relation to social life in general, but it is particularly significant in relation to social problems and social justice. Specifically, one aspect of hegemony is the notion of 'universalized interests'. This refers to the ideological process of presenting the interests of the few as the interests of the many. For example, in his important critique of 'the Establishment', Owen Jones explores various ways in which actions that benefit the power elite are presented as 'in the national interest'. He defines the Establishment in the following terms:

Today's Establishment is made up – as it has always been – of powerful groups that need to protect their position in a democracy in which almost all the adult population has the right to vote. The Establishment represents an attempt on behalf of these groups to 'manage' democracy, to make sure that it does not threaten their own interests. In this respect, it might be seen as a firewall that insulates them from the wider population.

(2015, p. 4)

A key part of this process of 'managing' democracy is the use of 'universalized interests' – convincing the general population that steps being taken are in their interests, when in reality that serve the interests of those who are already in positions of power. For example, tax cuts can be put forward as a means of giving 'hard-working families' more of their own money to spend, but such reductions in tax liability often benefit the rich more than they do 'hard-working families' and, in the process, leave far less money to be invested in public services (and, of course, 'hard-working families' rely much more on public services than do the rich). Such tactics are clearly in evidence in terms of the notion of 'austerity' where governments impose on citizens drastic cutbacks that are said to be in the interests of the 'economy' and thus of everyone. However, as writers like Blyth (2013) and Mendoza (2015) point out, it is highly dubious that such methods benefit the economy and what they actually do is to legitimize a shift of resources away from public services to private interests (from the many to the few). As Mendoza comments: 'Austerity is not a short-term disruption to balance the books. It is the demolition of the welfare state – transferring the UK from social democracy to corporate power' (2015, p. 7).

Hegemony, as dominance through ideas, involves winning the battle for hearts and minds. This reflects the ability of dominant groups (the 'power elite') to convince people that the interests of the elite are actually the interests of everyone ('universalized' interests). As we shall see, this process is a feature of the relationship between social problems and social justice.

Over-reliance on the market

As we noted earlier, current political thinking owes much to 'neoliberalism' and the assumption that the best results will be achieved by allowing free-market mechanisms to operate largely unchecked. The basic premise is that supply and demand mechanisms will automatically find the optimal balance for the economy. Governmental intervention in the economy is therefore seen as a bad thing and should be kept to a minimum. However, Chang (2010) makes the point that the notion of a free market unfettered by state involvement is a myth. Chang points out that there are restrictions on what can be traded (arms, for example), certain products have to be licensed (medicines, for example) and various other ways in which we can see that the market is not as free as its proponents make out. They also generally tend to neglect the huge government subsidies that are invested in private companies – for example, the research underpinning medication development that the pharmaceutical industry subsequently profits from.

What an over-reliance on the market produces is increasing inequality (Atkinson, 2015; Dorling, 2014). If the market is left to its own devices the result will be the old adage that the rich get richer and the poor get poorer. This has significant implications for both social problems and social justice.

> **Voice of experience 1.2**
>
> Too many politicians these days think that politics is just about the economy and the economy is just about the market. I know you have to have a sound economy to pay for public services, but politics is about society, not just the economy. It worries me that so many people can't see past the market as if it is some sort of god to be worshipped.
>
> **Chris, a county councillor**

Interconnectedness

This important term refers to the various ways in which social problems (and the social processes that give rise to them) interact and interrelate. It is not too difficult to see how social problems are connected to one another in various ways. Consider housing problems. These often have their roots in poverty (the poorer someone is, the less access they are likely to have to adequate accommodation). Poor-quality housing or homelessness can lead to problematic drug use problems, partly for psychological reasons of escapism, and partly for sociological reasons associated with networks of illegal drugs availability and, in some low-income neighbourhoods, cultures of drug use. Problematic drug use can lead to crime (for example, as a result of theft and burglary to feed a drug habit). In turn, this can lead to imprisonment (with prisons being largely privatized and thus creating an incentive to criminalize people) and subsequent difficulties in gaining employment due to the reluctance of many employers to recruit ex-convicts. From the unemployment that subsequently arises there is a greater likelihood of poverty and, therefore, a potentially higher risk of housing problems – bringing us full circle.

This theme of interconnectedness can be seen to apply locally, nationally and globally. For example, the underground economy of illegal drug production, distribution and sale is closely connected with organized crime across international boundaries (Hari, 2015).

One of the implications of this theme is that we need to recognize that social problems are not just isolated issues or concerns – they are parts of a broader nexus of social processes, institutions and structures. It is for this reason that it is important to adopt a *holistic* approach, one that encompasses a range of intellectual and professional disciplines so that we can see 'the big picture'.

Counterfinality

This refers to situations in which attempts to solve or alleviate a problem make it worse – that is, those attempts turn out to be counterproductive. This theme is included to acknowledge that efforts to address social problems and promote social justice can inadvertently produce negative outcomes. At times, they can:

> *Make the problem worse*: a child removed from their family because of abuse concerns may be more traumatized by the removal than by any possible abuse in the family home (note the word 'may'; I am not suggesting that they necessarily will be).

> *Introduce new problems*: the prohibition on alcohol in the United States in the 1930s created highly lucrative markets for organized crime. More recently, it has been recognized that imprisoning offenders can create problems for the children of those prisoners who are parents (Clewett and Glover, 2009).

> *Exacerbate other social problems:* slum clearance initiatives in the 1960s had the effect of destroying communities and increasing social tensions.

> *Increase inequalities and discrimination:* the sale of council housing designed to give more people the opportunity to own their own home has produced considerable inequality in terms of access to housing (Dorling, 2015a).

One of the important implications of this is that responses to social problems need to be carefully considered and well thought through. Social policy decisions based purely on political expediency or anticipated electoral gain can often produce significant counterfinalities.

Existential/spiritual implications

Many people automatically associate spirituality with religion, but, of course, religion is only one way of fulfilling spiritual needs or giving expression to our spirituality (Moss, 2005). Spirituality is concerned with questions of: identity formation (Who am I? How do I fit into the world?); meaning construction (Where do I get my sense of purpose and direction?); connectedness (Who are the important people in my life? What are the causes that matter to me?) and values (What are the beliefs and principles that guide me?).

Connectedness is an important concept in relation to social problems. This is because social problems can contribute to communities being divided and thus unsupportive, and a divided, unsupportive community can contribute to social problems – that is, there is a dialectical (mutually reinforcing) relationship between the two. Southerton expresses concern at the decline of a sense of community (one of the 'social evils' to be discussed in Chapter 2):

> People have become primarily focused on themselves, and the communities that once surrounded us and provided a sense of identity, belonging and security are systematically destroyed by this self-obsession. As communities are undermined, interpersonal relationships are rendered shallow and superficial.
>
> (2011, p. 138)

Irrespective of religious adherence, there are important spiritual or existential issues associated with social problems and social justice (not least the role of suffering – see Davies, 2012). For example, we need to consider the implications of both social problems and social injustices in terms of processes of identity formation, meaning making and connectedness and the potential detrimental effects on particular individuals and groups.

Consider, for example, how the oppression arising from discrimination can have such a detrimental effect on our sense of who we are. As Coleman and Ferguson argue:

> Oppression robs people of their identity as surely as exploitation robs people of the fruits of their labor. Oppression imposes rigid, stultifying identities on its victims. Often it imposes a deformed consciousness on the oppressed which helps to reinforce the very system of oppression which deforms them.
>
> (2014, p. 206)

Much of the literature on social problems is of a technical nature and does not really capture any sense of the *human* costs of such phenomena, or the important role of the human spirit in responding to the effects of social problems. Similarly, much of the literature on social justice has little to say on the existential/spiritual issues involved.

One of the features of the existential/spiritual dimension worth emphasizing is the role of anxiety and insecurity. Both social problems and social injustices can be seen to have the effect of increasing anxiety and insecurity and reducing trust. The personal, interpersonal and social consequences of this can be of major proportions at times. And, of course it is a common tactic used by many politicians to prey on people's anxieties and insecurities in order to 'sell' their worldview and their policies.

Practice focus 1.3

Sharon was a highly experienced mental health nurse. When her manager suggested she attend a training course on spirituality in mental health care she was not keen to go, as she was not a religious person and was not aware of religion being a major issue for any of her patients. However, she had not been on a training course for a while and needed to make sure that her continuous professional development record was up to date, so she decided to go after all. And she was glad she did. She was impressed with how the trainer made it clear that religion is only one way of expressing spirituality and that spirituality was a concern for everyone, whether religious or not. She was also quite taken with the idea that so much of the struggle that people with mental health problems have to contend with had its roots in spiritual issues: identity, (in)security, a sense of (not) belonging and so on. She realized that she would see her job in very different terms after this course. And to think that she nearly didn't go!

Social construction

Social construction refers to the ways in which social problems are defined and, to a certain extent, caused, by social processes. They do not exist in any absolute or predefined way; the situation is much more complex than that. We will be exploring the significance of this in much greater detail in Chapter 2, but its importance will be apparent throughout the book.

If there were no such thing as society, there could be no such thing as a social problem. We shall therefore be exploring how sociological factors (the influence of the media, for example) play a central role determining what is counted as a social problem and what responses to any such problems will be developed.

One implication of the social construction of social problems is that definitions of a problem (and thus strategies for addressing such problems) will vary from society to society and across history.

PCS analysis

The book is based on a multidisciplinary approach premised on the recognition that a holistic understanding is needed to avoid fragmentation and distortion. A theoretical framework that can help us achieve such a holistic approach is PCS analysis, as used in my earlier works on

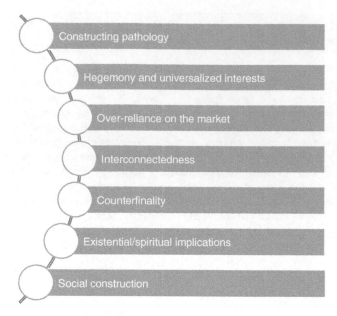

Figure 1.1   The seven themes

discrimination, oppression and inequality (Thompson, 2007, 2011a, 2016a).

PCS analysis is so called because its basic principle is that discrimination operates at three existential levels – **P**ersonal, **C**ultural and **S**tructural – and these three levels interact:

➤ *Personal* This refers to personal beliefs, values, actions and so on. This is sometimes referred to as our 'biography' – that is, the things that matter to us, and, to a certain extent, play a part in defining us, at a personal level.

➤ *Cultural* The personal level is 'embedded' in the cultural level (see Figure 1.2). The cultural level encompasses the unwritten rules, taken-for-granted assumptions and shared meanings that bind people together within what comes to be seen as a shared sense of cultural identity.

➤ *Structural* The cultural level is embedded within the structural level. The structural level relates to the sets of social divisions (class, race/ethnicity, gender and so on) that make up the social structure. With these divisions come structural power relations (some groups being dominant, other groups being subordinate). The structural level influences and shapes the cultural level (for example, it is no coincidence that we have sexist

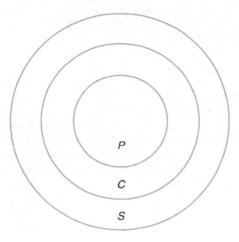

Figure 1.2 PCS analysis
Source: Thompson (2016a)

assumptions at a cultural level that place women in subordinate positions in societies that are patriarchal and male dominated at a structural level).

These levels form a 'double dialectic' – that is, the Personal interacts with the Cultural. An individual's beliefs, emotions and actions are shaped to a large extent by the cultural contexts in which they have been brought up and now live, while those cultures will also be shaped over time by the actions and choices made (individually and collectively) by the persons who subscribe to the cultures concerned. The Cultural level will also interact with the Structural level, in so far as cultural assumptions (the unwritten rules, shared meanings and taken-for-granted understandings that make up a culture) will owe much to the power relations (dominance/subordination) associated with the social divisions that make up the social structure. The cultural level, reflecting the power relations at the structural level, then supports and reinforces that structure (for examples, racist assumptions at a cultural level support and sustain racial divisions at a structural level).

Existentialism

PCS analysis developed from my theoretical development work in drawing out the implications of existentialist thought for professional practice. But, there are other elements of existentialism that are relevant to the present

> **Voice of experience 1.3**
>
> I learned about PCS analysis at university and thought it useful. But I must admit that when I qualified I forgot all about it. I had so much to learn about procedures and computer systems and which forms I needed to fill in that I lost sight of a lot that I had learned from my degree. But one day my manager criticized a court report I had done. She said that I was focusing too narrowly on the child concerned and not looking enough at the broader context of the child's life. It was then that I remembered about PCS analysis. It helped me to look at the bigger picture of the child's circumstances – to look at it holistically, as my tutor used to say.
>
> **Sam, a social worker in a children's services team**

analysis. Existentialism is often referred to as 'phenomenological ontology', referring to the two traditions of thought it encapsulates:

> *Phenomenology* This is the study of perception. It emphasizes that everything we perceive has to be interpreted (that is, the objective world 'out there' has to be interpreted subjectively in order for us to make sense of it. Nietzsche (2003) referred to this as 'perspectivism', reflecting the idea that no one sees the world in purely objective terms – we all see it from our own perspective. One of the implications of this is that meaning is an important factor to consider – meaning, in the sense of the interpretation we have to apply to make sense of the situations we find ourselves in.

> *Ontology* This is the study of being. It relates to such questions as: What does it mean to exist? What is the nature of human reality? A particularly significant concept is 'ontological security' (sometimes referred to as 'existential security'). It does not refer to a specific sense of security – for example, being safe from physical attack – but, rather, to a general sense of security, a feeling of being comfortable with who we are and how we fit into the world. It is therefore a spiritual matter. As we shall see, this is very relevant when it comes to social problems and social justice.

One of the basic tenets of existentialism is the human existence is a process of constant change. This is why the CHOICES themes are important – they spell out choices to emphasize that the current social arrangements do not have to be as they are. They have been socially constructed by a range of sociopolitical processes, and they can be reconstructed in the same way.

Bauman and Donskis (2016) remind us of the ideological assumption that the way things are is how they have to be – what is often referred to as the TINA approach, with TINA spelling out 'There Is No Alternative' – they refer to this as 'market determinism'. One of the key messages of this book is that there are alternatives – no easy answers, but there are definitely alternatives.

The structure of the book

Before clarifying the three-part structure of the book, I want to emphasize that this is not a book of facts and figures or policy details and specific contemporary debates. It serves a broader purpose in offering a critical analysis of some key issues relating to social problems, social justice and the relationship between the two. Anyone wanting up-to-date statistics or data will find that there is no shortage of information available in existing published materials and/or from online sources.

The book is divided into three parts. Part 1 comprises two chapters, the first of which clarifies in more detail the socially constructed nature of social problems. It lays down a foundation of understanding that will help to illuminate discussions in later chapters. The second chapter focuses on social justice and explores why this is an area of study that has very strong connections with social problems.

Part 2 contains nine chapters, each of which covers a specific social problem. Each of these chapters follows the same pattern of considering the causes and consequences of the problem; its relationship with social justice issues and other social problems; and some reflections on efforts to date to address the problem concerned.

Part 3 contains two chapters, the first of which provides an overview of how social policy initiatives to address social problems have fared to date. The final chapter explores future avenues for tackling social problems and promoting social justice. It does this by revisiting the seven themes outlined in this chapter.

Overall, the book presents a solid foundation of understanding that should both facilitate and encourage further study, learning and development around these highly important issues.

Points to ponder

➢ What do you understand by the term 'constructing pathology'?

➤ What is a 'counterfinality' and why is it important to be aware of this danger?

➤ In what sense can it be said that social problems are 'socially constructed'?

Exercise 1

What do you see as the three most important social problems facing us at the moment? What is it that makes them so important?

PART 1

Understanding Social Problems and Social Justice

Introduction to Part 1

In this first of three parts in the book, there are two chapters. These chapters provide a solid foundation of understanding that will be built upon in the remaining two parts of the book. The book covers complex sets of issues, and so it is important, right from the beginning, to be clear about what is involved and the approach that is being adopted.

It is essential to emphasize that the approach is multidisciplinary in two senses. In the first sense, it draws on a number of academic disciplines, and so there will be insights that are drawn from the literature base relating to psychology, sociology, political science, economics and philosophy. But, there is a further sense in which the approach is multidisciplinary, in so far as it draws on a number of professional disciplines: social policy, social work, youth and community work, and so on. Therefore, what is intended in this first part is a broad understanding of the range of issues involved. The part is divided into two chapters. In the first we focus in particular on the significance of social problems and how these are defined or 'constructed' by society and social processes. In the second chapter, our focus switches to social justice and ends with a discussion of how social problems and social justice are interrelated and need to be understood as such.

Part 1 incorporates issues relating to theory, policy and practice. My aim is not to give a definitive approach to any of these areas, but, rather, to illustrate how they are interrelated and to demonstrate how an adequate understanding of the issues involved requires an integrated approach that draws on these three elements.

It is to be hoped that these introductory comments in Part 1 will provide not only a basis of understanding, but also an appetite for learning more about these complex but vitally important issues relating to social problems and social justice and the relationship between the two sets of factors.

2

Making Sense of Social Problems

Introduction

In this chapter we trace some important defining features of the world of social problems. The aim is not to provide a comprehensive analysis, but, rather, to achieve the more modest objective of trying to lay down some foundations of understanding. We begin by considering what is meant by the key term of 'the social construction of social problems'.

It is essential to have a clear understanding of what is involved in social construction before proceeding to Part 2 where we will focus on a range of specific social problems. This chapter is therefore intended to give you a reasonably clear picture of what is involved in social construction and why it is so important in relation to developing a fuller understanding of social problems.

The social construction of social problems

To begin with, it is important to recognize that different societies define different things as a problem. For example, an adult having sex with a 15-year-old is considered sexual abuse of a child in some societies, but perfectly legal and acceptable in others. What a society defines as a social problem can also change over time. For example, it is not so long ago that homosexuality was defined as a mental illness, but we are now beginning to establish homophobia (or 'heterosexism') as a social problem in its own right, thereby turning the tables quite significantly. So, what needs to be understood is that there is no absolute definition of what constitutes a social problem. It is very much down to different societies in different geographical locations and at different historical times to come up with their own understanding and approach to what are seen as social problems.

As Heiner puts it:

> All around us are social phenomena which could possibly be seen as problematic; yet, only a few of these capture the public's attention for a brief period of time and these are replaced by another few in a subsequent period. The problems that capture our attention are not necessarily the worst ones and they are not replaced because they have gotten better. There must, therefore, be forces, other than the seriousness of these problems, that explain their procession through the public imagination.
>
> (2006, p. ix)

Some social problems remain the focus of public attention and concern longer than others, but it is certainly true that definitions of what is or is not a social problem vary from place to place, change over time and are given different levels of consideration and media coverage at different times (see the discussion below of 'moral panics').

To put it in technical terms, there are variations in the construction of social problems diachronically and synchronically. 'Diachronically' means throughout time – that is, over history – and 'synchronically' means at any given point in time. So, it is clear that there are significant variations, both from society to society and within individual societies over time.

Social meanings

Because social problems are socially constructed, we need to recognize that what is defined as a particular problem may well be construed in different ways by different people and at different times, depending on the

---

Practice focus 2.1

Peta was an outreach worker with a multidisciplinary drugs team. She had been involved in this type of work for over twenty years. One day she was asked to have a student spend the day 'shadowing' her. The student had lots of questions and Peta enjoyed answering them. One that really made her think was: 'What has changed in the drugs field during your twenty years?'. Peta could think of lots of things that had changed, but the one that she emphasized was how the public attention paid to drugs problems has varied considerably over that time – ranging from hardly getting mentioned in the media to being a major focus for a while. She put this down to the media being fickle, just chasing the latest sensational story and not having any genuine interest in tackling social problems like drugs.

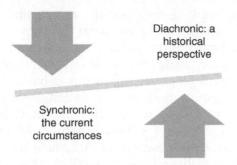

Figure 2.1 Diachronic and synchronic changes

circumstances at that moment – definitions are fluid to a certain extent. This relates to the idea of 'social meanings'. As individuals, we all develop our own understandings, our own sense of what things mean. However, these meanings are not entirely personal or individualistic – they reflect wider social meanings (instilled in us through our upbringing and reinforced through the media and other powerful institutions). To a certain extent they fit with 'cultural templates', established narratives at the **C** level that influence our understandings at the **P** level.

Societies involve cultures, and cultures are, in themselves, frameworks of meaning, preformed (but constantly evolving) patterns used to make sense of the world and our place in it. Those cultures will therefore contain different meanings and different understandings of what constitutes a problem. The technical term for this approach is 'phenomenology'. As we noted in Chapter 1, phenomenology is the study of perception and, as such, it involves acknowledging the central role of perception – especially *social* perception. That is, there are processes by which subjective perceptions are shaped by wider social frameworks of meaning. The term 'phenomenon' is derived from a Greek word that means 'that which is perceived'. So, the significance of this term is that it recognizes once again that there is no absolute sense of what is or is not a social problem. It will depend on how particular issues are perceived at a given time in a given society or cultural context.

However, such perceptions do not occur at random. As Heiner mentioned in the quotation above, there are other forces at work. Public perceptions reflect ingrained patterns of power relations within society. As Illouz puts it: 'meanings differ in their ability to constrain definitions of reality: some meanings are more powerful and binding than others' (2008, p. 9).

Phenomenology reflects the **C** level of PCS analysis, the set of institutionalized meanings that shape reactions at the **P**ersonal level and reflect structural power differences at the **S** level.

Phenomenology, and indeed social construction in general, can be understood as the opposite of what is known as 'essentialism'. Essentialism is the approach to social phenomena that is based on the assumption that the way things are is the way they have to be, that there is a 'fixed essence', with no possibility of things being different from how they are. Essentialist assumptions often manifest themselves in such comments as: 'That's just the way it is'; 'Life's like that'; or, more formally: 'This is the natural order'; or 'It's human nature'. All of these comments are based on the (ideological) assumption that how things are is how they have to be; there is no realistic alternative (TINA, as mentioned in Chapter 1). Essentialism, in distorting in this way the potential for social change, helps to conserve the status quo and thus serves the interests of dominant groups, the power elite.

This is why it is important to understand social problems as socially constructed, because, if societies define and, to a certain extent, create certain problems, then it leaves the door open for opportunities to change, and indeed, solve social problems. If, however, it is assumed that the way things currently are in terms of one or more social problems is the only way things can be, then we are allowing negativity and defeatism to creep in and thereby to create obstacles to making progress.

Moral panics and folk devils

Because of this process of social definition or social construction, what can easily arise is what is known as a 'moral panic' (Cohen, 2011). This is where a particular problem becomes, as it were, 'flavour of the month'. This is often driven by media coverage (a point to which we will return below) in which a particular concern is highlighted, often in a way that gives the problem more attention than it deserves. In this way, certain things can become a moral panic – that is, they become subject to greater focus than is merited. A contemporary example would be problems around terrorism and the threat posed by certain extremist groups. The media attention given to such problems leads to, in many circumstances, an exaggeration of the threat posed. We will discuss this idea further in Chapter 8 when we focus in particular on terrorism as a social problem.

A related term to moral panic is the idea of a 'folk devil'. Just as a moral panic is an exaggeration, fuelled by the media, of a particular social problem, a folk devil is a person, a group or an organization that becomes demonized in the process. That is, they are seen as more of a danger, threat or problem than they actually are. Again, the issue of terrorism is relevant here, in so far as the current practice in many sectors of society is for Muslims to be seen as an evil presence in society, a folk devil, in effect.

This, of course, is a gross distortion of the complex reality of the situation, but it is important to note that, in terms of social problems, these tendencies towards moral panics and folk devils are quite common and can be highly problematic and misleading.

Part of the problem related to moral panics and folk devils is a reliance on stereotypes. An example of a stereotype in terms of social problems would be to equate being homeless with being a rough sleeper. As we shall see in Chapter 6, homelessness is defined by not having a legal right to reside in the place you are currently staying or to not have access to a place to stay at all. But it is this latter element, the idea of not having any place to lay your head that tends to be understood as homelessness. The problem with this type of distortion or stereotypical view is that it underestimates the significance of homelessness as a problem. Of course, to be sleeping rough, we can fully understand, is much worse than to be staying somewhere indoors where you have no right to live, where you are, in a sense, just a guest. But, while homelessness in terms of sleeping on the streets is clearly a dreadful predicament to find yourself in, having no legal right to a home is also a significant problem, with highly detrimental consequences.

Voice of experience 2.1

For the most part I enjoy my job, but it can be very demanding at times. I meet so many people who are trying to get their lives together and need a firm base, a secure home, to do that from. But there just isn't enough housing to go round and some people just don't fit the criteria. It gets me down sometimes to see how much distress is involved and I wish there was more we could do. But at least I do what I can and I just have to hope that the government will pay more attention to homelessness at some point.

Clive, a housing officer

Multiple causation

What can also be helpful in terms of making sense of social problems is the notion of multiple causation. Oversimplified views of social problems tend to put them down to specific individual causes. For example, poverty is often seen as the failure of poor people to work hard enough and make enough effort to earn a living, but, in reality, as we shall see in later chapters, poverty is a complex phenomenon that has its roots in a number of causal factors. Therefore, if we are to develop an adequate understanding of social problems, we need to have an insight into this notion of multiple causation. In Part 2 we will explore a number of specific social problems and this will give us the opportunity to explore in more detail what this notion of multiple causation means and why it is important.

Social distribution

What is also significant in terms of social problems is social distribution. This is a technical term that refers to how certain social goods (that is, things that are deemed to be of value in our society) are not distributed evenly across the population. For example, there are significant discrepancies in terms of the level of wealth between the richest and the poorest in our society (Dorling, 2014; Jones, 2012). There are also huge differences in terms of the distribution of housing. While there are significant numbers of people who are homeless, there are many others who own several homes and may or may not be using those for accommodation purposes (Dorling, 2015a). Linked to this is the recognition that the level of security is uneven in terms of its social distribution. So, while some people have the wherewithal to feel quite secure, both physically and psychologically, there are others who lack those resources, and this can be a significant factor in terms of social problems. For example, some social problems (such as problematic drug use) can be directly linked to issues around security.

> ➤ CHOICES *Spiritual/existential implications* Social problems generate insecurity, a significant obstacle to well-being.

Marris discusses the significance of uncertainty as an existential feature of life:

> Uncertainty is a fundamental condition of human life. We try to master it by discovering the regularities in events which enable us to predict and control them. When they do not turn out as we expected, we look for ways to revise our understanding, our purposes and means of control. When we cannot foretell what will happen, we try to keep our choices of action open; and when none of those choices seems hopeful, we try to withdraw into familiar certainties or fall into despair.
>
> (1996, p. 1)

He goes on to argue that the power to control uncertainty is very unequally distributed across the population. There is a hierarchy in which the greatest burden of uncertainty tends to fall on the poorest, least powerful members of society. Attempts to regain a degree of autonomy and security can then, in some situations, lead to actions that compound the problems. This burden, he contends, robs the most vulnerable people:

> not only of security and a future they can plan for, but of hope and self-esteem. The rest of society then blames them for trying to make sense of their situation in the only terms they can. This is one of the cruellest consequences of unequal protection against uncertainty: it leads its victims to collaborate in the crippling of their life chances.

> (1996, p. 108)

Bauman also links issues of insecurity and uncertainty to the tendency to think in individualistic terms (atomism):

> The present-day uncertainty is a powerful individualizing force. It divides instead of uniting, and since there is no telling who might wake up in what division, the idea of 'common interests' grows ever more nebulous and in the end becomes incomprehensible. Fears, anxieties and grievances are made in such a way as to be suffered alone. They do not add up, do not cumulate into 'common cause', have no 'natural address'.

> (2001, p. 24)

Finally, in terms of distribution, there is the question of well-being, the quality of life that people experience. Once again, we can see that there are significant differences in terms of the distribution of well-being. This is a complex matter, but what is clear is that there are significant discrepancies across the social scale.

Who loses? Who benefits?

A further aspect of social problems worth considering is the recognition that some people actually benefit from social problems, in the sense that they have a vested interest that can be served by a particular social problem. If we take housing as an example, the shortage of housing that can be a major problem for significant numbers of people can provide a high level of income to private landlords in many circumstances (Dorling, 2015a). This is just one example of how inequalities in terms of the distribution of social goods across society can mean that social problems make certain groups of people 'losers' in a sense, while other people become 'winners' as a result of those social problems. One of the implications of this is that efforts to address social problems can often be met by resistance from some quarters, because, while many people who are misfortunate enough to be on the receiving end of social problems would welcome those problems being addressed, there may well be other groups of people whose vested interests mean that they want to resist that problem being solved or alleviated (consider, for example, the profits to be made from privatized prisons).

PCS analysis

In Chapter 1 I referred to my earlier work around discrimination and equality in which I developed a theoretical model that goes by the name of PCS analysis. This is an important theoretical framework for making sense of social problems. This is because one of the dangers associated with our current understandings of social problems is the tendency for there to be a blame culture or scapegoating. This is where individuals are blamed for the problems they experience. I have already given one example of this when I mentioned how poor people can often be blamed for their poverty, as if it is simply a matter that they do not work hard enough. Other examples are not too difficult to find, and so the oversimplified idea that people are responsible for their own problems is quite common. As Sprintzen puts it: 'The autonomous individual is a fiction. Individuality is always partial, embedded, historical, and transactional' (2008, p. 113). In other words, trying to understand the personal level without also considering the wider context of the cultural and structural levels is to fail to do justice to the complexities involved.

> ➤ CHOICES *Constructing pathology* Individuals are often held responsible for social problems. This distracts attention from the wider sociopolitical causal factors.

However, what is also important to recognize is that there may be ways at times in which individuals can make their problems worse through their own behaviour. For example, somebody who has been abused in some way can react to that abuse by developing a drink problem. However, to regard that drink problem as simply a matter of their own individual failing is to ignore the wider context in which problems around abuse and problematic alcohol and drug use need to be understood. PCS analysis is therefore useful to help us understand that, when it comes to social problems, it is likely that all three elements will be represented: personal factors, cultural influences and structural constraints and power relations.

What makes a problem a social problem?

Problems can be defined as situations that we do not wish to remain in, situations that we would like to get out of (Thompson, 2012a), but what is it that makes a social problem distinctively a *social* problem, rather than just an individual problem for the people who are experiencing it? One important factor to take into account here is that a social problem is generally recognized as a problem *for* society, rather than a just a problem *in* society. Therefore, it is not simply a problem for the individuals concerned, but, rather, a problem for wider society in one or more ways (or at least perceived to be so).

This introduces an important distinction in terms of how we are defining society. If we define 'society' as the *people* – the populace, as it were – then social problems can be seen as problems for those people. However, there is another dimension to this. If we understand 'society' to mean the *social order* – that is, the way things are currently arranged in society, then what we should be able to realize is that social problems can be a problem not only for people (for that proportion of the populace so affected), but also a threat to the social order. For example, our economy would break down if there were no limit or restriction on the use of drugs and alcohol. If large proportions of the population were to become addicted to drugs or to develop drink problems, then maintaining our industrial economy would prove extremely difficult. It is therefore important to understand that social problems need to be understood as not just problems for people *in* society but problems *for* society when that term is understood to represent the social order.

A key element of this is the need to recognize once again the vested interests of certain groups, particularly what is known as the 'power elite' – that is, those groups in society who have the most power. Social problems can therefore be understood as receiving more or less attention depending on whether they are more or less of a threat to the power elite and the current social order. Harris captures this point when he explains that:

> To become a "real" social problem, an issue needs to be legitimated by enough people. And it's not just the number of people: some individuals and groups (i.e., those with resources or power) can validate an issue more effectively than others can. Prominent politicians, religious leaders, journalists, or celebrities are among those who can generate concern and legitimacy.
>
> (2013, p. 5)

What this means is that we need to recognize that social problems are not just a matter of scale; it is not simply a matter of quantity (that is, if enough people have a problem, we see it as a social problem). For example, millions of people may have problems finding clothes that fit them

---

Practice focus 2.2

Zaf was a police officer with years of experience in a variety of policing situations. However, one aspect he had not come across was a death by suicide. But all this changed when he was called out to what was initially described as a domestic violence situation. When he arrived at the house he found a scene of considerable confusion and distress. He encountered a situation where a man had seriously assaulted his wife to the point of rendering her unconscious. He had done this in front of their two young children who became very distressed and cried incessantly. He then took himself into the garden shed where he used a kitchen knife to stab himself through the heart. Part of what Zaf needed to do was to arrange for social services to make arrangements for the temporary care of the children. Although he coped well with such a difficult situation he couldn't help thinking about it for weeks afterwards. It made him realize how significant a problem suicide is and how far-reaching its effects were. He kept coming back to the children's distress and wondered what impact the events would have on them in the longer term, given that they had seen their father assault their mother and were now aware he had subsequently killed himself. The ripples from this one incident, he realized, could be immense.

---

well, but the fact that this problem applies to millions of people does not make it a social problem. This is because it is in no way a threat to social institutions or the broader social order. So, to understand what makes a problem a *social* problem, we need to understand the notion of a threat – that it is a threat to some aspect of the existing social order and the vested interests of powerful groups within that social order.

One example of how social problems are more than just personal problems writ large is the significance of suicide. Emile Durkheim, one of the founders of sociology, was clear about the need to recognize suicide as a social problem, rather than just an individual one (Durkheim, 2006). This is because again there is an element of social threat. If too many people were to take their own life, then this would have a knock-on effect, not just for the people who know those individuals concerned, but for the wider social constituency of the social order.

Social policy and the role of government

This consideration of suicide brings us to the question of social policy and the role of the government of the day. When it comes to defining a social problem, as we shall see later, the media have an important part to play but so, too, does the government. Social policy is the process whereby governments and other powerful institutions develop laws and associated policies to address social problems and concerns. Governments therefore play a key part in terms of making a problem a social problem, in so far as the political shade of the governing party (or coalition) will have a significant influence on what is seen as a problem in the first place and how much priority is given to that particular problem.

Different political persuasions, of course, will result in different emphases and different levels of priority given to certain social problems. One of the important aspects of this arises from the work of the sociologist, Robert Merton (1996). He argued that many problems arise in society because of a gap between what society encourages and expects from people and what they are able to attain. For example, in a strongly materialist society there are very powerful expectations that people will have certain goods that they are able to enjoy. However, when social problems, such as poverty, unemployment and homelessness prevent many people from achieving those materialist goals, then the way they live their lives may create additional problems – for example, through crime.

Merton's analysis shows that much crime comes from the mismatch between the strong messages from society through the media that we must have a lot of material goods and the failure of our society and economy to enable all our citizens to be able to achieve that. That mismatch can then lead to crime and anti-social behaviour. In a sense, an emphasis on materialism sets many people up to fail – or to find illegitimate means of obtaining the materials goods they have been taught to aspire to (for example, through crime). There is therefore a link between wider social expectations in terms of the role of government and social policy and the nature of social problems. We will be exploring this issue in later chapters in relation to specific problems.

The political dimension of social problems is one that we need to bear in mind. As Isaacs points out: 'social problems are inherently political in that they are debates about the kind of society that we believe is just' (2015, p. 8). Recognizing this helps to lay the foundations for our discussion of social justice in the next chapter.

One other important aspect of social policy in the role of government is the question of counterfinality. As noted earlier, this refers to situations in which efforts to help to alleviate or solve social problems, for example, produce the opposite of what was intended. In other words, they are counterproductive. There are plenty of examples on record of how attempts to address certain social problems, either make those problems worse or introduce new problems and we shall be exploring particular examples of these in later chapters. For now, however, I simply want to emphasize the significance of this theme of counterfinality which highlights that there is a need for approaches to social problems to be carefully thought through to prevent the net result from being a worsening of the situation.

> ➤ CHOICES *Counterfinality* Efforts to address problems often lead to unanticipated negative consequences.

Other factors

Other significant factors that will influence what is counted as a social problem and what makes it distinctively a social rather than a personal problem, would include:

- ➤ *Political expediency* – politicians will often manipulate certain circumstances to highlight a problem because it suits their particular political goals;
- ➤ *Public opinion* – influenced by the media and, as mentioned earlier, moral panics and folk devils.

There is also the influence of the media more broadly and how the way in which issues are presented to the public in newspapers, television programmes and so on shapes a particular understanding of what counts as a problem. The media will also play a significant role in terms of determining how much of a priority a particular problem is given. For example, there have been many examples of issues around benefit fraud being strongly highlighted in the media and the stereotype of 'scroungers' receiving a great deal of attention. However, corporate fraud and tax evasion receive far less attention and far less public disapproval. What this means, therefore, is that there is an inbuilt bias as a result of how social problems are portrayed through media representations (Jones, 2012, 2015).

One of the consequences of this is that certain issues can be blown out of proportion; certain problems can be seen as involving a much higher level of risk than is actually the case (as in the example of terrorism mentioned earlier). This process of 'risk amplification' can be seen in such examples as the mental health field. The stereotype of the 'mad axe murderer' is a very common one, but it is a gross distortion of reality. If somebody is murdered, the chances are that the perpetrator will be somebody who is in no way defined as having a mental health problem. But, the fact that a very small number of people with mental health problems have become killers is blown out of proportion by media representation (and in some circumstances, political expediency). This then has a significant effect on how social problems are understood.

Voice of experience 2.2

It annoys me that the media feed this ridiculous idea that people with mental health problems are all a threat to our safety. The people who write this stuff blow it out of all proportion. They obviously have no real understanding of mental health problems. Of course, there can be incidents where harm occurs, but the reality is that if you were to be murdered, it is likely to be someone you know who is perfectly sane who does it. And anyway, in my experience, people with mental health problems are more likely to harm themselves than hurt others. All this distortion of the facts just creates more obstacles to recovery for people with mental health problems.

Angie, a community psychiatric nurse

Social decline?

A commonly expressed idea is that society is deteriorating, that moral standards are in decline, and thus, to a certain extent, social problems are seen to be getting worse. However, in 1975 an author by the name of Geoffrey Pearson published an important book in which he argues that social problems are in some respects improving in society. It is commonly assumed (another media distortion) that society is getting worse, that problems are getting worse over time. However, Pearson's interesting and thought-provoking analysis presents a different picture. He shows how, in Victorian times, there were large numbers of murders that were never investigated by the police, let alone resolved, because, at that time, police resources were so thin on the ground that any realistic chance of a conviction was not on the cards. Pearson argued that modern societies are far less tolerant of such crimes and difficulties. Another example of this phenomenon would be child abuse. We are now much more aware of abuse and invest much higher levels of resources into protecting children from abuse than was the case in the past. The idea of social decline is therefore an interesting and important one worthy of careful consideration, although limitations of space do not permit us to do that here.

Who decides and how?

This is a very significant question and the answers are no less significant. The short answer to the question is that it is powerful institutions that decide. This includes the government, as mentioned earlier, through their approach to social policy in terms of what is defined as an area of concern that merits legislation, policy development and the investment of resources through central and local government initiatives, for example. These are all defined through the political process of government. However, it would be a mistake not to recognize that the media also play a central role, because it is through the media that people's perception of what is and what is not a problem is generally portrayed. It is also important to be aware, while we are discussing powerful institutions, that the media not only form a powerful institution in their own right, but are also strongly representative of other powerful institutions, such as large corporations. Jones (2015), in his important text on 'the Establishment' (the power elite), gives examples of various ways in which the media represent the interests of powerful groups and not just of the general population. An example of this would be how profiteering and corruption, while reported in the media to a certain extent, are not generally defined as social problems and not seen as a threat.

Jones also highlights how there are distortions inherent in media coverage. He points out that such bias arises from the fact that the media are largely owned by a small privileged group who support the Establishment that they are part of:

> Rather than providing an honest view of British society, media organizations relish hunting down extreme examples that might be used to tap into widespread prejudices and insecurities – and in doing so, work in tandem with the political consensus. Newspapers routinely echo a mantra parroted by all political parties about social security: that taxpayers are subsidizing the feckless and the bone-idle.
>
> (2015, pp. 89–90)

This means that the media need to be recognized not as a neutral source of information about social problems, but, rather, a set of voices that speak, for the most part, from a privileged position (reflecting the **S** level of PCS analysis – indeed, the media play a key role in terms of the interaction between the **C** and **S** levels).

In considering who can define something as a social problem, we also need to explore the question of what are *not* defined as social problems. For example, corporate abuses (in relation to the environment and pollution, for instance), may be seen as undesirable, but they are generally not given the same status as a social problem. This brings us back to the notion of 'blaming the victim', perceiving social problems as the result of the failings of certain individuals. So, when the failing is of an organization or a corporation, for example, then the same rules tend not to apply.

Claimsmaking

Best (2002) helps us to understand a process he refers to as 'claimsmaking'. This involves identifying an area of concern and then making a claim that it is a social problem and therefore needs a social policy response. Such claims can come via the media in terms of editorial decisions made about what merits coverage, what type of coverage and how extensive. They can also come from activists and pressure groups – groups of people who are politically committed to highlighting and addressing one or more social problems (consider the work of Shelter in relation to housing problems). However, government policy is also a major source of claimsmaking.

This is not a simple matter of developing a policy and producing legislation accordingly. As Best and Harris highlight, policy developments can also trigger other claims:

> In constructing policies, policymakers have to make choices, choices that may, in retrospect, seem less wise than they might have appeared when the policy was first established. This means that policies often inspire new claims – policy outcome claims – about the effectiveness of the policies. Various critics argue that policies are flawed: some warn that policies are insufficient, that they don't do enough to deal with the problem; others insist that policies are excessive, that they go too far and in the process create new problems; while still others claim that policies are misguided, that an entirely different approach is needed. Evaluating how well a policy works, and deciding whether it needs to be modified and what the appropriate changes might be, can inspire heated reactions, and even new claimsmaking campaigns.
>
> (2013, pp. 229–30)

> ➤ CHOICES *Counterfinality* Efforts to address problems can make them worse or create new problems

Social evils and social institutions

In 2008 the Joseph Rowntree Foundation published an important report on what it called 'social evils'. This overlaps significantly with the idea of social problems, but, interestingly, includes things that are not generally incorporated into the idea of a social problem. They emphasize, for example, the way in which our society has become more and more materialistic, resulting in higher levels of inequality.

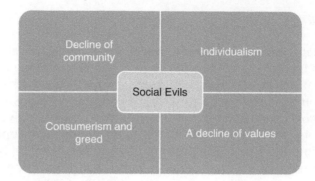

Figure 2.2   The four social evils

These 'social evils' can be seen to underpin various social problems and also contribute to social inequalities. We shall therefore discuss them in more detail in Chapter 3.

What this brings us to question is: whose interests are served by defining something as a social problem? The general tendency, because of this scapegoating and blame culture, is for the problems experienced by relatively powerless people to be defined as a social problem, whereas the problems inflicted on society by more powerful groups do not follow the same pattern. Power is therefore an important part of the process of the attribution of blame and the tendency towards scapegoating. This can be understood as an example of what is known in existentialist philosophy as 'bad faith', the failure to take ownership of our actions. Large, powerful organizations and interest groups, rather than taking ownership for the damage that they do to society and to the environment, are part of the distorted media process of presenting problems in terms of the failings of less powerful individuals and groups.

It is therefore important to recognize, when trying to understand who decides and how, that it is not simply a matter of relativism or 'anything goes', as it were. The power to define a problem is one that is vested in powerful institutions. A key concept here, as we noted earlier, is the idea of a 'claim' (Best, 2002). Who has the power to claim that something is a social problem? So, it is not simply anyone who can do that, but only people who have access to powerful channels of communication and influence. As we have seen, claimsmaking is a privileged process – it is not open to everyone.

One of those powerful institutions is religion. While religion can be seen in many ways as a positive element of social life, we have to recognize too that religion has played, currently and historically, a significant part in defining certain things as a social problem. To return to an example I gave earlier, the idea that homosexuality is a form of mental disorder owes much to its roots in religious beliefs around same-sex relationships (Paris, 2011).

Because of these powerful mechanisms of definition, some problems can become invisible. That is, they receive relatively little attention. For example, DeKeseredy et al. (2003), in an important study of poverty in Canada, argue convincingly that the extent and impact of poverty are largely unrecognized. The assumption portrayed through the media, and reinforced by powerful institutions, is that Canada does not have a problem with poverty, whereas the actual statistics paint a very different picture indeed.

Social causation

So far, we have seen that something becomes 'constructed' as a social problem because certain processes occur to give the entity in question the status of a social problem. However, we can also see that, in some ways, society can *cause* problems above and beyond processes of definition and construction. For example, if we move away from the ideological notion that poor people are poor because they don't work hard enough or try hard enough, we can see that poverty is a by-product of how our economy functions in terms of the distribution of wealth and how social policies relating to employment, taxation, benefits and so on help or hinder people in their efforts to secure a livelihood. In this way, we can understand poverty to be something not just defined by social processes (social construction), but also caused by social processes (social causation). This is an example of the notion of 'multiple causation' discussed in Chapter 1.

Similarly, the psychologist, Oliver James, describes mental health problems in terms of the various social processes that place undue strain on certain individuals:

> Like many before me, I have come to the conclusion that it is grossly inaccurate to depict depression, anxiety, or even schizophrenia and other psychoses, as physical diseases of the body requiring medical treatment. Although it is still possible that in some cases, sometimes, genes may affect our vulnerability to distress, the massive differences that exist between rates in different nations and different groups within nations strongly suggest that genes play a minimal role in the vast majority of cases. Cards on the table, I contend that most emotional distress is best understood as a rational response to sick societies. Change those societies, and we will all be less distressed.
>
> (2007, p. xx)

We shall be exploring this approach to mental health in more detail in Chapter 9. But, for now, it can be seen as a good example of the notion of social causation.

The role of ideology

In this part of the chapter we explore together some key aspects of ideology and how they affect social problems. To begin with, though, we need to be clear about what is meant by this key term of 'ideology'.

An ideology is a set of ideas that come to be established as normal and natural. For example, patriarchal ideology promotes the idea that women are 'natural' caregivers. Such ideologies are very powerful because they influence us without our knowing. They are presented as 'common sense' and are therefore largely taken for granted. They become part of the cultural 'fabric' (at the C level).

One feature of ideology is its role in justifying (or 'legitimizing', to use the technical term) the existing social order and the unequal power relations that are embedded within it. This relates closely to the idea of 'hegemony'. Hegemony means dominance, particularly dominance through ideas, and is therefore closely linked to the notion of ideology. The way this works in terms of social problems is that the interests of the powerful few can easily be portrayed as the interests of everybody. This process, as we noted earlier, is known as 'universalized interests'. So, what suits the powerful elite can be presented as something that is in the interests of the general populace. For example, many people have criticized the role of western powers in the Middle East and the resulting conflicts by arguing that a key factor has been access to oil resources. These oil resources have enabled the richest elements of our society to remain rich, and so there is an interesting argument that wars in the Middle East are only partly for political reasons, but also very much for economic reasons,

---

Practice focus 2.3

Ian was a youth justice worker in a busy team. He had training in handling aggression but had rarely needed to use it. However, one day he was confronted by a very angry and threatening young man who started throwing things round the office. It took three members of staff to restrain him. When he eventually calmed down, Ian tried to find out what had triggered off such a strong reaction. He had spoken to this young man before, but he had been very guarded and gave very little away. However, this time, he spoke freely about himself, his life and the challenges he was facing. Although Ian was very experienced, he was amazed to hear traumatic experience after traumatic experience. It really brought home to him just how grotesque a hand life had dealt this young man. It didn't justify his criminal behaviour, but it certainly went a long way towards explaining it.

with capitalist systems requiring considerable energy resources through oil in order to maintain their levels of profit. The interests of the powerful (profit through oil) are presented as the interests of people in general (national security and the terrorist threat).

Sharvit and Kruglanski help to cast further light on the significance of ideology:

> By ideology, one usually means a belief system centred around some social or collective ideal based on collectively valued causes such as justice or inalienable rights. Ideology's motivating power resides in its identifying a *discrepancy* from an ideal state and offering a means of removing the discrepancy through action. A terrorism-justifying ideology identifies a culprit presumed responsible for the discrepancy and portrays violence against that culprit as an effective and justified means for moving towards an ideal state. In this way, acts of terrorism involving extreme violence appear legitimate rather than deviant (Moghaddam, 2005)
>
> (2013, p. 316)

This illustrates how ideology is a significant factor in how social problems are defined and responded to. Indeed, ideology and power are highly relevant to our understanding of social problems. As Moloney explains: 'Everywhere we looked, every social research study we examined, suggested that major sources of human stress and distress generally involve some form of excessive power [Albee and Joffe, 1977]' (2013, pp. 207–8).

A further aspect of ideology worthy of note is the way certain powerful stakeholder groups, the institutions I mentioned earlier, play their part in determining what is and what is not a problem. This introduces Giddens' notion of the 'double hermeneutic' (Giddens, 1993). Hermeneutics is the study of meaning. What Giddens meant by a double hermeneutic was that the way things are defined and presented to the general public (via the media) can influence everyday thinking and public opinion. Then, in return (and this is what makes it a *double* hermeneutic), public opinion can subsequently influence those stakeholder groups – particularly at times leading up to an election when there are matters of political expediency to consider.

Pathologizing

Hegemony operates through what is known as 'interpellation'. This is a form of 'ideological seduction'. When interpellation takes place, ideas are presented that win us over, that convince us of certain things. For example, if we go back to the notion of the mad axe murderer, what we can see is that the presentation of people with mental health problems as a threat can lead us to adopt unduly negative attitudes towards that group of people. This process is known as pathologizing. We are seduced into seeing the victims of social circumstances as the perpetrators of those circumstances, and so we switch the cause-effect relationship around, or at least oversimplify it considerably. Interpellation is therefore an important issue; it happens largely through the media, whereby certain ideas, certain *dominant* ideas (for example the notion of benefit scroungers) distort the overall picture in terms of how powerful groups may be gaining far more undeserved income through tax evasion than benefit fraud accounts for.

Furedi adopts a similar approach to the dangers of pathologizing. He bemoans the tendency for certain social problems to be presented as emotional problems on the part of the individual: 'the distress that emerges from social conditions can be experienced as a problem of the self. Increasingly, we tend to think of social problems as emotional ones' (2004, p. 24). The ideological tendency to portray problems that have their roots in the wider social order as if they were purely individual difficulties serves to distract attention from the workings of the social processes that maintain the current balance of power and relations of dominance and privilege.

Medicalization

Another important issue to consider in terms of ideology is the tendency for certain social problems to be medicalized, for certain issues to be seen as symptoms of an illness. What happens then is that the pathologizing process begins to operate and certain difficulties come to be seen as a threat to society. They are seen as things that need to be fixed or put right through medical intervention. A classic example of this is the way in which the Soviet Union defined political dissidents as mentally ill, and used this as a justification for incarcerating them as psychiatric patients. That is, of course, an extreme example, but less extreme examples are far more prevalent today. For example, people who are involved in problematic alcohol or drug use are often seen as people who are experiencing an illness, and this then places all the emphasis on the personal level (the P level of PCS analysis), with little or no consideration of the wider cultural and structural factors that can play very significant roles in the development of problems associated with drugs and alcohol.

Moloney describes medicalization as a 'therapeutic outlook':

> The therapeutic outlook allows the more prosperous sections of society to put the yoke of responsibility for social problems (like impoverishment) straight upon the necks of the poor, the prime targets for parenting training, and many

... other interventions ... The implication is that they deserve what they get, because they are supposedly deficient 'in character, in integrity, in impulse control, when in reality what they are lacking is money.'

(2013, p. 137)

Voice of experience 2.3

I see this on a daily basis. People come to us with all sorts of poverty-related problems, huge challenges that most people wouldn't be able to manage. But what the general public hear is a very different story. They hear about scroungers and 'inadequate' people, about some sort of subhuman category of people. They don't know the half of it.

Will, a welfare rights worker

Consumerism

In the last twenty or so years, there has been a shift towards 'consumerism' in social policy. That is, there has been an increasing emphasis on service provision, rather than problem solving and empowerment (Thompson, 2016b). Therefore, in terms of enabling citizens to address their problems and difficulties, we have seen a more commercialized, capitalist approach to this in terms of an increasingly privatized, profit-making set of services. This neoliberal approach is very different from, for example, the traditional emphasis in the personal social services on empowerment, of working with people to help them solve their own problems, or public health approaches to health concerns.

Creating insecurity

Returning to the topic of moral panics and folk devils, an important ideological issue is the way in which the media can generalize irrational fears that can then feed – and feed upon – existential insecurities. That is, the process of media representation of social problems can 'up the ante' in terms of the risks involved (the risk amplification I mentioned earlier), and thereby create unnecessarily high levels of insecurity. As Lister and Lawson comment: 'Insecurity has become pervasive. It permeates the lives not just of the marginalised but also the reasonably well off. Our lives feel beyond our control' (2015, cited in Dorling, 2016, p. 132).

Of course, those high levels of insecurity thereby act as a buffer against any protests or criticisms in relation to the social order, as it is currently maintained in the interests of the power elite. This notion of insecurity and mistrust is one that will arise again in later chapters.

Clearly, then, there are various ways in which ideology plays a role in shaping social problems and public responses to them.

Conclusion

Of course, this chapter has not presented everything that there is to be said about social problems, but it is to be hoped that it has raised some important issues and thereby given you not only a better understanding, but also a desire to find out more. This sets the scene now for our discussion in Chapter 3 of social justice, and so it is to these issues that we now turn.

Points to ponder

➤ What do the terms 'synchronic' and 'diachronic' refer to?

➤ Essentialism involves assuming that things cannot change, that they have to be as they are now. Why is that an important notion to challenge?

➤ In what ways does the notion of ideology shape our perception of social problems?

Exercise 2

Who decides what is a social problem? What enables them to do that? What implications might this have for how problems are addressed?

3

Making Sense of Social Justice

Introduction

Social justice is a 'contested' term. That means that different people interpret, and use it, in different ways. Consequently, before exploring specific social problems and their relationship with social justice issues in Part 2, we need to be clear about how the term is being used for our own present purposes. This chapter has therefore been written to provide some degree of clarity about our understanding of social justice, establish why it is an important topic to study and examine its relationship with the concept of social problems in general and with a range of specific social problems in particular.

Social injustice

To understand social justice it is perhaps helpful to consider what we mean by social *injustice*. This is where the social arrangements in a given society at a particular time in history can be seen as unfair to particular sectors of the population, usually the least powerful groups. As Boswell (2008) reports Samuel Johnson to have said, a decent provision for the poor is the true test of civilisation. Similarly, Gandhi is attributed with the idea that a nation's greatness is measured by how it treats its weakest members.

Three dimensions of social justice

Social justice can be understood as comprising three main elements. The first is inequality. In an earlier work (Thompson, 2011a), I described equality as the absence of unfair discrimination. If someone is being discriminated against, they will suffer a 'detriment' (to use the legal term) – that is, they will lose out in some way: be denied access, be given less, be expected to accept disparaging treatment, and so on, depending on the context. Equality, in this sense, is not the same as 'treating everybody the same'. While equality in its literal sense implies sameness, in the moral, political and professional sense we are using it here, it is more a matter of equal fairness (Witcher, 2015). Where inequality arises, this is not simply about groups being seen as different from one another, but as representing some sort of hierarchy of rights and privileges, with certain groups being at the bottom of the heap and suffering a detriment because of it.

In terms of equality, then, social injustice can be seen to apply when an individual, group or category of people is discriminated against, treated unfairly in one or more ways.

Wilkinson and Pickett (2009) add an extra dimension to our understanding of equality by defining inequality as the gap between the richest and the poorest. The greater that gap is, the more problems there will be, and the more scope there will be for discrimination and injustice (see also Sayer, 2015).

The second area of social justice relates to the range of rights and responsibilities, particularly those that come with citizenship. Where such rights and responsibilities are not respected, we can be said to be in a position of social injustice. Promoting social justice therefore means recognizing people's rights and respecting them, thereby enabling people to carry out their civic responsibilities in a reasonable way. In this sense, therefore, promoting social justice means enabling people to be protected from any steps that in any way undermine or deny their citizenship.

Practice focus 3.1

Maggie was an equality and diversity adviser in a health trust. She was well informed on matters to do with racial, sexual and disability discrimination and had a lot of experience in helping colleagues deal with the issues involved. However, she had never explored issues of age discrimination until she was asked to deal with a grievance registered by an occupational therapist who claimed she had been discriminated against on the grounds of age. Aware that she had little experience in this area, Maggie decided to read up on age discrimination to make sure that she was well equipped to manage the latest case. She was amazed by what she read. She had never appreciated the breadth and depth of ageism and began to wonder why this aspect of inequality had never attracted her attention before. She soon worked out, though, that the fact that this form of discrimination had such a low profile was in itself an example of ageism, with older people being assigned a secondary position in society.

Related to this is the important role of human rights. People who are living in a country where they do not have the status of being a citizen of that country none the less have rights as human beings, citizens of the world, as it were. Social injustice arises when those rights are ignored, undermined or eroded.

The third element of social justice relates to the notion of merit. This relates to issues of how we determine what people are fairly and justly entitled to. It raises questions about what we attribute value to, what we reward and, conversely, what is disparaged or disapproved of. There is therefore a link with both equality and rights. In a society where there is a low level of social justice, people may not be rewarded for their merit – that is, there may be again a strong element of injustice. For example, people who do invaluable work in society may receive far less in terms of pay, status and other rewards as compared with, say, celebrities whose contributions matter far less, but which are far more highly rewarded. Social injustice involves giving certain people a message that they are less worthy than others, that they are of a lower level of merit.

Trust and (in)security

Traditionally, social justice is seen at a macro, broad level of society, but it is important to recognize that the impact of social justice issues also relates to the micro level – for example, in terms of the emotional impact of social injustice. This brings us back to the earlier discussion of the

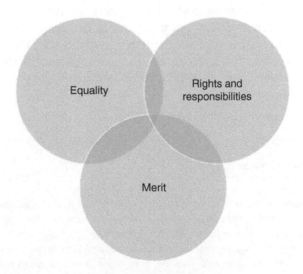

Figure 3.1　The three dimensions of social justice

significance of trust and insecurity. Dorling helps us to understand the significance of this when he argues that:

> Insecurity and mistrust rise as inequality rises. Those with resources have to
> look a longer way down to see where they might end up should anything go
> seriously wrong in their lives. Depression, unemployment and divorce feature
> highly as personal failings to be feared; fears of pandemics and atrocities, world-
> wide recession and large-scale immigration are more widely held fears that can
> be more easily stoked the more unequal the world as a whole becomes.
>
> (2015b, p. 137)

This echoes the point made in Chapter 2 about the insecurity associated
with social problems. Social problems are indeed social in their nature
and, as we have seen, it is a mistake to misconstrue them as just individual
matters. However, we need to acknowledge that there are none the less
individual, psychological consequences of both social problems and social
injustices – not least in terms of a sense of security and trust.

➤ CHOICES *Existential/spiritual implications* As Moloney puts it: 'Inequality is painful'
(2013, p. 108)

Dorling's comments are important because they highlight that everyone faces some degree of existential uncertainty in their lives, but it is not
a level playing field in this regard. The least powerful, most disadvantaged
groups (and, of course, the individuals and families within those groups)
will face greater insecurities and have fewer resources to fall back on if or
when adverse circumstances arise.

Voice of experience 3.1

The people I work with have to rely on public services and all their bureaucracy. I know
people who have similar problems to the ones I come across in the community I work
in, but the difference is they are people who can afford to get their problems sorted elsewhere – they can go to solicitors, accountants, therapists and God knows who else to get
their problems sorted and their needs met. So, they face a lot less stress than the people
on my patch who haven't got such luxuries and the confidence and security they bring.

It is important to be fully aware of trust and a sense of security as part of the measure of social justice. A society cannot be said to be fair and just if it leaves its most vulnerable citizens in a state of insecurity and mistrust. Ballat and Campling relate this to the important concept of well-being:

> Our sense of well-being is very much influenced by how much we are able to put our trust in other people. This is most obvious when we are ill and vulnerable and highly dependent on the care of others.
>
> (2011, p. 38)

Well-being is about quality of life, and so what Ballat and Campling are proposing is that low levels of trust (and, conversely, higher level of insecurity) have an adverse effect on our levels of life satisfaction. They are focusing, in their work, on the significance of this in a health context (that is, how low trust affects health outcomes), but we can also see how the same argument would apply more broadly to social problems. That is, it is not only vulnerability brought about by poor health that can be affected by low trust. A sense of vulnerability associated with such problems as poverty, homelessness, unemployment, abuse and so on can also be of significance when it comes to matters of trust and (in)security.

➤ CHOICES *Existential/spiritual implications* Having a sense of security and trust is an important part of spirituality

Defining social justice

Having discussed social injustices, we should now be in a better position to appreciate what social justice is all about. I mentioned earlier that it is a contested notion – that is, something that is defined in different ways by different people. I am not going to try and come up with some sort of all-encompassing final definition. But what I am going to do is give some sense of what ideas are encompassed within the concept of social justice. Mooney and Scott echo my comments on the variability in how social justice can be understood:

> Certainly social justice is an ambiguous, contested and changeable idea, the focus of many different theorisations, subject to competing claims and used in a myriad of different ways to promote and legitimate government policies, not least social policies (McLaughlin and Baker, 2007; Christie et al, 2008; Craig et al, 2008; Newman and Yeates, 2008; Hattersley and Hickson, 2012).
>
> (2012, p. 1)

This is not to say that 'anything goes' and anyone can interpret social justice as they like, but it does mean that, in approaching the topic we need to be aware that there will often be competing understandings that can complicate matters.

There are, though, some important recurring themes, a certain degree of common ground. For example, Bell offers what I regard as a helpful definition:

> Full and equal participation of all groups in a society that is mutually shaped to meet their needs. Social justice includes a vision of society in which the distribution of resources is equitable and all members are physically and psychologically safe and secure.
>
> (1997, p. 3, cited in Bordere, 2016)

For me this is helpful because it highlights some key elements:

➤ *Participation* Citizens should not be just the passive recipients of decisions made by powerful groups who prioritize their own interests over those of the wider society.

➤ *Meeting of needs* This was a major feature in the development of the welfare state – a recognition that the needs of all citizens must be of concern.

➤ *A vision of society* Contrary to the essentialist idea that 'There Is No Alternative', we have choices, individually and collectively, about the society we are constantly in the process of shaping and reshaping.

➤ *Distribution of resources* Inequality, as we have seen, relates to the gap between the richest and the poorest. If that gap is too great, the unfairness and suffering can be of immense proportions. Wilkinson (2005) notes the tendency for societies with greater levels of inequalities to display more discrimination against certain groups, such as women, ethnic minorities or religious groups.

➤ *Safety and security* We have already noted on more than one occasion the significance of security and trust and how their absence can prove to be a major obstacle to well-being and thriving. Social injustices contribute to social problems. Social problems contribute to low levels of security and trust.

Social justice also needs to be linked to diversity, based on the recognition that: (i) human societies are characterized by differences of various kinds and at various levels; and (ii) such diversity is an asset; it offers an enrichment of our lives through the breadth of perspective it brings. As Sen, in a highly respected study of inequality, puts it: 'Human diversity is no secondary complication (to be ignored, or to be introduced 'later on'); it is a fundamental aspect of our interest in equality' (1992, p. xi). In other words, we need to see equality and diversity as two sides of the same coin.

Sen also points out that equality issues are multidimensional – that is, equality in one area can easily lead to inequality in other areas. For example, respecting diverse cultures as part of a commitment to anti-racism can lead to concerns about gender inequalities and sexist aspects of certain cultures. We should not therefore expect issues of equality and diversity to be straightforward and without elements of conflict and complexity. Again, we are dealing with contested areas.

It should be clear, then, that discussions of social justice run the risk of being misunderstood due to different people's understanding of what the concept means. For present purposes, therefore, I want to reiterate the three elements of social justice that I regard as particularly important, namely equality and diversity; rights and responsibilities and merit. We shall be focusing in particular on equality and diversity – particularly in terms of freedom from unfair discrimination.

Equality, diversity and discrimination

Although I have outlined three different elements of social justice, for the remainder of this book our primary (but not exclusive) focus is going to be on issues of equality and inequality – that is, to do with fairness between groups. This is in large part because these issues underpin to a large extent the other two main dimensions. That is, inequality relates closely to rights and responsibilities on the one hand and merit on the other. Inequality and discrimination will so often undermine rights and contribute to negative evaluations of (self)-worth.

As I indicated earlier, it is important to distinguish between equality in its literal sense of sameness and to understand it as being more closely linked to the idea of equity which is to do with fairness.

Diversity

One of the problems with understanding equality to mean sameness is that there is then a contradiction between equality and diversity, the latter being characterized by difference and variety, of course. That is, if a commitment to equality amounts to working towards treating everybody the same, then difference and diversity become a problem to be solved. Given that the diversity approach is premised on the key idea that the variety of perspectives, insights and understandings that diversity brings is an asset, a resource to be valued and celebrated, then a notion of treating everybody the same becomes highly problematic.

Practice focus 3.2

Carol was a counsellor in private practice. Her training had included important issues to do with 'cultural competence' and the dangers of making discriminatory assumptions. However, she had always been confused by the idea of equality, which she associated with the idea of sameness. She remembered the old adage of 'We believe in equality, we believe in treating everybody the same'. She couldn't see how that squared with diversity and the idea of valuing difference. It seemed to be one big contradiction. However, it all made sense for her when the subject came up in supervision. Her supervisor helped her to understand that it would make more sense if she thought of equality as meaning equal fairness, rather than sameness. That proved to be a significant light bulb moment for her.

However, if we understand equality as equity, and therefore as a matter of fairness, rather than sameness, then equality and diversity can be recognized as highly compatible and mutually supportive concepts. As I mentioned earlier, promoting equality and valuing diversity can then be understood as two sides of the same coin.

The role of discrimination

Where equality is lacking, we will encounter discrimination. Discrimination, in its literal sense, is the ability to identify a difference and that, of course, can have positive aspects as well as negative ones. We would be in great difficulty if we were not able to discriminate between, for example, what is safe and what poses a danger to us. However, in its moral, political and professional sense, discrimination refers to the process of identifying a difference and then using that difference as the basis for treating an individual, group or category of people unfairly. This process results in certain people suffering a detriment because of discriminatory attitudes, practices, processes and assumptions (Thompson, 2016a).

One example of this can be the cultural filters relating to the background of professional practitioners in a variety of work contexts. Where there are professional staff involved in addressing social problems, they will not, of course, be operating in a purely objective way. Inevitably, as phenomenology teaches us, there will be a subjective element to how they perceive the situation, and this can be at times a source of unfair discrimination. It is therefore important that professional practitioners, whatever their background, are able to rise above the situation and be able to see it from other people's points of view, rather than just support an ideological hegemony that involves powerful people imposing their views on less powerful people. This is why, for example, being non-judgemental is a core value of social work and social care, counselling and so on.

Dorling's five tenets of injustice

To develop our understanding of social injustice further, it is worth considering Daniel Dorling's five tenets of injustice. In an important and wide-ranging text (Dorling, 2015b), he offers a helpful analysis of inequality by identifying five taken-for-granted assumptions or 'tenets' that characterize the ideological underpinnings of 'common sense' understandings of inequality. These can be seen as important features of the C level of PCS analysis, dominant cultural assumptions that influence individual thoughts, feelings and actions at the P level, while also reflecting structural power relations at the S level. It is worth exploring each of these in turn:

➤ *Elitism is efficient*

This is based on the misleading notion that allowing certain groups to have privileges above and beyond others enables the economy and the workplace in general to operate more efficiently. In reality, inequalities create significant tensions in a workplace and in broader society and are therefore not a source of efficiency, but, rather, a source of difficulties, conflicts and significant problems (Johnson, 2009; Singh, 2009).

Despite the logical flimsiness of this assumption, it is one that is widely held. This is indicative of how ideology works – hegemony is achieved not through rational argument or the provision of evidence, but, rather, through the 'ideological seduction' of interpellation based on the various subtle ways in which ideas that serve the interests of dominant groups are disseminated.

➤ *Exclusion is necessary*

Implicit in the notion of elitism is the idea that it is acceptable for certain groups in society to be excluded, to be treated less favourably than others (to regard one group as inherently superior to others is, by definition, to regard other groups as inferior by comparison). This then has significant implications in terms of the three elements of social justice being considered here, namely equality; rights and responsibilities; and merit.

However, the ideology underpinning elitism argues that exclusion is not only acceptable, but also necessary. This is an essentialist argument – that is, one based on the idea that the current situation is how it has to be. This is how hegemony operates: certain ideas that could potentially produce a fairer outcome are excluded from consideration because the current arrangements are portrayed as 'necessarily so'.

➤ *Prejudice is natural*

This is another assumption that is highly questionable. It is commonly assumed that prejudice is part of 'human nature' (another example of essentialism). However, in reality the situation is far more complex than this. Discrimination often arises at not just the level of personal prejudice but also at cultural and structural levels (see the earlier discussion of PCS analysis). Prejudice is neither natural nor necessary; it is, however, a common feature of cultural assumptions at the C level.

Part of the C level is a set of stereotypes that are powerful and pervasive (but distorted) representations of reality. It is often through such stereotypical assumptions that prejudice manifests itself. Prejudice is therefore something that needs to be understood by reference to culture rather than 'nature'.

➤ *Greed is good*

The idea behind this is that it is understandable that people should want as much for themselves as possible. But, more than this, it is also assumed that this is a good thing, that greed will feed the economy, will fuel progress and development because people will be motivated to achieve as much as possible for their own personal gain. Once again, this is a gross distortion of a complex phenomenon, a gross oversimplification of something that needs to be understood in a more nuanced way. 'Greed is good' is an idea that again reflects hegemony. It is an idea that is presented as if people as a whole will benefit, rather than just those who are privileged enough to benefit from an economy and a society based on greed (rather than based on fair reward for fair contribution – taking us back to the notion of merit).

Greed is good is a feature of neoliberalism, with its emphasis on the role of the market and the scaling down of the role of the state. The idea that greed is good implies that it is acceptable for some to acquire vast sums of wealth, leaving many people to struggle to make ends meet. This is therefore contrary to the idea of a welfare state and social justice. As Morelli and Seaman comment: 'Any conceptualisation of social justice requires recognition of the importance played by income and wealth equality' (2013, p. 55). Jones (2012) highlights how the gap between the earnings of those at the top of the organizational hierarchy and ordinary workers has been increasing significantly over the years: in 2000 the pay of top executives was 40 times the average wage for workers in their companies; by 2011 it had increased to 185 times.

➤ *Despair (for some) is inevitable*

This is another example of hegemony: an idea that benefits the privileged few is presented as 'necessarily so'. The (essentialist) idea that it is inevitable that some people (those at the bottom end of the social hierarchy in a variety of ways) will inexorably suffer is another gross oversimplification and a misleading distortion of reality. There is nothing inherent in the nature of society that makes it inevitable for some people to be excluded to the point of despair.

Perpetuating the notion that the suffering of the least powerful members of our society is inevitable serves to maintain the existing social order, with its highly unequal social and economic arrangements.

Voice of experience 3.2

I work with some very deprived families and see how much they miss out on. I see parents struggling to bring up their children and give them a decent life despite their poverty. I see all sorts of problems that are not the fault of the individuals concerned. The problems are *social* problems, but the net result is that it is some very vulnerable people who lose out in so many ways. It doesn't have to be like this, but politicians don't seem to care about anything but votes.

Lou, a children's centre worker

These five tenets of injustice, as presented by Dorling, reflect and critique an essentialist view of social reality. As we noted earlier, this is the opposite of a social constructionist approach which recognizes that the way things are is not written in tablets of stone. The way things are is as the result of historical, social and political processes that have produced the current social arrangements.

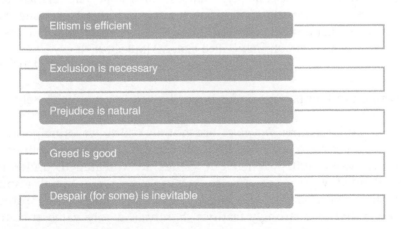

Figure 3.2   Dorling's five tenets

➤CHOICES *Social construction* Things can be different; we have choices.

The role of values

It would be a serious omission to try to understand social justice without considering the role of values. Values are the beliefs and principles that matter to us; they guide us, influencing our thoughts, feelings and actions. The very notion of 'social justice' is, of course a value statement in its own right. To be committed to promoting social justice is to express a value.

Furedi also discusses the significance of values and links these specifically to the idea of being threatened:

> Social responses to threats are experienced and mediated through taken-for-granted meanings about the nature of social reality and in particular of personhood. One of the most insightful sociologists of the twentieth century, C. Wright Mills, has argued that people's consciousness of being threatened is mediated through their system of values. Mills claimed that whether or not people feel well or insecure is influenced by their relationship with the prevailing sense of meaning. So, 'When people cherish some set of values and do not feel any threat to them, they experience *well-being*'. In contrast, 'When they cherish values but *do* feel them to be threatened, they experience a crisis'. 'And if all their values seem involved they feel the total threat of panic,' adds Mills. Mills also projected a scenario that captures an important dimension of the construction of social anxiety: 'suppose, finally they are unaware of any cherished values, but still are very much aware of a threat,' he states before concluding, 'that is the experience of *uneasiness*, of anxiety, which, if it is total enough, becomes a deadly unspecified malaise' [Mills, 1959].
>
> (2007, p. 98)

This is an important passage and it is worth examining more closely:

➤ *Threat mediated through values* are not just abstract principles. They are very concrete in how they shape our thoughts, feelings and actions (Moss, 2007). When our values are threatened, undermined or offended we can experience a very strong emotional response. Consider, for example, the anger that is generated when someone whose value base strongly features dignity as a core value encounters an example of a person being treated in an undignified way.

➤ *Security and meaning* We have already noted the significance of security as an existential/spiritual issue and therefore as a matter of meaning. A key part of our frameworks of meaning is the 'messages' we receive from society. For the least powerful groups in society those messages are predominantly negative and stigmatizing – messages of low worth (see, for example, Jones's, 2012, treatise on the unduly negative media representations of working-class people).

➤ *Threat and crisis* A threat to our values can reduce well-being; having our values constantly undermined can provoke a crisis. This can lead to panic, which in turn reinforce a sense of insecurity and mistrust.

➤ *Uneasiness and anxiety* This can be linked to our earlier discussion about the insecurity and mistrust associated with social problems and, in part at least, deriving from social injustice.

Constantly receiving messages of inequality and inferior worth can then place significant and persistent pressures on certain groups of people. This is reflected in the comments of Sutton et al. when they argue that:

> High levels of inequality cause distress by violating widely shared values such as justice and social cohesion. They elicit destructive feelings of relative deprivation, foster selfishness and prejudice, cause higher-status groups to be hypocritical, and lower-status groups to disengage from education while pursuing self-defeating and sometimes anti-social means of advancement. Many of the ill effects of inequality appear to aggravate inequality further – meaning that, if left unchecked, inequality has a self-perpetuating power.
>
> (2013, p. 132)

What is being described is a dialectical process that produces a vicious circle (or set of vicious circles). Circumstances of inequality create negative and destructive thoughts, feelings and actions which, in turn, can contribute to social problems. The dominant atomistic approach to social problems that pathologizes people on the receiving end of social problems reinforces the inequality. All this happens through the medium of values.

Social evils

In Chapter 2 I made reference to the four social evils identified by the Joseph Rowntree Foundation (2008) research. It is worth revisiting them here to consider each of them in relation to social justice.

A decline in community

Neoliberalism's emphasis on allowing the market free rein can be seen as a direct precursor to this (albeit not the only contributory factor). Placing a primary emphasis on the economy places all else in the background, out of focus. Therefore, a sense of community, a sense of shared endeavour takes a back seat. The divisiveness of social injustices can be seen as both a reflection of, and contributor to, a decline in community. This in turn leads to a loss of solidarity and sense of security (see Stepney and Popple, 2008).

Individualism

This is another direct and explicit feature of neoliberalism and its market emphasis. The focus on the market and the primacy of the economy distracts attention from wider social processes of exclusion, marginalization, discrimination, oppression and exploitation. By focusing primarily on individuals (the P level), questions about what is happening at the C and S levels are strongly discouraged.

Consumerism and greed

It does not take much working out to realize that consumerism is also a by-product of neoliberalism. The market emphasis encourages consumption, as consumption produces profits. And, of course, an increased level of consumerism promotes greed. As we noted earlier, we have now reached the point where, in many quarters, greed is seen as acceptable, if not actually desirable.

A decline of values

In a sense, values are an inescapable aspect of human existence, and so the issue is not whether values have declined, but whether they have changed. Allowing the market free rein is a value position in itself. Its primacy, as I have already indicated, pushes other important issues. So, the values of tolerance, compassion and respect the report mentions have not disappeared; they have just been put in the shade by the dominance of neoliberal thinking.

It would be both naïve and intellectually unsound to claim that these evils are purely and simply a consequence of neoliberalism and the inequality it spawns. Indeed, these social evils existed in some form long before neoliberalism came to the fore. However, it should be clear that neoliberalism is a common theme and a factor that has contributed strongly to the sense of malaise that the survey on which the report is based highlights.

The effects of (growing) inequality on the production and maintenance of social problems

A key argument underpinning this book is that it is no coincidence that, as inequality grows, the significance and detrimental impact of social problems also grow.

In this regard, Wilkinson and Pickett (2009) provide two interrelated arguments, one concerned with health inequalities and the other with the prevalence of violence:

> It has been known for some years that poor health and violence are more common in more unequal societies. However, in the course of our research we became aware that almost all problems which are more common at the bottom of the social ladder are more common in more unequal societies. It is not just ill-health and violence, but also, as we will show in later chapters, a host of other social problems. Almost all of them contribute to the widespread concern that modern societies are, despite their affluence, social failures.
>
> (2009, p. 18)

In a similar vein, Dorling goes so far as to say that: 'Growing income and wealth inequality is recognised as the greatest social threat of our times' (2014, p. 1).

We also need to consider the significance of social exclusion and its impact on self-esteem, security and anxiety. This returns us to our earlier discussion about how social problems need to be understood at a macro level in terms of wider social processes and institutions but also at a micro level in terms of the psychological impact on individuals, families and communities. Inequality contributes significantly to social exclusion. The greater the gap between those at the top of the social hierarchy and those at the bottom, the greater the harm that is likely to be experienced, not only by those at the bottom, but across the social range as indicated by the research of Wilkinson and Pickett.

Dorling has also highlighted how significant social inequality can be in terms of a wide range of social problems. He argues convincingly that significant inequality can be damaging to human abilities, curbing our potential and blocking progress. They can also affect our performance in and out of work and our levels of happiness and well-being. They can also be significant in relation to health and violence as we have already noted but, as Dorling adds, also in relation to educational attainment. This last point is particularly significant, as educational attainment, as a basis for social mobility, can make such a difference in terms of avoiding certain social problems such as poverty, unemployment, housing problems and so on.

It should be clear, then, that there is a strong relationship between inequality and social problems. This is what we shall now explore further.

The relationship between social problems and social justice

As we work our way towards the end of Part 1, it is important to emphasize that a key argument being presented is that there is a dialectical relationship between social problems and social justice. By dialectical what I mean is that these two aspects of society influence once another in significant and powerful ways. They interact and influence one another: social problems reinforce social injustices and social injustices reinforce social problems. This relationship merits closer attention.

Social problems can be seen to contribute to social injustices in a number of ways. For example, consider crime and the victims of crime and how these matters reflect social injustices. In particular, there is considerable statistical evidence to support the notion that, despite the greater level of affluence in certain areas, burglaries are far more likely to take place in lower income working-class areas.

Practice focus 3.3

Andrea was a police community service officer. She had always thought that crime was a fairly simple matter: there are certain people who are criminally inclined and therefore have to be carefully policed. However, it didn't take her long to realize that there was much more to it than that. The more she worked with local communities, the more she could see how ingrained the social problems were, and the more she could appreciate how much of a role inequality was playing in creating those problematic circumstances in the first place. She had been brought up in quite a privileged background and had had no idea of the extent and intensity of the social problems she encountered in the community she served. She was intelligent enough to work out that crime wasn't just a matter of some sort of moral inadequacy on the part of certain people.

Certain social problems, such as mental health problems and racism, can also be associated with social justice. Discrimination against people with mental health problems and against people from minority ethnic backgrounds can combine in a number of significant ways as we shall explore in greater detail in a Chapter 9.

Social problems also contribute to social injustice in terms of the abuse of power. In Chapter 8, where we explore abuse issues in more detail, we will note that a key aspect of abuse is precisely the abuse of power, something that is closely associated with social injustice.

We can see, then, that social problems contribute to social injustices in a number of ways. However, we can also note that the relationship flows in the opposite direction, in the sense that social injustices can contribute to social problems. For example, poverty is strongly linked to inequality. The fact that certain groups of people are struggling to live at income levels that are below their level of need is not a sign that they are not hardworking enough but rather a reflection of an unequal society that allows certain groups to earn massive amounts of money while others struggle to meet their basic needs.

Similarly, as we shall examine in more detail later, the fact that so much of our housing stock is used as an asset for further financial gain, rather than as homes for those who need them, is a significant contribution to our problems of housing and homelessness (Dorling, 2015a).

Voice of experience 3.3

Four of the children in my class are from the homelessness hostel at the edge of the estate. It's really upsetting to know what they have been through and all the uncertainty they face. It's hard not to feel sorry for them, even though I know that pity doesn't help. It just makes me wonder why, as a supposedly civilized society, we can't do more to make sure that children – or adults – don't have to live like this.

Kelly, a primary school teacher

Social injustices are also significant in relation to the destruction of our habitat – that is, in relation to our environmental problems and challenges. The fact that we have an unequal, unjust society based on materialist values geared towards maximizing profit at the expense of other important considerations – such as our environment – is a significant source of problems in relation to maintaining a liveable habitat.

Therefore, if we are to develop an adequate understanding of social problems or social justice, we need to be aware of the interrelationships between the two. To explore social problems without considering the social justice implications is to tell a less than full story of the significance of contemporary social problems and concerns. Similarly, by the same token, to explore social justice without exploring its impact on social problems and how social problems both reflect and contribute to social injustice is to give only a partial account.

Conclusion

Chapter 2 set the scene for the examination in Part 2 of specific social problems by exploring what we mean by social problems and establishing why it is important to appreciate the implications of the fact that they are socially constructed. In Chapter 3 I have sought to complement that understanding by laying down foundations of understanding about the role and significance of social justice. As part of this I have discussed the relationship between social problems and social justice, highlighting how important it is to take account of the key links between these two aspects of social life.

This is not the end of the story when it comes to social problems or social justice or the important connections between them. I will have much more to say about them as you work your way through the book, but what these two chapters in Part 1 have, I hope, done is to set down a platform of understanding that you will be able to build on in the remaining two parts of the book and, indeed beyond that as you continue your studies of these vitally important issues.

Points to ponder

➤ What are the three dimensions of social justice?

➤ What problems does the notion that 'greed is good' create for society?

➤ How does inequality contribute to social problems?

Exercise 3

Social justice is concerned with values. What are your values in relation to social justice? How did you learn them or who did you learn them from?

PART 2

Analysing Social Problems and Social Justice

Introduction

In Part 2 of the book we sharpen our focus by narrowing it down to looking at specific social problem areas. So, while Part 1 had a broad focus on common themes across, first of all, social problems, then social justice, then finally the relationship between social problems and social justice, we now focus down on particular problem areas.

There are nine chapters in total in Part 2. Each concentrates on a social problem or set of related problems, seeks to cast some light on the key issues involved and to relate these to social justice issues. Each chapter adopts the same basic structure, beginning with a short introduction followed by sections on: the causes and consequences of the problem(s) concerned; how they relate to social inequality and injustice; how they relate to other social problems; what responses there have been to date; and a short conclusion.

By adopting this structure I have been able to facilitate comparing and contrasting the different problem areas. This helps to give us an overview of the social problems field and how it intersects with social justice concerns, thereby avoiding a common criticism of other analyses of social problems that they are too narrow and lack any sense of a holistic understanding of the sets of issues involved and how they relate to one another.

Although the nine problem areas explored are by no means the only ones worthy of our attention, the insights gained from Part 2 should give you sufficient understanding (and, I hope, enthusiasm) to take your learning forward by considering in the same terms other problems not covered here – that is, asking the same questions about causes and consequences, relationship with inequality and so on.

4

Poverty, Deprivation and Debt

Introduction

The three elements of the title of this chapter are closely related in a number of ways, but they are also different. So, in this chapter, we will begin by considering poverty before relating this to the related concept of deprivation and then to debt – a problem closely linked to poverty, but also something that can cause great harm in its own right, regardless of poverty.

Understanding poverty, deprivation and debt

As poverty is such a significant factor in so many ways, it would be wise to begin with a definition of precisely what we mean by poverty. However, this is more difficult than it might originally seem. We have a number of competing definitions of poverty, and government policies often show elements of different definitions at different times.

Defining poverty

One way of defining poverty is what is referred to as an 'absolute' definition. This is used in relation to situations in which levels of income and financial resources are such that they do not allow for physical survival. Absolute poverty is therefore quite an extreme notion. It refers to circumstances where people may, for example, literally starve to death, where they do not have enough funds or other resources to meet their basic survival needs. Of course, in some countries in the world absolute poverty remains a reality, even in the twenty-first century. However, it is not entirely absent in the industrialized western world, despite attempts over many years to eradicate it.

To understand poverty more fully, though, we also need to consider what is known as 'relative poverty'. This is a complex concept and one that is often misunderstood. It does not mean, for example – despite the common misassumption – that, if I am earning a reasonable living, but I live across the road from a millionaire, then relative to that person, I am poor. It is not that simple. The notion of relative refers to relative to the social norms in that particular society at that time. It is linked to the idea of social exclusion. For example, if it is the norm to have a house with indoor toilet facilities, anybody who cannot afford indoor toilet facilities and has to rely on an outside toilet could be deemed to be living in relative poverty.

This has psychological and spiritual consequences. For example, if a person is made to feel that they do not belong, that they are not part of their society, then this has implications in terms of rights and responsibilities (for example, the undermining of citizenship) and merit (instilling feelings of inferiority and inadequacy) as well as inequality, and is therefore an important consideration. Much of the social policy response to the challenge of poverty has therefore been based on a relative definition, to a certain extent at least. It asks questions such as: How can we make sure that all our citizens feel that they are part of our society and are not excluded from it in significant ways because of a lack of income or other resources?

> ➤ CHOICES *Spiritual/existential implications* Poverty creates feelings of not belonging – consider, for example, the impact of having to rely on food banks.

Practice focus 4.1

Reena was an educational psychologist who, since qualifying, had worked for three years in an affluent area. However, she was now working in a very different area, providing services for a number of schools that had significant areas of deprivation within their catchment area. Of course, she had been aware of the significance of poverty, as that was part of her training. However, coming face to face on a daily basis with some of the worst consequences of poverty was a very different experience from reading a textbook or having a seminar discussion. Two things really stood out for her. First, she could see how debilitating it was trying to cope in such difficult circumstances. Second, though, she really appreciated the resourcefulness and resilience that so many of the families she met were able to demonstrate. She was both dismayed and impressed.

Another widely used definition of poverty is a statistical one. This is where poverty rates are calculated on the basis of average earnings. Therefore, a common definition of poverty would be based on the idea that, where somebody earns, for example, less than 60 per cent of the median income within their particular society, they can be deemed to be 'below the (statistically defined) poverty line'.

Sen explains:

> The mainstream approach to identifying poverty specifies a cut-off 'poverty line', defined as the level of income below which people are diagnosed as poor. The conventional measure of poverty, still widely used, proceeds from here to count the number of people below the poverty line – the so-called 'head count' – and defines the index of poverty as the proportion of the total population that happens to be below the poverty line (i.e. the fraction of the population identified as poor). This gives a neat and well-defined measure, and it is not hard to see why it has been so widely used in the empirical literature on poverty and deprivation.
>
> (1992, p. 102)

What this shows is that poverty is a contested concept. That is, different stakeholders or interest groups will have different theoretical and political perspectives on poverty, and will therefore treat the issues and challenges involved differently, according to their own perspective.

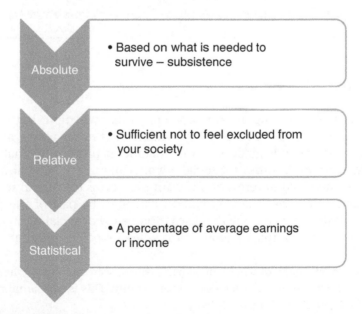

Figure 4.1   Definitions of poverty

Trapped in poverty

One important concept in terms of poverty is what has come to be known as 'cycles of poverty'. What this refers to is that people who are living in poverty are likely to produce children who grow up to live in poverty. This is partly because people who live in poverty are likely to have lower levels of education, fewer opportunities for advancement in terms of career and so on, and so it can easily become the case that, for example, being brought up in a housing estate that is characterized by high levels of poverty and related social problems can lead to the next generation of people continuing to live in poverty. Unfortunately, some people have used the notion of a cycle of poverty to pathologize poor people, regarding them as a sort of 'underclass', thereby failing to take account of wider cultural and structural factors.

This sort of cyclical effect is also sometimes referred to as 'the poverty trap'. It relates to the idea that some people will find it difficult, if not impossible, to get out of poverty because poverty is not simply a lack of resources, it has the related problems of lower levels of educational attainment, greater health problems, higher levels of crime and problematic drug use and so on – issues that we will be considering in later chapters.

> ➤ CHOICES *Interconnectedness* Social problems tend to reinforce one another.

Deprivation

Poverty is, of course, a significant problem in its own right, but it is also important to link it to the idea of deprivation. It is not simply a matter of struggling to make ends meet on a low income; it means also that people can be denied opportunities for social advancement in a number of ways. They may be deprived in terms of, for example, access to cultural resources, facilities and amenities. This deprivation can then be part of the poverty trap and a cycle of poverty. See the discussion below of social capital.

Isaacs gives an example of deprivation when he points out that:

> The poor today, many of whom are elderly, will be scared to put the heating on in case it costs too much. They count every penny. This is how around 20 per cent of the population of the UK live.

(2015, p. 51)

Deprivation, then, is, in a sense, a knock-on effect of poverty. Certain doors remain firmly closed for people living in poverty.

Social exclusion

The term 'social exclusion' is one that has been used extensively over the years, and is closely associated with poverty and deprivation. However, it is not identical with poverty because people can be socially excluded for reasons unconnected with poverty – for example, in relation to their sexuality or their ethnic origin. None the less, it would be a mistake not to recognize that poverty is a factor that has a central role in many aspects of social exclusion. As Isaacs clarifies:

> Socially excluded now generally defines any individual who is disadvantaged in multiple ways so that they are excluded from 'normal' course of life expectations, particularly in education and work. What 'normal' might mean is open to interpretation and debate.
>
> (2015, p. 54)

According to Green and Clarke the concept of social exclusion 'was intended to capture the complex interactions between material deprivation and some of its consequences, such as poor health, educational outcomes and housing, and increased criminality' (2016, p. 21).

Social exclusion has also been linked to the concept of 'social capital' (Lin, 2001). Just as people can accumulate economic or financial capital, it is possible to develop 'social' capital. This refers to social contacts and connections, membership of groups and so on. Just as financial capital is unequally distributed, so too is social capital. People living in poverty may therefore face additional barriers.

Voice of experience 4.1

I have been involved in studying social capital for over a year now. I find it really interesting how different groups of people have differential access to resources. So, we have all sorts of capital to consider – not just financial, but also social, cultural, even emotional. These different types of capital are interlinked in complex ways. Fascinating, really fascinating.

Chris, a university-based researcher

Daly and Silver (2008) make an interesting link with trust. Social capital can give rise to trust through the various networks and interconnections concerned. A lack of social capital can therefore be associated with a lack of trust (and the attendant insecurities).

The development of social exclusion can be seen to have its roots in the wider sociopolitical context. Heiner makes the point that:

> By its very nature, capitalism engenders inequality and, at least, relative poverty, if not absolute poverty. In order to quell those in poverty, rather than slicing up the pie differently, the poor are assured that the whole pie will expand and their lives will improve. "Capitalism's need for growth", writes Hertsgaard, "coincides with a way to satisfy the demands of the poor majority for a better life would be to share existing resources more equitably. Privileged classes throughout history have been less than keen on that idea".
>
> (2006, p. 161)

The dominance of neoliberal thinking, as discussed in Chapter 1, emphasizes the primacy of the market, thereby reinforcing the social exclusion inherent in the current socioeconomic arrangements.

> ➤ CHOICES *Over-reliance on the market* A narrow focus on the market distracts attention from social exclusion.

Debt

It is understandable that poverty is so often closely associated with debt. People who are struggling to make ends meet because of poverty will face the risk of debt far more than other people will. For example, there is what is often referred to as the 'poverty premium' – that is, the various ways in which poor people are called upon to pay more (people who do not have a bank account and cannot therefore pay for their electricity by direct debit are likely to have to rely on a pre-pay meter which involves paying a higher rate for their electricity). However, it is important to recognize that debt is a problem in its own right across the income spectrum and not just for people in poverty. This is because there is a strong ideology of consumerism that encourages people to spend money on, for example, luxury goods and other indicators of status within society ('conspicuous consumption', as it is often called). Many years ago the sociologist, Robert Merton, argued that there is often a mismatch between society's cultural expectations (in terms of purchasing power, for example) and people's ability in financial terms to live up to such expectations (Merton, 1996). In this respect, people can often be set up to fail by consumerist values that are prevalent in a neoliberal society. This then has implications for debt.

People whose level of income places them far above the poverty line may none the less face significant problems with debt because they are – or have been – spending beyond their means. They are trying to live up to consumerist ideals without having the financial resources to do so. The consequences of this can be quite disastrous in terms of, for example, homelessness, loss of employment and other knock on effects associated with excessive use of alcohol or other drugs, and so on. Therefore, while debt is sadly a common accompaniment to poverty, we need to be aware that debt can be a social problem in its own right, with its roots in a consumerist ideology in a society where levels of inequality mean that a significant proportion of the population do not have the resources to live up to the consumerist ideals that are presented to them by the media and other powerful institutions.

So, whether we are talking about poverty, deprivation or debt or any combination of the three, what we have to take into account is that there will be significant consequences in terms of, for example, people's ability to achieve a level of reasonable living standards, but there will also be

Practice focus 4.2

Dawn was an advice worker who initially specialized in housing issues. However, for the sake of variety, she volunteered to get involved in debt advice work. Her housing work had mainly involved working with people from the more disadvantaged sectors of the community. However, what surprised her about debt work was that it seemed that anyone can get into debt. She found herself working with people who were in debt because of poverty and unemployment, but also with people who had a really good income, but had somehow got to the point where their outgoings greatly exceeded their income. Regardless of social background, what was apparent to her was that debt could be crushing. She could see the sense of powerlessness and hopelessness that it could create. Once people found themselves in the vicious circle of debt, it took an awful lot of work to get them to see what they needed to do to get out of it, however difficult that was going to be. The more involved she got in this type of work, the more she could see that consumerism was such a problem. Everywhere you turn you get messages that you need to spend money, you need to get the latest and the greatest – whether you can afford it or not. No wonder, she thought, so many people get sucked in by this and then wish they hadn't.

potential psychological consequences in terms of self-esteem, self-respect, aspirations and so on. This brings us back to the issue of trust and insecurity and how a decent society rooted in social justice would not allow certain groups of people to lack a reasonable level of trust and security in the context of the society they are part of.

Moloney captures the wide-ranging implications well when he comments that:

> Impoverishment is soul sapping. It can mean exposure to a range of material and personal threats that come with living in substandard or slum dwellings. Aside from low pay, the poor are also more likely to be trapped in unregulated labour markets comprised of sweatshops, meagre piece-work rates, and abusive supervisors. [Scott et al., 2012] They are subjected more often to traumatic experiences such as accidents at work, in the home, or on the street, and to infections and other illnesses, as well as bereavement, job loss or insecure work, unsanitary and overcrowded housing, urban noise, and violent crime. [Tombs, 2004] The children of the poor have few safe or pleasant places in which to play, and are more at risk of being run over by motorists. [Road Safety Analysis Group, 2010]
>
> (2013, p. 101)

This amounts to a seriously worrying set of consequences, and this partly explains why poverty reduction has been such a prominent feature of social policy for many governments.

Finally in terms of causes and consequences, it is important to be aware that poverty can have a significantly adverse effect on health. There are various reasons for this, but the common thread across these is that poverty is highly detrimental to our health in the present and in terms of future expectations in terms of freedom from illness and, indeed, life expectancy in itself. Moloney again makes apt comment:

> First, in concentrating upon individual responsibility for health and illness, we lose sight of the bigger picture, of how pervasive problems like poverty can cause or exacerbate health problems. In disguising this reality, the health care system bolsters and protects those aspects of society that manufacture illness in the first place. Secondly, age-old aspects of the human condition, especially emotional and spiritual suffering, come to be seen as the province of professionals upon whom lay people come to depend in their efforts to understand and manage what they now take to be illness.
>
> (2013, p. 30)

Overall, then, it should be clear that poverty, deprivation and debt can be highly significant in terms of the adverse consequences they lead to. We are now going to move on to consider how these matters interrelate with inequality.

How poverty, deprivation and debt affect, and are affected by, inequality

To a certain extent the relationship between these factors and inequality is self-evident, particularly with poverty and deprivation, because they are direct consequences of an unequal society. If we return to the definition of inequality as the unacceptable gap between those at the top of the income scale and those at the bottom, we should be able to recognize how poverty stems from that gap being too great. That is, while certain groups of people have extreme wealth, one of the consequences of this is that other groups have far less than they need to feel comfortably part of their society and not to feel socially excluded.

Materialism

A key aspect of this is the materialism I mentioned earlier. Social expectations within a materialistic neoliberal society lead to strong aspirations towards affluence. We are constantly bombarded with messages that state that we should be aiming for wealth as a key factor in our lives. However, there is considerable evidence to suggest that this is highly problematic for us in a number of ways. As Barry puts it:

> The more materialistic a society – the more that it is generally believed that money is the only significant goal in life – the more that people with a lot of money will feel like winners and those with a little will feel like losers. This feeling will intensify if those who are better off than others believe that they are more virtuous and those who are worse off share this belief.
>
> (2005, p. 78)

What is apparent, then, is that a materialist culture, with its emphasis on wealth as the defining feature of happiness and well-being, is not only rooted in inaccuracy, but also positively dangerous in terms of its negative consequences.

Discrimination and inequality

A further factor in terms of the relationship between poverty and inequality is the discrimination associated with the job market. For example, someone who is from a housing estate associated with poverty, deprivation and related social problems, may well face active discrimination in terms of not being considered for a job they may be perfectly capable of doing very well (DeKeseredy et al., 2003). This sort of built-in discrimination based on culturally shaped prejudices is a particular concern for many people who are struggling with the poverty trap we focused on earlier.

There is also the issue of secondary poverty to consider. This relates to the way in which many families may not be in poverty when the overall level of income and financial resources is considered relative to their needs. However, it is not uncommon, in certain families, for the breadwinner to retain a significant proportion of the family income for their own needs – to pay for alcohol, betting or other expenses that are specific to that breadwinner. The result can be that, while the overall level of financial resources is sufficient, the actual amount left after these indulgences leaves the remainder of the family in a situation of poverty (Pascall, 1997). Generally, but not exclusively, that breadwinner is a man, and this reflects patriarchal assumptions about rights and responsibilities along gender lines in families. We are therefore dealing with a social justice matter as well as a social problem.

Voice of experience 4.2

It saddens me that so often I meet families whose level of income should be plenty for their needs, but where one member of the family – usually the man, I'm afraid – is spending far more than their fair share. It might be in the pub or the betting shop or on expensive hobbies. One man I came across not so long ago was a member of a gun club. He was spending a fortune on guns and equipment, but his family were really struggling to make ends meet. It's so sad because it creates so many problems and tensions.

Clare, a community nurse

Also important in terms of the relationship between poverty, deprivation and debt and other forms of inequalities is how inequalities can, in a sense, beget further inequalities. Wilkinson helps us to understand this when he proposes that:

> Socioeconomic inequalities often lead to differences in ethnicity, race, religion, or language, which might otherwise be easily accepted, becoming infected with social prejudice. However, where material inequalities are smaller, issues of social superiority and inferiority are less in the foreground of social relations and religious, ethnic, racial, and linguistic differences are less likely to cause friction.
>
> (2005, p. 228)

That is, the preponderance of inequality can be seen to contribute to a lack of acceptance of difference and diversity, with the knock-on effect of creating further discrimination.

In addition, there are considerable inequalities in how debt matters are managed in our society. For example, consider the quite low interest rates that corporate entities are able to rely on in order to run their businesses compared with the very high interest rates that people in debt or poverty need to pay (if, for example, they are relying on 'pay day lenders') in order to make ends meet. This has the effect of reinforcing inequality, in the sense that it becomes much easier for affluent sectors of society to retain their positions of wealth and privilege, while people in debt and poverty face ever greater difficulties because of interest rates that prove to be punitive and at times unmanageable.

How poverty, deprivation and debt affect, and are affected by, other social problems

These problems do not exist in a vacuum. They can be seen to connect with a wide range of other problems in various ways. As Heiner explains:

> Poverty increases the likelihood of marital instability, alcoholism among parents, and child abuse. Compared to non-poor children, poor children are one-third as likely to have had adequate prenatal care, almost twice as likely to be born prematurely, almost twice as likely to be of low birth weight, twice as likely to repeat grade in school, and about three and a half times more likely to be expelled from school. [Arloc, 1997] State health officials in Kansas report that low-in-come children are three times more likely to die before reaching age 18 than higher-income children. According to the same report, before reaching age 18, low-income children are four times more likely to die from fires and five times more likely to die from infectious diseases and parasites.
>
> (2006, p. 89)

Here we shall focus on three sets of interconnections in particular.

Housing and homelessness

Perhaps one of the clearest links is between housing and homelessness, on the one hand, and poverty on the other – for example, as a result of the way poverty limits access to housing. Someone who is in a position of wealth will no doubt have various options when it comes to housing choice. For someone in poverty or debt the opportunity to purchase a property is likely to be severely limited, and, in a time of increasing use of private sector housing as profitable assets, and the decreasing amount of social housing available, those people at the bottom of the financial hierarchy are likely to

---

Practice focus 4.3

Martin was a youth and community work student who was looking forward to his first placement in the field. He was placed with a special project helping homeless young people to try and get back on their feet. He thoroughly enjoyed the placement, but it made him realize just how challenging the work could be. He could see how one set of problems (family conflicts) were linked to others (poverty and family stress), which then led to further problems (family breakdown and homelessness). Being homeless, Martin realized, then created all sorts of obstacles to progress, not least being able to get a job and avoid further poverty. When you add the escapist temptations of drugs and alcohol to the mix, you get an incredibly complex situation. Martin was disheartened at first, but, in the end, this challenging experience made him all the more committed to playing his part in doing something positive about the situation.

---

face huge difficulties in securing adequate accommodation for their needs. This can create a cycle of poverty once again, especially where a person becomes homeless and therefore struggles to gain employment to enable them to earn the wherewithal to break out of this cycle of poverty.

Environmental problems

There are also issues relating to the destruction of habitat to consider – for example, the consumerist ideology of neoliberalism places great emphasis on consumption, as consumption at increasing levels is necessary to maximize profits. This sort of economic growth comes at the expense of natural resources. An emphasis on profit at all costs means that those costs can often include a contribution to the destruction of our habitat through the worsening of environmental problems.

Linked to this is the idea of the throwaway culture in which goods are so often created to meet the latest fashionable need (therefore with built-in obsolescence), rather than to have any more lasting effect in terms of the ability to make use of those goods on a longer-term basis. This is significant in connection with the destruction of habitat for obvious reasons, but one implication that is often not considered is that the financial resource difficulties associated with poverty and debt often mean that certain sectors of society do not have the financial resources to buy durable goods that are likely to be more expensive. They therefore have to rely on buying something that is cheaper, but will not last as long. It will therefore need replacing sooner at the expense of our natural resources.

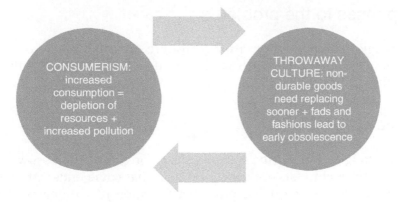

Figure 4.2   Poverty and environmental problems

Problematic drug use

Poverty also has strong links with problematic drug use. This is partly because of availability issues. While it is a mistake to assume that illegal drugs are only available in low-income areas (which is certainly not the case) we do have to acknowledge that access to illegal drugs reflects broadly the pattern of income distribution in our society.

A further factor linking poverty and debt, on the one hand, and problematic drug use on the other, is escapism. When people are faced with significant problems as a result of poverty or debt or both, then the tendency to rely on alcohol or other mind-altering substances is understandable and well documented.

Voice of experience 4.3

It starts off with peer pressure, just wanting to do what other group members are doing – just to fit in, to feel that they belong. Then they get the enjoyment, the slight euphoria from being inebriated. Next comes the sense of escapism, the feeling of leaving all your concerns behind. Before you know it, they are into drink in a big way – and it's one hell of a job getting them out if it. They generally have to hit rock bottom before they bounce back up again.

Alexis, a social worker in an alcohol problems team for young people

---

The examples featured here illustrate how there is a significant link between poverty and other social problems, very strong links indeed in fact.

Responses to the problems

Poverty alleviation has been a major feature of social policy for a considerable period of time. This has included a wide range of initiatives, including the following.

Welfare benefits

We have long had a benefits system with its origins in the post-war welfare state. In recent years our benefits systems has come under attack with prejudicial notions that it has produced 'a nation of scroungers' (Jones, 2012). Unfortunately, in our highly unequal society, many people are forced to live on a benefits system that often barely meets their needs. There is also considerable stigma associated with having to rely on benefits. The 'blame the victim' mentality that we discussed earlier is widely prevalent in relation to the benefits system, while the huge abuses associated with corporate tax levels receive relatively little attention and much lower levels of social disapproval. As Chomsky puts it:

> There's strong public opposition to welfare. On the other hand, there's strong public support for what welfare does. So if you ask the question, "should we spend more on welfare?" No. "should we spend more on aid to women with dependent children?" Yes. That's successful propaganda. Welfare has been successfully demonized.
>
> (2012, p. 82)

Workfare

Another approach to poverty that has had mixed results is what is known as 'workfare'. Workfare refers to attempts to create working opportunities for unemployed people so that they are, in effect, being made to provide services in exchange for their benefits. These are generally paid at levels far below what would be received in regular jobs and there is no guarantee of future employment, nor is there the potential for advancement associated with other types of work. It is for this reason that workfare schemes have been highly criticized by a number of commentators.

The minimum wage

A further attempt to address poverty has been the introduction of the minimum wage and more recently the notion of a living wage. This is based on the idea that people in employment should be earning at least enough to meet their needs. It is telling us that there is something seriously wrong if people are in employment and yet they are still not able to meet their basic needs in terms of feeling a part of their society. There have been many discussions around the significance of a minimum wage or a living wage and what level it should be paid at. However, despite the criticisms it is clear that it has gone some way to reducing some aspects of poverty. However, it relates only to the poverty for those people who are in work and therefore does not address the wider problem of people who are denied opportunities to work.

Overall, then, there have been attempts to address poverty in a number of ways but the overall effect has been largely of a very limited nature. There is still far more that can be done to address issues around poverty and debt, but, unfortunately, a neoliberal society rooted in the idea of austerity and the limiting of public services means that poverty, deprivation and debt are likely to be with us for some considerable time yet (Blyth, 2013; Mendoza, 2015).

Conclusion

Poverty is not a matter of there not being enough money to go round. Rather, it is about how that money is distributed across society. As we have seen, poverty leaves huge detrimental consequences in its own wake – not just deprivation and debt for so many, but also so many other harmful effects that can, and often do, ruin people's lives.

Poverty is not only a devastating social problem in its own right, but also – as we shall see further in later chapters – a major contributory factor to various other social problems. The common tendency to present poverty as simply the inadequacy of poor people is therefore highly problematic and a significant barrier to progress.

Points to ponder

➤ What are the three main ways of defining poverty?

➤ What do you understand by the term 'social capital'?

➤ How might poverty contribute to problematic drug use?

Exercise 4

What reasons do you think there are that poverty persists in wealthy industrial nations in the twenty-first century? List as many as you can.

5

Unemployment

Introduction

In Chapter 4 we examined the significance of poverty as a social problem. One of the main causes of poverty is unemployment. Except for
the privileged few who are independently wealthy, earning a living is a
key challenge. While many will launch their own businesses to generate income, most people will need to rely on paid employment. Where
such opportunities are not available or otherwise prove elusive, poverty
will often be the result. While the benefits system provides a safety net to
avoid absolute poverty, benefit levels are generally not generous enough
to avoid some degree of relative poverty – especially for people who are
unemployed on a long-term basis. So, we can already see a link between
the subject matter of the previous chapter and this one.

While unemployment is indeed a major contributory factor to poverty, poverty is not the only unwelcome consequence of unemployment.
As we shall see, unemployment brings with it a range of difficulties and
challenges. We shall also see, once again, that there are significant links
between unemployment as a social problem and social justice – or, more
specifically, social injustice.

Understanding unemployment

Many years ago the UK Labour Party leader, Neil Kinnock, made the
point that regardless of percentages quoted in unemployment statistics,
for someone who is unemployed, the problem is one hundred per cent.
Unemployment is therefore both an individual and a social problem. As
a personal problem, for people who are unemployed there are significant
implications in terms of such matters as identity, self-esteem, self-respect,
plus, as we have discussed in earlier chapters, there is the importance of
sense of security that comes with having employment. We also need to
recognize unemployment as a social problem because of the threat to the

economy and potentially to the social order if numbers of unemployed people reach a level where the current social arrangements come under threat in some way. High levels of unemployment feed social unrest.

One of the basic sources of unemployment is there simply being more people looking for work than there are jobs available. This is known as 'structural scarcity' – that is, the employment arrangements are structured in such a way that there are not enough jobs to go round. This is similar to the idea of 'structural unemployment' which refers to circumstances where there may be jobs available, but not where the labour force is. For example, there may be jobs available in the capital city of a particular country, but high levels of unemployment in provincial and more rural areas.

Globalization

However, the overall picture is more complex than this. It is not simply a matter of a shortage of jobs *per se*. We need to take cognizance of the fact that there are at least three other sets of factors that influence unemployment. The first is globalization. This refers to the way in which, in a sense, the world is getting smaller. We now have international markets, international finance systems, and therefore global issues in terms of employment. One of the direct consequences of this is that jobs that were previously

Practice focus 5.1

Mair was a welfare rights officer helping people to make sure they received the benefits they were entitled to. Most of the people she encountered were unemployed. Some had been out of work for so long that they had more or less given up on ever finding employment. There were far more, however, who kept on trying, constantly striving to find a job, despite knock back after knock back. She was so glad she had a job as she could see how difficult it was to cope with unemployment, whether you had become resigned to it or were facing rejection after rejection – either way, it was so disheartening. One evening she and her partner attended a party given by one of their neighbours. She was enjoying the festivities until one of the other guests, someone she hadn't met before, started to talk about 'the great unwashed' and made disparaging comments about unemployed people and what a drain they were on the economy. Mair was aware that he was talking about something he clearly knew nothing about and was basing his comments on pure prejudice. She wanted to say something, but she knew her blood was boiling and she might regret what she said. So, she and her partner made their excuses and left. For quite some time after she regretted not saying anything, as she felt those comments were just so unfair and so ill informed.

located in the western world are now often to be found in developing countries where the cost of labour is significantly lower (because the cost of living in those particular countries is significantly lower).

While globalization opens up new markets to large multinational corporations, it shifts the employment opportunities to those areas where living costs are lowest, leaving unemployment problems in its wake in those areas where employment was previously on offer. While it is a positive development that developing nations have an influx of income through these employment arrangements, it creates greater inequality 'back home', as the stakeholders who benefit from increased profits do better, while ordinary working people lose out.

Technological development

The second significant change is in the use of technology. We now have so many computerized systems, so many technologically advanced ways of completing tasks that previously required direct human labour. This means that technology has reduced the number of jobs available, often in quite startling ways. Some factories that previously employed literally hundreds of people can now be run with simply a handful of technicians. This change in the basis of modern life has forced us to reconsider the very nature of work, a point to which we shall return below.

Globalization and technological change are both important factors, but they are not unconnected. For example, India is a country that now offers services to large multinational corporations. What has facilitated this has been the development of low-cost telecommunications technology that allows, for example, call centres to be based thousands of miles away from the callers, but at a very low price, with call quality more or less the same as a local call. The circle is then complete when we recognize that India now has a burgeoning IT industry that is fuelling further technological change at a lower cost than would have previously been the case (thereby raising profit margins). This then creates further inequality – for example, when you compare the relatively affluent lifestyles of people involved in India's IT infrastructure and the ordinary people who face major poverty problems on a large scale.

Business process re-engineering

The third significant change is a particular philosophy in management thinking that has proved to be quite influential. The idea of 'business process re-engineering' (Becker et al., 2011) has resulted in organizations (in the business sector) trying to maximize profits by minimizing the number of employees they need, and organisations (in the public service sector) relying on the minimum number of staff in order to reduce costs to the taxpayer (consistent with the neoliberal principle of minimal state provision). The result of this business process reengineering philosophy has been a major emphasis on what has euphemistically come to be known as 'downsizing'. This has created major problems in terms of not only directly increasing levels of unemployment, but also adding stress to those employees who are left behind. For example, if an organization employs the minimum number of staff, there is no allowance for special circumstances, such as illness, temporarily increased demand or whatever. This can lead to considerable problems for both the organization itself and its wider stakeholder group, but especially for the staff who are then faced with what often amounts to oppressive working conditions.

Voice of experience 5.1

I've been in HR for over 15 years now and I have seen a lot of changes – and they are generally not for the better. Organizations seem to expect people to do the impossible these days. They want to pare staff back to the bone, but still keep the same level of productivity if not better. No wonder we see so much stress these days.

Ceri, a human resources officer

Oppressive workplaces

This leads us on to the question of not only a lack of employment, but also employment that is detrimental in one or more ways. Where levels of unemployment are high, there is a greater opportunity for unscrupulous employers to abuse and exploit their staff in a variety of ways – for example, by giving them unreasonable workloads. In circumstances of high unemployment the chances of the workforce challenging their employers, taking out grievances or exploring industrial action options will tend to be significantly less. As a result of this, there are further pressures placed on those who are in employment. Therefore, one of the consequences of unemployment is that it acts as a foundation for oppressive employment (Schnall et al., 2009). Indeed, oppressive employment could be regarded as a social problem in its own right.

Self-esteem and self-respect

As mentioned earlier, work needs to be recognized as an important source of self-esteem and self-respect for a significant proportion of the population. As the existentialist writer, André Gorz, has helped us to understand,

Figure 5.1 Oppressive employment

work is a key part of most people's identity (Gorz, 1999). We have an affinity with the type of work we do in many circumstances. When we are denied the opportunity, through unemployment, to connect with that affiliation, the result can be quite detrimental in a number of ways, not least to our level of well-being (Dorling, 2016).

Work is something that people can put their heart into and get great satisfaction from. Ironically, it is often people living in poverty who work the hardest. As Isaacs comments:

> One of the first things that the social research tells us is that poor people tend to work harder than anyone else. Polly Toynbee (2003) documents this well in her turn-of-the-millennium study, *Hard Work*. In this book she presents quantitative and qualitative evidence to suggest that the poor work longer and harder now than they did forty years ago. Comparing the wages of some of the lowest-paid workers, she illustrates how the poor have seen their wages rise more slowly than the rest of the population.
>
> (2015, p. 49)

What this illustrates is that work is not simply a matter of earning a living. There is much more to it than this, of course. Consequently, unemployment is not simply a financial challenge in terms of making ends meet.

How unemployment affects, and is affected by, inequality

Unemployment is closely linked to inequality in so far as being unemployed tends to place a person at or near the bottom of the social hierarchy, partly in terms of income and related resources and partly in terms of social status and respect (given that unemployment is stigmatized to a certain extent). However, this is not the only link between unemployment and inequality.

The importance of comparisons

There is now a considerable body of research showing the significance of comparisons across employment (see, for example, Shore et al., 2006). One of the key implications of this research is that what matters most is not so much direct levels of recompense for work carried out, but, rather, comparison with others. That is, a person who is being paid well but who is on a lower rate of pay than someone who does a similar job is likely to be dissatisfied. This has significant implications in terms of how working life is experienced.

Another element of comparison relates to how people perceive themselves in relation to others in terms of income. That is, having little or no income matters more when others around have higher levels of income. In an important text, Tew draws links between this phenomenon and mental health:

> International comparisons would suggest that there is relatively little adverse impact on mental wellbeing if one is poor within a context where everyone is poor, or within a culture where one is valued for who one is rather than what he owns. Instead, it is suggested that it is experiences of injustice, in terms of *relative* disadvantage (and the negative social connotations that may go with this), rather than *absolute* levels of deprivation, that may be more pernicious in their effects on mental health (Dohrenwend, 2000).
>
> (2011, p. 37)

One of the implications of this is that what will create significant problems for people wrestling with unemployment is not so much their direct

Practice focus 5.2

Marcus had been involved in mental health work for many years when he was appointed to the post of development officer. A key part of his new role was to look at ways of reducing a reliance on medication and explore more community-based ways of addressing mental health needs. He therefore set about making appointments to speak to key people in the mental health field, professionals, survivor groups and patient representatives. He was trying to find common ground to move forward on. One area that struck him was the fact that so many people with mental health problems were living in areas of high deprivation – something that exacerbated their difficulties because of the stresses and strains involved. He also remembered the social comparisons research he had read at university. He knew there would be no magic answers but he could see that there were plenty of issues he would be able to explore in an attempt to alleviate the difficulties involved.

income level, but how this is perceived in terms of their implied worth. Therefore, if a worker is paid less than someone else, the implication is that they are worth less than that person. This is an important issue for all people, whether in employment or not. However, when we consider this from the point of view of unemployment, we can see that it is particularly significant, in so far as someone who is unemployed – particularly on a long-term basis – is being given a highly negative and problematic message. This means that differential rates of pay, while they give messages about worth and value, are relatively insignificant compared with the message about worth and value that is given by unemployment.

> ➤ CHOICES *Existential/spiritual implications* Unemployment is dispiriting in a society in which so much of self-worth is associated with employment.

Racism

An important factor in terms of inequality in relation to unemployment is the higher rates of unemployment among minority ethnic groups. There has been considerable research carried out in relation to racism and unemployment and the message from this research is not a positive one. For example, Kapadia et al. (2015) summarize the ways in which members of minority ethnic groups are disadvantaged. While the factors involved in this are bound to be complex, racial discrimination in the recruitment process is likely to be chief among them (Heath and Cheung, 2006).

Drawing on the work of Brynin and Guveli (2012), Kapadia et al. also point out that some minority ethnic groups are also more likely to be employed in insecure, low-paid jobs. Another significant factor in terms of race and ethnicity is that, in the current climate, there can be significant workforce tensions when numbers of migrants are employed in a particular setting. This can be a combination of genuine concerns about job opportunities being lost to immigrants and racist attitudes towards any outsider group. However, what can easily happen is that anxieties about low wages and insecure employment are transposed on to immigration – that is, immigration becomes a scapegoat for problems generated by neoliberalism.

Discrimination against unemployed people

Returning to the theme of constructing pathology, we can see that unemployed people are often dismissed as workshy, feckless individuals who are not making any effort to find work. While such individuals may well exist, it is a gross exaggeration to assume that unemployed people *in general* fall into that category. This is an example of one of the ways in which stereotyping works – by taking some (generally negative) characteristics associated with a small minority of members of a particular group or category of people and overgeneralize this to the whole group or category. For example, some people living in social housing may lack pride in their community and behave in ways that adversely affect other residents. This can then be overextended to become seen as a characteristic of social housing occupants in general. It also serves to deflect attention from the fact that there will also be a minority of residents in owner-occupied accommodation who do not take pride in their community and behave in ways that adversely affect other residents. Of course, this type of simplistic thinking represents a gross distortion of the reality, but then stereotypes generally do. Despite such distortion, stereotypes are quite common.

> ➤ **C**HOICES *Constructing pathology* Unemployment is not simply a matter of laziness.

Assuming that unemployment is down to individual inadequacy or lack of effort is to: (i) distort the **P** level and totally disregard the **C** and **S** levels, thereby producing a partial and misleading picture of the situation.

Jones argues that: 'If you think poverty and unemployment are personal failings rather than social problems, then why have a welfare state at all?' (2012, p. xiii).

This links closely with the theme of neoliberalism and the over-reliance on the market, with its commitment to reducing the role of the state to a minimum. It is no coincidence that neoliberal arrangements at a structural level are supported by an ideology of individualism at a cultural level which influences behaviour and attitudes at a personal level. Such behaviour and attitudes then serve to sustain the cultural ideology which then continues the social arrangements and power relations at a structural level. This is an example of the double dialectic of PCS analysis I mentioned in Chapter 1.

How unemployment affects, and is affected by, other social problems

Unemployment is particularly significant as a social problem because it connects in major ways with various other social problems. Here we shall focus on three in particular.

Poverty

There is a strong link between unemployment and poverty. This is partly because a reliance on benefits as a result of lack of employment is likely to result in a low level of income, which, of course, is then, potentially at least, a major source of poverty. This is especially the case for people who are unemployed on a longer-term basis, as the benefits system does not generally factor in longer-term costs. For example, if a particular benefit covers ongoing housing and food costs, this may be just about sufficient in the short term. However, if clothing and/or furniture need to be replaced on a longer-term basis, this can result in considerable poverty, particularly the type of poverty referred to earlier as relative poverty, whereby a family may, for example, have to make do with furniture that has broken due to long-term wear and tear due to the fact that there is no funding available to arrange for a replacement to be provided.

Jones (2012) notes that almost 6 out of 10 households in poverty have at least one person working. This indicates that unemployment is not the only source of poverty. There is also a problem of low pay and/or underemployment – that is, part-time work that does not provide sufficient income for the individual's or family's needs.

There are significant issues we have already mentioned in terms of self-esteem in relation to both poverty and unemployment. Being poor and unemployed can have an adverse effect on our sense of self-worth. This can mean that where people are applying for jobs, the strength of their

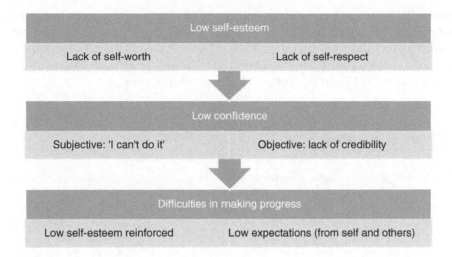

Figure 5.2   The importance of self-esteem

application is not as great as it should have been because of low levels of confidence as the result of the self-esteem issues associated with both poverty and unemployment. This can produce an unemployment trap whereby people who are living in poverty struggle to find the confidence to present well at interview, for example.

Abuse

Abuse is also a significant social problem that has links with unemployment. For example, home-based tensions as a result of unemployment can be a trigger factor in terms of domestic violence. If, for example, a couple are living together and spending almost all their time together on a very limited income, with a sense of hopelessness, it is quite understandable that violence will at times be the result (although this is not to say that it is acceptable).

Unemployment can also be seen to be linked to child abuse, partly for the reasons of family tension already mentioned, as these can also apply to situations in which children and young people are physically abused for example. However, there is also the issue of access to children, what is sometimes referred to as 'pathways of abuse'. Someone wanting to abuse a child and who is unemployed is going to have greater opportunities to have access to children compared with someone who is in full-time employment in a role that does not involve contact with children.

Unemployment is also relevant to issues relating to the abuse of vulnerable adults – for example, older or disabled people. This can be particularly the case in relation to financial abuse where somebody who is unemployed (and therefore living on a low income and with the consequent psychological effects of that) may be more likely to capitalize on opportunities to gain financial advantage unfairly from someone who is in a very limited position to prevent that from happening.

Voice of experience 5.2

Abuse is abuse wherever it happens. In my work I have come across it so many times and in so many guises. It sickened me at first and I thought of changing career direction, but over time I suppose I got used to it, but not in a complacent way. In fact, it made me all the more determined to make a positive difference wherever I could. There is so much I have learned about the common themes, like unemployment, low self-esteem, family tensions and so on. It's all very complicated, nothing like the simplistic picture you read about in the press.

Lynn, a safeguarding adviser in a local authority

Crime and anti-social behaviour

Crime and anti-social behaviour can also be linked to unemployment, partly because of the low-income issues already mentioned, and partly because of the self-esteem concerns that so often accompany unemployment. These factors can lead to a higher likelihood of offences being committed. While it is certainly not the case that unemployment is a direct cause of crime and anti-social behaviour, it would be naïve not to recognize it as a significant causal factor amongst others.

However, it can also work in the opposite direction, in the sense that someone with a criminal record is going to find it more difficult to find employment and thereby escape the trap of unemployment. Hari captures this point well when he comments that this is particularly the case if the offence involved drugs:

> But perhaps most important, once you have been busted for a drug offense – at fifteen or seventeen or twenty – you are virtually unemployable for the rest of your life. You will never work again. You will be barred from receiving student loans. You will be evicted from public housing.
>
> (2015, pp. 95–6)

While not all ex-offenders will face this problem to this extent, the difficulties faced by people with a criminal record are not to be underestimated.

Practice focus 5.3

Caitlin was a probation officer who had worked mainly with young offenders. She was used to dealing with school-related issues and problems to do with employment. However, there were various apprenticeship and youth employment schemes she could draw on, and quite a few of the young people she supported entered the armed forces. However, when she transferred to a new team and found herself working with adults, it was a different picture. The level of employment support was nowhere near the same for adults as it was for adolescents. Added to that were the ingrained prejudices against 'ex-cons'. She had met plenty of prejudice against young offenders, but that was tempered to a certain extent by some people's willingness to give young people a chance. She could see that helping more seasoned offenders to find employment was going to be a major challenge, while she also recognized that unemployment would only serve to make reoffending more likely.

Responses to the problem

There have been numerous attempts to tackle unemployment. For example, various governments have come up with job creation schemes of one description or another. There has similarly been considerable government investment in various industries in order to try and boost the success of various organizations so that they are in a position to take on more staff.

There have also been various retraining or skills development schemes that have tried to tackle what has often been referred to as the skills gap. For example, there may be opportunities for employment in a particular industry, but only for people who have the relevant skills. Teaching unemployed people various skills can therefore be seen as a way of reducing unemployment.

In the past two decades, there has also been a significant expansion of higher education. This not only increases employment chances, in principle at least, but also provides opportunities for people to be engaged in worthwhile activities, rather than being unemployed.

Despite the significance of unemployment, the scheme developed by the UK government to reassess the ability of people who are currently registered disabled to enter the workforce has created a number of significant difficulties for people whose disability is of such an extent that it is unrealistic for them to be expected to be in the workforce. While it is important for disabled people to have the right to enter the workforce where feasible, this is very different from pressurizing certain individuals into work that they are unable to carry out safely. This approach reflects the tendency to blame the victim mentioned earlier, the fall-back position of pathologizing people – for example, to see them as lazy and as scroungers, rather than as people who, for legitimate reasons, struggle to compete in the employment world.

This is highly problematic because, as Dorling points out:

> Research published at the end of 2015 demonstrated that for every 10,000 assessments the DWP [Department for Work and Pensions] undertakes in just one of the programmes designed to cut benefits (the Work Capability Assessment), an additional 7,020 antidepressants have to be prescribed and an additional six suicides result. In the four-year period 2010–13, some 1.03 million claimants were reassessed (3% of the working-age population). The number of suicides associated with this programme was 590, and the number of additional antidepressants prescribed was 725,000 [Barr et al., 2015].
>
> (2016, pp. 38–9)

> ➤ **C**HOICES *Constructing pathology* Pressurizing disabled people into employment has created a significant backlash.

Voice of experience 5.3

It makes me very angry to see so many disabled people lose out and have insult added to injury because of some short-sighted political dogma that expects everybody to be able to find work. Some of the people I work with really struggle just to live an ordinary life, getting up, dressing and so on, so the idea that they can hold down a job too is just absurd. Some people have no idea how challenging a severe disability can be.

Sandy, a disability rights worker

Rethinking the world of work

Overall, there have been various attempts to address unemployment, but each one of them has tended to be relatively superficial. They have tended not to recognize the significant changes in the workplace that were outlined earlier in this chapter. Returning to the work of Gorz (1999), we need to consider alternatives to the current model of employment and the assumption that we should expect everybody to be in employment and earning their living in that way. The current rates of globalization, technological advancement and other changes in working life raise the question of how long we can continue to maintain our current expectations of the role that work should play in people's lives and in relation to how societies are run. McDonough explains Gorz's view as follows:

> According to Gorz, a conception of 'real work' ought to encompass the broad creative scope of human activity and not be limited to what we do when 'at work'. Rather, socially we must move beyond the constraints and exploitation of the wage relation and beyond the wage-based society in order to achieve a system in which there is a decent livelihood for all.
>
> (2015, p. 75)

Why, Gorz asks, do we need to base our expectations on a traditional, industrial model of securing a living through paid work? As technology continues apace to make many traditional forms of work redundant, how long can we sustain a model of the economy that is premised on paid work as the primary means of meeting our subsistence needs. McDonough again offers helpful comment:

> Gorz has a radical vision which points to a society beyond capitalism. For him, it has to be recognised that 'neither the right to an income, nor full citizenship, nor everyone's sense of identity and self-fulfilment can any longer be centred on and depend on occupying a job' (Gorz 1999: 54).
>
> (2015, p. 75)

As technology accelerates its tendency to reduce job opportunities, the challenge of finding full employment will continue to get more and more difficult. The more unemployment there is in a world that equates being employed with being a decent, worthwhile human being, the more social problems there will be and the more distress and 'diswelfare' there will be for a growing proportion of the population. Consequently, Gorz is right that there will be increasing pressures over time to rethink our societal expectations of employment and explore other models of social organization.

Conclusion

Unemployment, in simple terms, is just a matter of not having a job. However, what this chapter should have demonstrated very clearly is that there is much more to it than this. Unemployment not only fuels other social problems, but also undermines self-esteem and self-respect, giving the people so affected the message that they are of little worth to society.

This is neatly summed up by a trade unionist who is reported to have said: 'the problem with being unemployed is that you never get a day off' (Corrigan, 1982).

While social policy over the years has included various attempts to address the problem, it remains a significant concern. What is also concerning is that some of the factors that have contributed to unemployment (globalization and technological development, for example) are likely to accelerate, rather than slow down, placing a much sharper focus on the question of how long we can continue to maintain an ideology of full employment while the social exclusion costs of doing so are likely to affect growing numbers of people over time.

Points to ponder

➤ What do you understand by the term 'structural unemployment'?

➤ How can unemployment contribute to an oppressive workplace?

➤ How can unemployment contribute to crime?

Exercise 5

Have you ever been unemployed? What feelings did it evoke in you? If you have never been unemployed, what feelings do you imagine it would evoke in you? How might those feelings be different after, say, over 12 months of being unemployed?

6

Housing Problems and Homelessness

Introduction

Home is such an important foundation for our well-being for virtually all of us. Not having a home or being forced to live in substandard accommodation is therefore a considerable source of distress and difficulties for anyone so affected, which is, in reality, large numbers of people. Once again, we see that such problems are not distributed at random across the population – they are closely linked to the social structure and thus to inequality. It is the poorest, least powerful members of our communities who are most likely to face such challenges – and, in some ways, the least likely to have the resources to address them.

It is also the case that these problems do not occur in a social vacuum – they are closely intertwined with other social problems. This chapter will therefore help us to develop a fuller understanding of what is involved when it comes to housing problems and homelessness, how these relate to social injustice and to other social problems. We begin by considering some key issues relating to housing-related problems.

Understanding housing problems and homelessness

In this first section of this chapter I am going to explore the issues in terms of three levels of seriousness, beginning with the most serious. This relates to people who are homeless and entirely without shelter, what are often referred to as 'rough sleepers' or 'street homeless'. I will then move on to look at the question of homelessness in terms of people who have a roof over their head, but have no security of tenure in relation to that roof. Thirdly, I will explore some issues relating to people who are not homeless, but who none the less have problems relating to their housing needs.

Street homelessness

Barry makes the point that homelessness is an extreme form of social exclusion that is connected with other social problems:

> Homelessness is the most extreme form of social exclusion (with the possible exception of being in prison) in contemporary western societies. Those with 'no fixed abode' (whether sleeping rough or in temporary shelters) have no mailing address, which is a minimum condition of participation; they have no way of exchanging hospitality (so it is hardly surprising that they hang out with other people in like circumstances) and they occupy the most despised social status. They thus illustrate strikingly the dependence of behaviour on circumstances. Faced with a bleak and meaningless existence, can it be wondered at that homeless people resort to some reliable means of attaining oblivion? 'The research will exacerbate concern that it may be almost impossible for homeless people to kick addictions to drugs and alcohol' [Summerskill and Mahtani, 2002]. So once again, instead of holding individuals responsible, we should apply the public health model and change the circumstances in which they find themselves.
>
> (2005, p. 161)

This echoes comments I made earlier in terms of the need for a more holistic perspective on social problems. It also illustrates our theme of interconnectedness, showing how an aspect of one problem (not having an address due to homelessness) can contribute to another problem (not being able to obtain employment) which can then lead to yet another problem (poverty) and possibly even to others, such as problematic drug use and/or crime.

> ➤ CHOICES *Interconnection* Housing problems are closely linked to other social problems and to social injustice.

Practice focus 6.1

Kaye was a development worker for a large national housing charity. She had previously worked as a fundraiser for another charity. But in her current post was the first time she had been actively involved in the charitable work in the field. What took her by surprise was how housing issues seemed to be so inextricably linked to so many other problems. Before taking up her post she had assumed that the focus of the work would be on housing issues pure and simple. But, by the time she got settled

▶

◄

into the job she was well aware that housing was like a focal point for so many other problems: family breakdown, domestic violence, drugs and alcohol problems, mental health concerns, poverty, unemployment and more. It made her realize how important it was to develop partnership working – that is, for workers from different fields to work together and support one another in trying to provide a seamless service and prevent citizens from being passed from pillar to post, from one support agency to another.

One of the great difficulties with addressing homelessness is the set of stereotypes that are applied to homeless people. For example, it is commonly assumed that being homeless is a simple matter of choice, rather than the result of a more complex set of circumstances. This relates to the C level of PCS analysis whereby dominant ideas become part of our everyday understanding, our so-called 'common sense'. It is an example of how complex, multilevel problems become reduced to a single, simplistic explanation and, in the process, reinforce the ideological notion that individuals are to blame for their own difficulties.

➤ CHOICES *Constructing pathology* A subtle process of blaming the victim

The consequences of rough sleeping are of major proportions. First of all, we need to consider the health impact. Without putting too fine a point on it, many people die from sleeping rough particularly in a severe winter. But, without going to this extreme, there are also other significant problems in terms of the exacerbation of existing health conditions and the development of new ones as a result of the conditions in which they are living (for example, pneumonia).

There is also the question of crime to consider. This can be seen to apply in two directions. First of all, people who are homeless and rootless may well have to rely on crime in order to survive – for example, to steal food that they are not able to pay for by conventional means. However, the other side of the coin is that people who are homeless and sleeping on the street face a significant risk of being victims of crime. In fact, this is a serious problem that is often given minimal attention in the media. It does not fit comfortably with media stereotypes of homeless people.

A further consequence of rough sleeping is that a vicious circle can develop – and, indeed, often does. For example, as we have noted, in order to get a job it is necessary to be able to provide an address. But, if a person does not have an address because they are homeless, this can make it

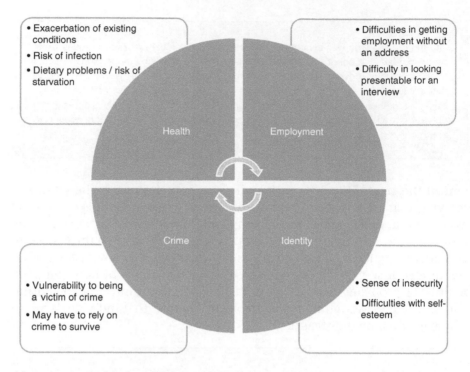

Figure 6.1 The consequences of rough sleeping

difficult, if not impossible, for them to find employment. Similarly, being homeless can lead to the escapism associated with problematic drug use becoming more appealing, but such use will then make it more difficult to break out of the trap of homelessness. There is therefore a further vicious circle to be contended with.

We should also not forget that people who are homeless are likely to be vulnerable, not only because of their housing status, but also because of the range of reasons that commonly contribute to homelessness in the first place: family breakdown, mental health problems, trauma, drink and drugs problems, and so on. As Isaacs explains:

> There are also particular personal problems that rough sleepers tend to suf-fer from that distinguish them from the majority of homeless people. Rough sleepers are often drug addicts and alcoholics. They may have mental health problems too. In a sense, the fact that rough sleepers are on the streets is not primarily a problem of not having a home, but it is a condition brought about by much more deeply rooted personal issues.

(2015, p. 58)

They are also deeply rooted *social* issues.

Voice of experience 6.1

A lot of people say to me that my job must be depressing, working with homeless people all the time, but I don't find it depressing at all. It's certainly not an easy job, but when you get to know what people have been through, you can't help but want to do something positive, something that can make a difference. And, I'll tell you what, it certainly makes me appreciate what I have got going for me in terms of a home, a stable family and a steady job.

Mike, a hostel worker

The psychological and spiritual consequences of rough sleeping should also be taken into consideration if we are to develop an adequate understanding of the problem. The implications in terms of self-esteem and the challenge of maintaining a positive identity are both profound and far reaching. Similarly, imagine the challenges involved in maintaining a sense of security and a feeling of belonging to your society when you do not have a roof over your head. Add to this the stigma and discrimination and we begin to get a picture of how existentially challenging being homeless is.

Insecure housing

Insecurity of tenure is also a form of homelessness. That is, while the common sense tendency is to think, in general terms, of a homeless person as someone who is literally sleeping in the open, there are also significant numbers of people who are in hostels, in temporary accommodation that they have no right to remain in, or who are what is often referred to as 'sofa surfing' (that is, they are relying on favours from friends or relatives to prevent them from becoming rough sleepers).

Having insecurity of tenure is a significant factor in terms of the insecurity, confidence and self-respect that we have discussed in earlier chapters. When we add to this the feelings of powerlessness that can come from having no security of tenure, we can see that this is a situation that is highly significant. Unfortunately, there can be a marked tendency to downplay the significance of this, because it is assumed that someone who has a roof over their head (even if they have no right to that roof) does not face serious problems. What we need to appreciate, then, is that homelessness is much more of a problem than is generally understood or presented by the media.

One of the main reasons for homelessness is generally assumed to be the lack of housing availability. However, Dorling (2015a) makes the point that

Practice focus 6.2

Chloe was a local authority housing officer covering a mixed area, with pockets of significant deprivation rubbing shoulders with some very high-value property areas. When she started the job, she assumed that the long waiting list for housing was down, purely and simply, to a shortage of available flats and houses. She felt the solution was down to the government investing more in the provision of social housing. However, one day a comment from someone on the waiting list made her rethink. One of the applicants became upset when she realized that she was still a long way from the top of the waiting list. She started complaining vehemently about all the houses in the area that were not being occupied, that were just, as she put it 'toys for the rich to play with'. This was something Chloe had not considered before, but it certainly gave her food for thought.

what is more significant is not so much the lack of availability of housing, but its distribution and its use as an asset in terms of wealth management. He explains that, in absolute terms, there is no shortage of housing stock. The problem comes from the availability for those who need it, because so much of the housing stock is not in use for its intended purpose. This is because it is worth more as a property asset to its owners than it is as a source of rental income, particularly in those areas where property prices rise quickly.

What also contributes to homelessness is the question of 'unaffordability'. This can be related to the problem of debt mentioned in Chapter 4, whereby a person's financial problems can spiral into a situation in which they are no longer able to pay their rent or meet their mortgage repayments and they are consequently evicted. The house price rise that has been the result of houses being seen as assets, rather than as homes, has meant that attaining the first rung of the housing ladder becomes harder to achieve, if not impossible. This is illustrated by the fact that so many people are now leaving the family home at a much later age than was traditionally the norm, because it takes so long for them to find a way out of their home circumstances and on to the housing ladder (in terms of saving for a deposit, for example, and/or reaching a stage in their career where their salary is sufficient to fund a mortgage).

Substandard housing

In addition to the problems related to homelessness, there are, as I mentioned earlier, problems relating to the quality and suitability of existing housing accommodation. This can be as the result of poor conditions, such as dampness, that can exacerbate health problems (asthma, for example) and lead to damage to cherished belongings, and so on. We have again to recognize the psychological and spiritual consequences of this in terms of any sense of insecurity that can arise from it. Not having adequate accommodation can be seen as a form of social exclusion.

Another problem can be overcrowding, where there is literally a roof over people's heads, but, for whatever reason, there is insufficient space for the individual's or family's needs. This leads to a lack of privacy and personal space, and the family tensions involved can at times contribute to family breakdown.

Voice of experience 6.2

Every couple that comes to us is different; they all have their own particular issues. But that doesn't mean that there aren't common themes that keep coming up. One of them is poor housing. We see so many couples who are in housing that is just not right for them. It creates all sorts of tensions, leaves people feeling miserable and struggling to cope. That's enough to put a strain on any relationship, but where there are already cracks in the relationship housing stress can be the last straw.

Marie, a marriage guidance counsellor

There are also health issues to consider – for example, in terms of infection rates and the overall effects on the immune system of living in stressful circumstances. When we add to this picture the question of mental health, we can see that overcrowding is quite a significant problem. Where people are struggling with emotional and/or spiritual challenges, not having space for themselves can mean that they have no safe haven, nowhere to retreat to when things are getting too pressurized.

What is important to acknowledge is that poor housing conditions are not distributed equally across the social spectrum. What will tend to happen is that there will be a clustering of problems in what have come to be known as problem estates or 'sink' estates. Poor housing can indeed be in isolated pockets, but also whole neighbourhoods associated with severe housing problems have arisen in various parts of the country. These then become 'breeding grounds' for other problems for some of the reasons already outlined.

Housing ideology

In terms of the causes of housing problems and homelessness, a key factor is the ideology of 'a nation of homeowners' put forward by Margaret Thatcher in the UK. She introduced policies that allowed council tenants to buy their properties at highly subsidized rates. While this was a boon to the individuals and families concerned, one detrimental consequence of this was that social housing came to be in short supply for those who could not afford to buy, and the existing stigma relating to 'council housing' became even greater. Housing that was already associated with low-status families (people who could not afford to buy their own home in the private housing market) came to be seen as associated with even lower status families (people who could not even afford to buy highly subsidized council housing).

Such policies reflected a neoliberal ideology (minimizing the role of the state – in this case, in the form of council-provided housing stock) premised on the assumption that owning a home is to be preferred to renting one. The fact that this assumption tends to go unquestioned, uncritically accepted as a normal or natural approach to adopt, indicates that this is ideology at work. The fact that many other countries (Germany, for example) have approaches to housing that are not biased in favour of ownership shows that there is an implicit value judgement underpinning the 'nation of homeowners' rhetoric.

> ➤ CHOICES *Counterfinality* The 'nation of homeowners' policy has created and exacerbated a range of other problems

Added to this, the current tendency for housing to be seen as an investment resource, rather than primarily as a source of homes for people, increases the difficulties. There is also the problem of private sector profiteering to consider. One of the implications of the nation of homeowners and the consequently significantly reduced availability of social housing is that it subsequently produces a greater reliance on private sector rental accommodation for people who cannot afford mortgages. Although there is some degree of rent control, it is still possible – and quite common – for rents to be at high levels that many people cannot afford; can afford only by making sacrifices in terms of their quality of life; or manage to afford by getting into debt.

This needs to be understood in the context of the point made by Jones (2015) who highlights that a significant proportion of MPs are private landlords: a quarter of Conservatives; 15 per cent of Liberal Democrats and 12.5 per cent of Labour (www.insidehousing.co.uk/quarter-of-tory-mps-are landlords-says-research/6524104.article).

The welfare state focus on ensuring that, as far as possible, the basic needs of all citizens are met can therefore be seen to have been largely replaced by a neoliberal approach that reduces public service protection for the least powerful groups, while creating significant profit opportunities for the wealthy few.

Consequently we can see that neoliberalism has (at least) two detrimental effects: (i) it means that there is limited (and more stigmatized) social housing for people who cannot afford to buy; and (ii) where people come to rely on the private rental sector, they are faced with high rent levels (and higher profits for the landlords, thereby contributing to further inequality).

> ➢ CHOICES *Over-reliance on the market* A market focus in housing puts profit before meeting citizens' housing needs.

When it comes to the consequences of these problems, one of the major ones is the sense of existential insecurity that is generated. Such psychological and spiritual consequences in terms of self-esteem, confidence and the challenge of sustaining a positive identity are not insignificant. Linked to these issues are behavioural responses that can prove to be problematic in some circumstances – for example, the problematic alcohol or drug use, aggression and/or other forms of anti-social behaviour that often arise when people are personally and spiritually diminished by the negative social circumstances that are forced upon them.

> ➢ CHOICES *Spiritual/existential implications* 'Home is where the heart is', so it is not surprising to note that housing problems affect people profoundly.

Practice focus 6.3

Lisa was a chaplain in a hospital that covered some notorious 'sink' estates. She had previously worked in a highly rated university and so the difficulties she was used to dealing with were mainly the problems of affluence. Now, however, she faced a very different picture. On a daily basis she came face to face with serious social problems and major personal challenges for the people she was trying to support. What she could see in particular were the spiritual challenges involved. How, she thought, did so many people in such straitened circumstances manage to hold themselves together? She could also see how some people didn't manage to hold themselves together and she had to work very hard to help them through some very spiritually challenging experiences.

How housing problems and homelessness affect, and are affected by, inequality

First of all we need to consider the significance of poor housing quality and its effects as they relate to inequality. One of the major consequences is the reduction of life chances or opportunities for people whose life is already limited in various ways for other reasons. This means that people living in poor-quality accommodation can feel trapped in a world of social exclusion.

Stigma

Supplementary to this is the stigma associated with social housing. As mentioned earlier, there has always been some degree of stigma associated with 'council housing' deservedly or not, but since the ideology of a nation of homeowners came to the fore, the availability of social housing has been severely restricted, one of the consequences of which is that the stigma associated with social housing has unfortunately increased. This 'postcode prejudice' can again create a vicious circle in which such stigma acts as a barrier to social advancement, thereby reinforcing a sense of low worth and powerlessness. In such circumstances people can feel trapped and therefore not highly motivated to make positive changes where possible. The next phase of the cycle can then be for such people to be demonized and stereotyped as feckless and lacking commitment to doing something positive with their lives (Jones, 2012).

Ethnic group differences

In terms of inequality, a further factor to consider is that there is clearly a disproportionate effect on minority ethnic groups in terms of housing and homelessness. This can be a combination of lower incomes and the prevalence of racism. Finney and Harries (2015) highlight, in relation to the housing circumstances of minority ethnic groups, that:

➤ There are stark and persistent inequalities in housing tenure and density of occupation (that is, higher levels of insecurity and overcrowding); and

➤ Between 1991 and 2011 the proportion of Indian, Pakistani and Black Caribbean people relying private renting more than doubled.

These are just some of the examples of housing inequalities that are not simply class based (in terms of income levels), but also relate to differences in housing resource distribution across ethnic groups.

These factors are worthy of much fuller consideration than we are able to give them here, but it is worth emphasizing that this is a sad, but clear, example of how housing and homelessness problems are not distributed evenly, but have a much stronger effect on certain groups in society – mainly the least powerful groups.

Discrimination in employment

There are also issues relating to discrimination in employment to note. I have already mentioned the difficulties of finding employment for a person who does not have an address, but there is also discrimination due to having a certain address – that is, one that is stigmatized and devalued in some way. This can then create yet another vicious circle whereby people are trapped in a low-income environment and thereby faced with the challenges of the attendant problems.

Ideological assumptions that people who face social problems are responsible for their own difficulties can lead to negative, stereotypical assumptions being relied upon in recruitment processes. Of course, this will not happen in every case, but it would be naïve to go to the other extreme and say that it never happens.

> ➤ **CHOICES** *Constructing pathology* Assuming that people are responsible for the social problems they face adds insult to injury.

Debt

Returning to our subject of debt, there is also the problem of negative equity to consider. Because of the use of housing as an asset in terms of wealth management, the escalating house price rises have produced a situation where many who people bought their home at an inflated rate now find themselves in circumstances where they have negative equity – that is, their home is now worth less than the mortgage they had to invest in to buy the property in the first place. This can be a major source of debt problems, and has therefore created various difficulties associated with that, both financial and psychological.

In sum, then, we should be able to see that there are significant imbalances in terms of the adequacy and quality of housing; issues relating

Figure 6.2   Housing problems

to tenure and security; and access to amenities. In a nutshell, housing is an aspect of social policy that reflects considerable inequality and discrimination.

How housing problems and homelessness affect, and are affected by, other social problems

We could explore a wide range of potential links in this section of the chapter, but I am going to limit myself to three in particular. The first of these is that of crime and anti-social behaviour.

Crime and anti-social behaviour

There are clear and well-established links between housing problems and crime. The two tend to reinforce one another – that is, there is likely to be more crime in those areas associated with poor-quality housing and poor-quality housing is likely to be a significant causal factor in terms of crime and anti-social behaviour.

This is not to say, in a simplistic way, that housing problems 'cause' crime, but they are clearly among the key factors. Housing difficulties affect health, employment and earning power, self-esteem, security, family relationships and various other important aspects of life. Crimes are committed for a wide variety of reasons, but the disadvantages associated with being homeless or in inadequate housing are no doubt part of the picture in very many cases.

Alcohol and drugs

There is also the problem of alcohol and drugs to consider. Clearly, the pressures and tensions associated with housing difficulties can be linked very firmly with issues of escapism. It takes very little effort to imagine how appealing substances that distort reality and create a sense of euphoria are likely to be for people who have to wrestle with homelessness or poor-quality housing. This is not, in any sense, intended as a justification for problematic drug use, but, rather, a recognition that drug-related escapism is likely to appeal to many people when they are faced with such huge hardships and struggles.

Voice of experience 6.3

Trying to keep young people off drugs is a big part of my work. I'm really committed to it because I have seen the harm that can be done, the sheer devastation that comes with dependency. But, on the other hand, I can see how easy it is for young people from bad areas to get involved in doing drugs. You've got all the crap they have to deal with on the one hand and the good feelings, the tension release and the feeling of belonging to a subculture on the other. It's so sad that so many people get into drugs, but it's not surprising really.

Ayotunde, a youth worker

Nor should we forget the question of availability ('opportunity pathways', to use the technical term), in the sense that drug dealers are much more inclined to target those areas of poor quality housing where they are likely to make far more sales than trying to ply their wares in leafy suburbs (although this is not to imply that drug problems are limited to housing problem areas).

Destruction of habitat

A further link in terms of social problems is with the destruction of habitat. The development of ghettos and sink estates has had major consequences when it comes to the use of natural resources. The 'concrete jungles' that emerged from the 1960s and the rehousing plans of that era are testimony to the disrespect to the natural environment that has become a common factor. Also, the use of property as a financial asset means that there is then pressure to build more accommodation, often on greenbelt sites, when this is not necessary if we accept Dorling's argument about the current distribution of housing stock (Dorling, 2015).

> ➤ CHOICES *Counterfinality* Mass demolition of 'slum' areas in the 1960s resulted in large numbers of high-rise tower blocks, many of which became significant problem areas.

Responses to the problem

The primary response has been for there to be a plea for greater house building. However, as Dorling has already highlighted, the problem is not in the availability of housing stock, but in terms of the difficulties of accessing it, because so much of the housing stock is not in use as homes due to its higher value as a financial asset to those in the upper echelons of the financial income bracket.

Until that situation changes, the development of more housing will at best alleviate the problems, rather than address them more holistically. However, in doing so, as I have already suggested, this will contribute to other problems, such as the destruction of habitat. It is therefore clear that a considerable rethink of housing and homelessness as a social problem area is very much needed.

Conclusion

'There's no place like home', the saying goes. For many people that statement has a high degree of poignancy. There are many people who have no home at all; they sleep wherever they can. There are many others who have a roof over their head, but do not have a home they can call their own; they are relying on the good will of others and have little security in a legal or a psychological/spiritual sense. And there are many, many more who have a home, but it is one that has huge problems associated with it – poor conditions, overcrowding, poor amenities and so on.

We have seen that these problems relate closely to other social problems, creating various vicious circles that can be very destructive. But, significantly, what we have also seen is that these problems are firmly rooted in inequality. Part of the development of the welfare state was the idea of 'homes fit for heroes' in recognition of the poor housing conditions (and associated health problems) that became apparent in World War II. What we have now, for the most part is a neoliberal state approach rooted in the idea of homes fit for those who are wealthy enough to afford them.

Points to ponder

➤ Why is the housing problem not simply a matter of demand exceeding supply?

➤ What psychological impact is homelessness likely to have?

➤ How might housing problems and crime affect each other?

Exercise 6

What possible options might be open to a government to address housing-related problems? Please list as many as you can. What differences might the political ideology of that government make to what options are chosen by them?

7

Crime and Anti-Social Behaviour

Introduction

Crime is a major social problem in terms of the harm it can do to individuals, families, groups, communities and even whole societies. It can range from relatively minor infringements of the law to mass murder. Anti-social behaviour is a relatively recent addition to the crime terminology and refers to those behaviours that are on the fringe of the crime seriousness spectrum, but which can none the less make some people's lives a misery.

Understanding crime and anti-social behaviour

The topic of crime and anti-social behaviour brings us firmly back to the idea of social construction. This is because these matters are very clearly socially constructed – that is, they are determined within the context of social norms.

Social variations

One example of this is the fact that crime is culturally and historically variable. For example, there are significant variations in terms of what is regarded as a crime. Some countries forbid particular activities and count them as crimes (for example, homosexual behaviour), while they are perfectly legal in other societies. There are also significant variations in terms of penalties. For example, the use of marijuana in some contexts may result in a fairly minor penalty, if any at all, whereas in others the consequences can be very severe, resulting in imprisonment. As Croall explains: 'While often linked to criminal law, activities legally defined as crime change over time, and what people perceive to be "criminal" is dependent on a cultural context' (2012, p. 179).

➤ CHOICES *Social construction* There are significant differences across societies and over time in terms of what is deemed to be a crime.

There are also variations in the reporting of crime. This variation can come from citizens themselves in terms of which crimes are reported to the police. For example, in a high-crime area people may not bother reporting crimes if they feel that the chances of any redress are limited, or they feel that there may be reprisals if they do bring a crime to the police's attention and a local person is convicted. But, there will also be variations within the police system in terms of which crimes are seen as worthy of detailed recording and others which do not appear in the statistics. Croall points out that these can not only distort formal statistics, but also skew how policy responses to crime are viewed and evaluated: 'Official statistics about crime are therefore notoriously unreliable (Maguire, 2007; Croall, 2011) although they are often, misleadingly, used as an indicator of the success or otherwise of policies' (2012, p. 180).

We should also not forget about the question of moral panics and folk devils discussed earlier. Consideration of these issues needs to include the focus on the distortion of risk I identified – that is, the way in which certain criminal behaviours can receive more or less attention, depending on variations in media coverage and the extent and intensity of attention given to them. These media distortions can then affect how certain crimes are viewed, both in general terms and specifically in terms of the level of risk involved.

Further social variations are linked to the effectiveness or otherwise of sentencing practices. While some approaches may produce a reduction in crime, the reliance on, for example, imprisonment as a major sentencing option is highly dubious, as the research consistently indicates a relatively low level of effectiveness in terms of rehabilitation and reduction in offending (Roeder et al., 2015).

White collar and corporate crime are aspects of the crime picture receive relatively little attention, but we should not exclude them from our overview of crime as a social problem. The way crime is presented in the media and through other channels is biased towards certain types of crime. There is relatively little emphasis, for example, on corporate fraud or other such issues, compared with an emphasis on what could be called working-class crime. Jones highlights the discrepancy between these different types of crime:

British prisons are full of people from deprived backgrounds, mostly suffering from mental distress: over 6 in 10 male prisoners and 5 in 10 female prisoners suffer from at least one personality disorder, according to the Prison Reform Trust. Benefit fraud – costing an annual £1.2 billion, or 0.7 per cent of social security spending – is treated as a despicable crime, while tax avoidance – worth an estimate £25 billion a year – is even facilitated by the state, with accountancy firms that promote such tax avoidance seconded to government to draw up tax laws.

(2015, p. xv)

This further reinforces the idea that crime as a social problem, as presented to the public, is very different from the reality on the ground, as it were.

> ➤ CHOICES *Social construction* How problems are perceived depends on social processes of definition.

It should be clear, then, that these variations add up to a complex picture that is far from straightforward. So-called common sense ideas about crime are therefore to be treated with some degree of criticality and scepticism.

Alienation

In terms of trying to make sense of the causes and consequences of crime, it is important to consider issues such as alienation and disaffection. This brings us back to the concept of social exclusion; if people feel that they are not valued as part of their society, then their engagement with that society will be limited. This can result in crime and/or anti-social behaviour where there is a lower level of commitment to the social order. The same issues of alienation and disaffection can also lead to an acceptance of, and resignation to, crime and anti-social behaviour. For example, as mentioned earlier, people may not report issues to the police or other authorities because they have come to an acceptance that there is little that can or will be done in response to such problems – particularly in high-crime areas. This means that the psychological effects of crime can work both ways: both cause and consequence of disaffection.

In considering alienation, we should also give some thought to the issue of powerlessness. Coleman and Ferguson make the important point that, while power corrupts, so too does powerlessness:

Rosabeth Moss Kanter reminds us that it is not just power that corrupts. Relative powerlessness can also corrupt by increasing "pessimism, learned helplessness, and passive aggression".

(2014, p. 30)

Practice focus 7.1

Yasmin was a youth justice worker in a multidisciplinary team. She was asked to supervise a student on placement, which she was happy to do. The student was given a small number of cases to manage under Yasmin's supervision. Yasmin was also encouraged by the university tutor to set up some sort of project for the student to engage in. Yasmin was quite interested in media representations, so she asked the student to prepare a project report comparing and contrasting how crime issues were presented to the public by the media with what he was learning about crime on the placement. This proved to be a really good idea as the student embraced the idea enthusiastically and came up with a really interesting report that highlighted some major differences between the media rhetoric and the criminal justice system reality. Yasmin decided she would set a similar project for any students she supervised in future.

When we are addressing issues of power and powerlessness, once again we are engaging with complex issues, far removed from the media representations of crime which tend to be largely oversimplified.

The wider picture

What also is of significance in terms of media coverage of crime is the way that the major emphasis is on crime carried out by individuals (and normally individuals within certain social groups) with relatively little emphasis on wider issues of crime. Thus, issues related to organized crime, gangs and, of course, the corporate crime mentioned earlier receive little or no coverage. We therefore need to understand that crime is a much bigger, wider issue than is generally portrayed. There is an undue emphasis on individual, working-class crime to the point that many people conceive of crime primarily, if not exclusively, as an activity limited largely to working-class individuals – a perception far removed from the reality.

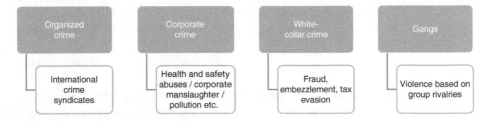

Figure 7.1   The wider picture

Anti-social behaviour

Anti-social behaviour is certainly not new as a phenomenon, but it is a relatively new term in the criminal justice field. It refers to behaviour that is not sufficient to be treated as a full-scale crime, but sufficiently troublesome to warrant a police and criminal justice system response. Rodger (2013) refers to it as 'incivility'. Similarly, Davie (2014) uses the term 'social rowdyism'.

More formally, the Anti-social Behaviour, Crime and Policing Act 2014 defines it as:

(a) conduct that has caused, or is likely to cause, harassment, alarm or distress to any person,

(b) conduct capable of causing nuisance or annoyance to a person in relation to that person's occupation of residential premises, or

(c) conduct capable of causing housing-related nuisance or annoyance to any person.

(p. 2)

On the one hand, the significance of anti-social behaviour should not be underestimated. While some people see it as 'crime-lite', this is misleading as being on the receiving end of ant-social behaviour can be extremely distressing and even traumatizing. From my professional practice in various communities over a number of years I was made very aware of how anti-social behaviour could make some people's lives a misery, in some cases leading to self-harm or even suicide. I also saw how it could contribute to mental health problems and, especially, to exacerbating existing mental health conditions.

On the other hand, however, the focus on anti-social behaviour has had the effect of criminalizing certain forms of behaviour, giving many people criminal records, which, as we shall see below, can lead to problems gaining or sustaining employment. As Croall comments:

The introduction of Anti-Social Behaviour Orders (ASBOs), for example, effectively criminalised a whole range of incivilities', not hitherto regarded as crime, which were predominantly associated with areas of social housing (Burney, 2009).

(2012, p. 184)

While anti-social behaviour is clearly an issue that merits attention, given, its detrimental effects, we need to be cautious about attempted policy responses that have negative consequences – not least the reinforcement of stereotypes of working-class communities (Jones, 2012).

> ➤ CHOICES *Counterfinality* Attempts to address problems can sometimes lead to new problems.

How crime and anti-social behaviour affect, and are affected by, inequality

The classical sociologist, Emile Durkheim, was interested in the issue of crime, but instead of asking the usual psychological question of 'What causes crime?', he turned it on its head and looked at it from a sociological perspective. This led him to ask 'Why do people *not* commit crimes for the most part?' (Durkheim, 2014). If crime can lead to advantages (financial gain, for example), then what is it that stops the majority of people from committing crimes most of the time? He therefore questioned individualized explanations of crime and helped us to understand that we need to look more holistically, at not only crime and anti-social behaviour, but also social problems in general.

Discrimination

This more holistic perspective introduces the significance of inequality. If we are to develop this wider, sociologically informed perspective on crime, then we need to take account of inequality and discrimination. This takes us back to the topic of alienation and disaffection. It is not too difficult to work out that these can arise from discrimination and can also contribute to discrimination. These are therefore very important concepts in helping us to understand the links between crime and anti-social behaviour, on the one hand, and inequality and discrimination on the other.

Voice of experience 7.1

Traditionally probation training included a strong emphasis on discrimination, especially racism, but a lot of people high up in the criminal justice system didn't like that, so we took a lot of flak over it and were put under pressure to tone it down. But, in reality, you can't equip people to work in the criminal justice system without getting them to understand the significance of discrimination.

Pat, a training officer in a probation service

Jones also alerts us to differential patterns in sentencing and decision-making processes about who is prosecuted, patterns that reflect considerable discrimination. He puts it succinctly as follows:

Steal bottled water and end up in prison for six months. But help push the world into the worst economic crisis since the 1930s and expect to face no legal sanctions whatsoever.

(2012, p. xxi)

The topic of such corporate crimes and how they are presented in the media will also reflect significant inequality. For example, newspapers that are owned by large-scale corporate bodies are less likely to focus on corporate crimes than they do on the crimes of less powerful individuals in a wider range of social circumstances.

Further discrimination can be seen in the impact of crime. All sectors of society are potential victims of crime, but while more affluent groups may possess more and better items worth stealing, it is actually poorer groups who are more plagued by crime, partly because they are less well equipped to protect themselves (Croall, 2007).

Added to this is the discrimination apparent in relation to how the legal system operates. As Croall comments:

there are clear indications that lower-class suspects and defendants are disadvantaged in relation to legal representation, making credible representations in court and receiving more interventionist sentences. In some respects the more affluent can 'buy' themselves out of heavier sentences, illustrated in aspects of monetary penalties.

(2012, p. 184)

Finally, in terms of discrimination, there is the question of the use by the police of the stop and search procedure, usually but not always, when a crime is suspected. Drawing on official statistics, Jones (2015) reports that black people are six times as likely as white people to be stopped and searched. It was also found that, in the West Midlands, under the Public Order Act 1994, a black person was 28 times more likely to be stopped and searched than a white person. This should leave us in no doubt, then, that the criminal justice arena is not a discrimination-free zone.

Practice focus 7.2

Ross was a youth justice worker in a busy inner-city office. He had been brought up in a rural area that was predominantly white in population. His professional training had covered racial discrimination issues and he felt they were important. However, as he had no direct personal experience of dealing with racial discrimination issues, he did

▶

◀

not feel confident in addressing such matters. Consequently, he had a tendency to play them down in his work. However, that all changed when, one day, he was asked to write a court report about a young man of Pakistani origin who had been arrested for drugs-related offences. It turned out that this was one case where Ross could not play down the racial discrimination issues. When he interviewed the young man concerned, he was given so many examples of direct and indirect racism, both within the criminal justice system and in his life more broadly, that he could not discount the significance of racism in this person's life. Ross realized he would need to give much more prominence to such issues in his work from now on and wondered whether there was a suitable training course he could ask to be nominated for.

The decline of community

Alienation and disaffection as a form of social exclusion can, of course, lead to a lack of social cohesion. The Joseph Rowntree Foundation report on social evils mentioned earlier identified the decline of a sense of community as one of those evils (Joseph Rowntree Foundation, 2008). This can be seen, then, as a significant factor in terms of crime and anti-social behaviour. If people do not feel that they are a valued part of a society or a community, then their faith in that community will be restricted and the likelihood of their respecting that community will also be significantly diminished. This will be particularly significant in those communities where poverty and deprivation are to the fore. In this regard, MacLeod et al. (2009) offer an important insight when they state that people from such areas are more likely to report feeling unsafe and to have concerns about crime as a growing problem. Similarly, Croall comments that: 'The clientele of police stations, courts and prisons are largely drawn from the most deprived groups and crime has a disproportionate impact on the poor' (2012, p. 179).

Social comparisons

In an earlier chapter, we discussed the significance of social comparisons, and this is again something that is quite significant in terms of inequality and crime. If people perceive that they are being treated unfairly in terms of how they are being valued in society, their reaction to that perception of injustice could well be behaviours that can be seen as anti-social. With the advent of social media and the internet more broadly, people now have access to a much wider range of information and are therefore much better placed to have information about how their communities are viewed in comparison with others. Such problems as stigma and demonization (Jones, 2012) can therefore be seen to have the potential to be even more damaging in the digital age.

Crime pathways

This links in with the idea of crime pathways. If someone is to commit a crime, then they need to have the opportunity to do so. People will have different opportunities or pathways to follow depending on their social circumstances. The opportunity to commit certain crimes will depend on where you are located in the social order. For example, corporate fraud is not something that offers a pathway generally open to manual workers within an organization. What this means is that which crime pathways are available will depend on a person's location in the social hierarchy.

This is why there has been a focus in recent years on identifying and registering people who have committed sexual offences against children, so that the information to the effect that someone's name is on that register can be used to try and deny them access to children (for example, by using the register to prevent sex offenders from being offered employment in schools or other such places where they would have access to children).

How crime and anti-social behaviour affect, and are affected by, other social problems

There is a complex web of interconnections between crime and other social problems. As in previous chapters in Part 2, we will be focusing on three problem areas in particular.

Poverty

The first link I want to make is between crime and anti-social behaviour, on the one hand, and poverty on the other. This is because crime is potentially a way out of poverty. Crime for financial gain of course can be a significant factor in terms of trying to escape from the clutches of a poverty-stricken lifestyle. Poverty can also be something that is brought about by crime – for example, as a result of imprisonment, in so far as not only the loss of a job, but also the greater difficulty in finding jobs subsequently as an 'ex con' add to the steep challenges involved. Crime can also be a cause of poverty if we consider corporate crime and the way in

Practice focus 7.3

At the last election I heard a party political broadcast where someone was arguing that we need to be tough on crime and anti-social behaviour and make sure that the punishment should fit the crime. It was quite obvious that this person was just vote catching, as he showed that he had no knowledge whatsoever of how these problems arise and what needs to be done about them. He was clearly living in a different world from the one I work in.

Ronnie, a community worker in a community enhancement project

which significant sums of money that should go into taxation and public services are hived off into the bank accounts of people who are already of a very wealthy status.

Poverty can also be significantly linked to anti-social behaviour, in so far as the stresses and strains of poverty can be understood as significant causal factors in terms of behaviours that show no respect for, or commitment to, one's community.

Abuse

Abuse can be understood as a crime in its own right – for example, when an assault is carried out on a child or a vulnerable adult. Domestic abuse also amounts to a crime in many circumstances, particularly where violence is involved.

Conversely, we can also recognize criminal gain as a potential source of motivation for abuse – particularly in relation to the financial abuse of, for example, older people.

Crime and anti-social behaviour can also be seen as significant sources of tension within families and communities, and that tension can then be a significant contributory factor to various forms of abuse, whether child abuse, abuse of vulnerable adults or domestic violence. We shall return to these points in Chapter 9.

Destruction of habitat

The question of crime – particularly corporate crime – is also relevant in relation to another social problem namely the destruction of habitat.

Illegal land deals and various other examples of corporate crime are not too difficult to find. The pursuit of profit at the expense of all other considerations can have significant detrimental implications for the environment, and therefore for our longer-term habitat. For example, the flaunting of pollution regulations by factories is not only a crime, and therefore part of a social problem in its own right, but also a contributory factor to the social problem of the destruction of habitat.

Responses to the problem

What is perhaps seen as the classic response to crime and, to a lesser extent, anti-social behaviour is imprisonment. While some nations are relatively reluctant to imprison their criminals, other nations have a much higher rate of imprisonment. Consider, for example, that the United States has five per cent of the world's population, but houses 25 per cent of the world's prisoners (www.apa.org/monitor/2014/10/incarceration.aspx)

The primary way imprisonment works in reducing crime is by keeping offenders off the streets, placed in a secure environment where their opportunities to commit crime are severely limited. But, also underpinning the idea of imprisonment is the notion of rehabilitation. This means that prison is seen not simply as a form of punishment, but also as a form of training environment to help inmates learn the necessary skills to be able to secure employment and to live a decent law-abiding life. The effectiveness of these efforts is rather mixed (Roeder et al., 2015), but it is an indication of changes historically in the prison system from what was originally purely a punitive matter to one that is now a mixture of punishment and rehabilitation.

Practice focus 7.4

Gary was a prison officer in a medium-security prison. Before entering the prison service he had always been a firm believer in a punitive approach. After he took up his post his attitude was reinforced by being insulted and sworn at by various prisoners at times – 'these people deserve what they get', he thought. However, he began to soften his approach after attending a training course on which a video was shown. The video involved hearing the stories of a number of ex-prisoners who had managed to make a huge change to their life as a result of the rehabilitation efforts made on their behalf. It was not some sort of epiphany that changed his attitude overnight, but it did open up the possibility of him recognizing more fully the value of shifting the focus from punishment to rehabilitation.

As an alternative to imprisonment, there now exists a wide range of community sentences. These include a Community Order whereby an offender may be required to contribute a number of hours on an unpaid basis to some sort of community project. This can be helpful in terms of trying to create a greater sense of social inclusion and to help offenders to appreciate the consequences of their actions. However, an approach that more firmly emphasizes the consequences of a person's offending behaviour is what is known as 'restorative justice'. This involves offenders being required to do something to, in a sense, make up for the crime that they have committed. One example of this is to work with victims of crime. For example, a professional, such as a probation officer, may be involved in bringing together the offender and their victim so that the offender can appreciate how much distress their behaviour has caused, in the hope that this will make such offending behaviour less likely in future.

Another significant response to the problem of crime and anti-social behaviour is in the field of prevention. We have seen various aspects of this over the years. For example, there have been Neighbourhood Watch schemes developed in a wide range of areas, so that neighbours will keep an eye out for any suspicious behaviour or movements within their local community. Technology has taken this a step further through the widespread use of closed circuit television (CCTV). The basic idea is similar, in so far as the intention is that greater vigilance around crime will make it less likely that crimes will be committed.

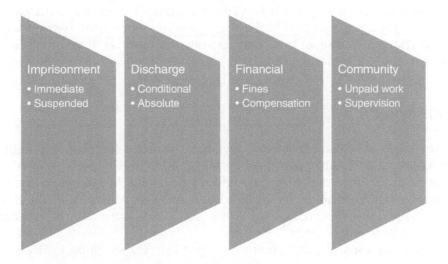

Figure 7.2 Types of sentencing options

However, two problems emerge with the increasing use of CCTV (producing a potential counterfinality). First, there is the impact on civil liberties and the erosion of privacy. It seems that, wherever we walk along an inner-city street, 'big brother' may be sitting in a remote-control room watching us. Second, there is the problem that installing CCTV in one area may help reduce street crime there, but inadvertently divert the crime elsewhere. This could result in more crime in neighbouring communities where CCTV is not available.

Voice of experience 7.2

Technology has been a mixed blessing really. On the one hand, theft prevention has become easier in a number of ways due to various developments in security equipment. But, on the other hand, there are now all sorts of new crimes that have emerged with the new technology too. Cybercrime, as it tends to be called, is just one example of that; online bullying would be another. It's difficult to keep up.

Alex, a crime prevention officer

One further important factor in terms of prevention has been improved technology. For example, car theft is now a far less common crime than was previously the case for the basic reason that stealing a car is now much more difficult due to the technology involved in, first of all, gaining entry into a car and, secondly, starting it without having the keys.

Overall, then, there have been various attempts to respond to the problems of crime and anti-social behaviour. However, once again we find that these efforts are targeted in a fairly narrow way and take little or no consideration of the wider social picture.

Conclusion

Crime and anti-social behaviour, as we have seen, are complex and highly problematic areas. Although there are huge differences between how such matters are presented ideologically and what actually happens in communities and in the systems set up to address them, it remains the case that crime and anti-social behaviour create immense distress for significant numbers of people.

Huge amounts of public money are put into the criminal justice system (consider, for example what is involved in terms of the ongoing costs of the courts, prisons, the probation service, the police and youth justice services). We can see, then, that there are significant costs – both human and financial – arising from these problems. To this we must add the costs – again both human and financial – associated with the way in which crime exacerbates other social problems.

Monahan and Maratea make an interesting point when they state that:

> Crime enjoys unrivalled prominence as a social concern. The perpetuation of our collective concerns about crime is attributable in large part to its unwavering presence in news and entertainment media. The torrent of coverage produces a vast array of patterned messages about crime, criminals, and the criminal justice system. The problem, of course, is that a great many of these messages are errant – if not downright false – and thus contribute to a flawed understanding of crime that promoted punitive solutions and ever more expansive social control policies.
>
> (2013, p. 226)

This reflects the gap already identified between the ideology and the reality. While that ideology remains to the fore, the focus will continue to be a narrow one that does not do justice to the complexities involved.

Points to ponder

> In what ways does crime vary from place to place and through history?

> How might the decline of community contribute to crime?

> In what ways might the media distort perceptions of crime and anti-social behaviour?

Exercise 7

I have used the term 'high-crime area' in this chapter in the sense that it is usually used. However, what difference would it make to our understanding of crime if we were to describe corporations and financial institutions as 'high-crime' areas? What issues does this raise for crime as a social problem?

8

Abuse

Introduction

In this chapter I am going to focus on three particular types of abuse, namely child abuse, the abuse of vulnerable adults and domestic abuse. Although these three different forms of abuse are quite distinct in a number of ways, they also have much in common. All three of them create significant harm and distress, generally for people who are vulnerable in some way – indeed the exploitation of vulnerability and the abuse of power involved is a central feature of abuse.

Understanding various kinds of abuse

Of course, there is no simple or straightforward cause of something as complex as abuse. Rather, it arises from a multifaceted set of interacting factors. Similarly, the consequences of abuse are many and varied. Our discussion here is therefore far from comprehensive, but it should provide at least a foundation of understanding to be built on over time. I begin by exploring some key issues underpinning the phenomenon of abuse.

Power

A significant theme that runs through each of these three different types of abuse is the abuse of power. For example, when we are looking at issues in relation to child abuse, what we can quickly recognize is that a key factor is the abuse of power on the part of an adult perpetrator in relation to the child or children concerned. Sexual abuse is based on the power of adults to lure or force a child into sexual activity that they are not emotionally ready for yet in terms of their psychosexual development. Similarly, physical abuse generally involves the use of physical violence against a child or young person in order to secure compliance, or as a result of an adult losing their temper and thereby abusing their greater physical strength.

Similar issues can be seen to apply to vulnerable adults. 'Vulnerable adults' is a term used in social policy to refer to people whose circumstances render them vulnerable to abuse and/or exploitation. This would include frail older people, people with physical and/or learning disabilities or people with mental health problems – that is, people who are less able to defend themselves and are therefore more likely to be targeted by unscrupulous people seeking to exploit them (Mandelstam, 2013).

What should be quite apparent is that power is a recurring theme. Whether that power is used deliberately against vulnerable adults or is misused unintentionally (through neglect, for example), the detrimental results are the same – ranging from distressing to devastating. It is no exaggeration to say that abuse can have hugely damaging effects that will often last a lifetime (see the discussion of trauma below).

A similar pattern relates to the significance of domestic abuse. This can include domestic violence. Violence is, of course, an extreme form of the (ab)use of power. However, domestic abuse can often be of a more subtle, indirect nature than direct physical violence. The abuse can arise from, for example, persistent emotional pressure. The perpetrator may be constantly undermining their partner's self-esteem, constantly creating and reinforcing pressures and tensions. In some respects, the harm done by emotional

Practice focus 8.1

Mared was a social worker who had worked for several years in a child protection team. She enjoyed the work and felt she was doing an important job. However, it was very demanding work, physically, mentally and emotionally. She reached the point where she felt she needed to do something different, something less exhausting. So, when she saw a vacancy advertised for a social work post in an older people's team, she decided to apply. She thought she would probably come back to child protection work at some point, but needed some time out from its demands to prevent herself from becoming worn down. She was successful in her application and looked forward to her new challenges. After a month in her new post she felt she had made the right decision and was feeling refreshed by the change. However, what she hadn't realized was that abuse issues would feature so strongly in her work with older people. It would not be an exaggeration to say that she was quite shocked by how often abuse issues arose – and some very severe abuse too. After years of tackling child abuse she had developed a mindset that equated abuse with children, and so getting used to the idea of elder abuse was going to take a little time.

abuse can be more severe and longer lasting than physical abuse. It can destroy confidence and create a sense of (misguided) guilt: 'I deserve this. I am not worth anything better. It's my own fault for being so weak'.

Emotional abuse can also engender far less support, mainly because it is less visible. Perpetrators will often be skilled enough to make sure that their abusive comments are not witnessed by others: sweetness and light when there is anyone else present, but a harsh and cruel bully when there is no one else around. Sadly, some perpetrators of physical abuse are also skilled enough to hide their tracks – for example, by making sure any cuts or bruises will be hidden by clothing.

While the phenomenon of 'wife beating' is generally recognized and represented in media coverage and forms part of common cultural understandings, what has received far less attention is the domestic violence that men can experience at the hands of women, or men or women can experience in same-sex relationships (Silvers, 2014). The problems of domestic abuse are therefore much broader than is generally recognized.

This theme of the abuse of power is therefore a significant one. Any attempt to make sense of abuse that does not consider the power issues involved is therefore likely to reach a far from adequate understanding of what is involved.

Undervalued groups

What is also significant in terms of the causes and consequences of abuse is the fact that, to a major extent, the people who are on the receiving end of such abuse represent undervalued groups in society. Children, older people, people with disabilities and, for the most part, women are generally less powerful within social settings. Abuse is therefore something that can be understood sociologically in terms of complex social processes, and not just psychologically in terms of individual attempts to benefit from an abusive relationship. This fits with PCS analysis, in so far as experiences at the personal level (P) are shaped to a large extent by cultural assumptions, shared meanings and taken-for–granted assumptions at the cultural level (C), dominant ideas which reinforce power relations of dominance at the structural level (S).

Munro reinforces the point that abuse – specifically child abuse from her point of view – needs to be understood sociologically:

> Child abuse is a phenomenon shaped by its social context. It is quite unlike a specific disease entity, such as measles, where it can be hoped an understanding of its cause and treatment that has universal application can be developed. A

society's views on child protection are a reflection of its view on children and families generally.

(2008, p. 5)

A key issue here is vulnerability. Abuse generally involves the exploitation of vulnerability. To a certain extent everyone is vulnerable; as human beings we are all quite fragile in many ways. However, some people are, for sociological reasons, in circumstances that render them more vulnerable, more open to abuse. Children and frail older people are two examples we have already mentioned.

Trauma

The consequences of abuse are quite severe in very many cases. For example, one consequence of abuse that is now receiving considerable attention is that of psychological trauma (Thompson et al., 2017). We are now much more aware of how child abuse, for example, can have a lifelong effect in many cases in terms of traumatic reactions on the part of the children or young people who have experienced such abuse. As we shall see in Chapter 9, we are also now developing a fuller understanding of how mental health problems in adulthood have their roots, to a large extent, in childhood trauma experiences.

Trauma comes from the Greek word for wound. It can be used in a physical sense – for example, when someone who suffers a head injury is described as having a head trauma – or in a psychological sense when a devastating experience produces potentially long-term psychological consequences ('sequelae', to use the technical term). The term 'psychological trauma' is generally used in such circumstances, but a more accurate term would be 'psychosocial trauma' as the causes and consequences are sociological as well as psychological (Thompson and Walsh, 2010).

Voice of experience 8.1

When I started working with children traumatized by abuse I was well aware from my training of how much harm abuse could do. But what I hadn't appreciated was just how many different ways abused children can express trauma destructively: self-harm, sexualized behaviour, anxiety, depression, aggression and violence, voluntary mutism, masochism, sadism – I've seen them all. It's tragic really to think how much harm comes not just directly from the initial abuse, but also indirectly from the actions of many of the children and young people concerned.

Lee, a specialist child trauma therapist

Cycles of abuse

Another consequence is what is often referred to as the 'cycle of abuse'. This refers to how children who have been abused may grow up to be abusers in adulthood, or even to abuse other children while they are still children themselves. This is quite a worrying phenomenon that has detrimental consequences for a significant number of people.

Of course, this does not apply to all abused children, but it is certainly common enough to be an area of concern. It can be linked to trauma, as one of the potential consequences of trauma is destructive behaviour towards self or others (Wilson, 2006a).

Death and physical injury

In some cases, whether our concern is with children, vulnerable adults or domestic abuse settings, the result of such abuse can be death. Sadly, there are many such cases on record (Marshall, 2012).

There will also be the significance of physical injuries to people as a result of abuse. While such incidents are clearly not as serious as those resulting in death, they can still be of major proportions, partly because of the physical harm inflicted and partly because of the psychological harm that can accompany it (a further example of the significant role of trauma).

Psychological and spiritual harm

Indeed, it is important that we should not neglect the psychological and spiritual consequences of abuse in terms of the negative effect on self-esteem and confidence and the impact on a person's sense of identity. For example, people who have been abused will commonly refer to themselves as feeling dirty or soiled or, in a sense, less than fully human. Of course, what this means for the individual concerned in terms of their quality of life and the opportunities available to them is of quite significant proportions.

We have already noted how social problems can undermine security and destroy trust. Unfortunately, abuse situations are characterized by precisely such destructive processes. We have noted that abuse is abuse of power, but we should also be aware that is it is abuse of the *person,* an undermining of our sense of who we are, how we fit into the world and whether we are safe within it. These are clearly fundamental spiritual issues.

> ➤ CHOICES *Existential/spiritual issues* Abuse generates considerable insecurity and mistrust

Depending on the circumstances, some incidences of abuse can have short-term effects and a full recovery can be achieved. However, it is sadly the case that, for many people who have experienced abuse, the harm can be permanent unless specialist help is provided (Rymaszewska and Philpot, 2006; Tomlinson and Philpot, 2008).

Situational vs planned abuse

It can also be helpful to understand the distinction between situational abuse and planned abuse. This is parallel with the distinction in criminal justice circles between manslaughter and murder. Murder is defined by having an intention to kill that is subsequently carried out, whereas manslaughter refers to bringing about death, but not necessarily in a planned or premeditated way. Similar issues can be seen to apply to abuse situations. For example, in the sexual abuse of children there may be a process of grooming whereby the perpetrator of abuse has deliberately developed a trusting relationship that can subsequently be abused in order to receive sexual gratification (another example of the abuse of power – the power of an adult to win the trust of an impressionable child). However, there may be other circumstances where abuse occurs in the spur of the moment and was not in any way planned or premeditated. Of course, the consequences of the abuse can be just as devastating, regardless of whether the abuse was planned or not, and the perpetrator remains no less responsible for their actions. However, in terms of the criminal justice response to abuse, whether it was situational or planned will often have a bearing on the court's decision with respect to sentencing options.

It is also important for practitioners in the field to be aware that not all abuse is planned. The absence of any signs of grooming does not mean that abuse is not a possibility in any given situation.

This reflects the inherent uncertainty and complexity inherent in safeguarding work of any kind, as Munro indicates specifically in relation to child abuse:

Child protection work inevitably involves uncertainty, ambiguity and fallibility. The knowledge base is limited, predictions about the child's future welfare are imperfect, and there is no definitive way of balancing the conflicting rights of parents and children. The public rightly expect high standards from child protection workers in safeguarding children, but achieving them is proving problematic.

(2008, p. 1)

As we shall note later, these are issues that are not reflected in media reporting of safeguarding interventions, particularly those by social workers.

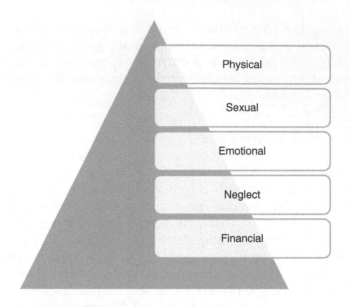

Physical

Sexual

Emotional

Neglect

Financial

Figure 8.1 Main types of abuse

Practice focus 8.2

Kevin was a police officer with extensive experience of child protection work and had received specialist training in undertaking joint interviews with social workers of alleged perpetrators of abuse. Before he undertook the training he couldn't understand why social workers seemed to get abuse issues wrong so often. Surely, he thought, it is just a matter of recognizing the signs of abuse and acting accordingly. However, partly as a result of the training itself and partly through working more closely with social workers, he came to realize that his initial views had been harsh and unfair. He now realized that abuse issues are highly complex, with no clear cut or straightforward ways of responding to the problems involved. He could appreciate how difficult it is to handle a situation when, on the one hand, you can often have abuse occurring without any signs or indicators being apparent and, on the other, you can have indicators of abuse present (bruises, for example), and yet it turns out no abuse has taken place. There is no guaranteed, scientific way, he realized, of being sure about abuse, so he now knew these situations had to be handled very carefully and sensitively.

> ➤ **C**HOICES *Constructing pathology* Professionals, as well as citizens, can be pathol-
> ogized – see Jones (2014).

How abuse affects, and is affected by, inequality

As we have seen, inequality and its attendant problems can generate considerable tensions in families and communities. These tensions can then,
in their own right, be significant factors in terms of the development of
abusive situations. For example, in terms of violence, whether domestic
violence or physical abuse of children or vulnerable adults, the level of
tension can be a key factor.

Sexism

Inequality, in the form of sexism, can also be significant, whether this
is directly in relation to sexual abuse or in the form of expectations in
relation to gender roles. For example, part of the common socialization
patterns for men in modern societies is often the assumed necessity to be
strong and tough, and this can then be, in some circumstances, a precursor to violence. In addition, the competitiveness instilled in boys and
young men can combine with a strong sense of frustration in certain circumstances to produce potentially explosive results.

Wilkinson and Pickett link violence to feelings of humiliation:

> acts of violence are 'attempts to ward off or eliminate the feeling of shame and
> humiliation – a feeling that is painful, and can even be intolerable and over-
> whelming – and replace it with its opposite, the feeling of pride'. Time after
> time, when talking to men who had committed violent offences, [Gilligan, 1996;
> 2001] discovered that the triggers to violence had involved threats – or perceived
> threats – to pride, acts that instigated feelings of humiliation or shame.
>
> (2009, p. 133)

Nor should we forget that there is also the issue of men as victims of
domestic abuse to consider. There is at present a significant gap in our
understanding of how domestic abuse can affect men in terms of their
self-esteem and identity. So, whether it is men or women who are the
recipients of domestic abuse, or, indeed, any other form of abuse, the psychological and spiritual consequences can be quite significant.

This goes some way towards explaining cycles of abuse. People who have
been humiliated by abuse may, in certain circumstances, resort to violence
because of the humiliation involved in that abuse. However, violence is not

the only response to humiliation. It can also provoke depression, social with-drawal and self-harm, even to the point of suicide.

Voice of experience 8.2

Over the years I have come to recognize more and more how significant abuse is in the mental health field – not only how it is disgusting that people with mental health problems are often subject to abuse because they are seen as odd or different, but also how, when you get to know a patient properly, you start to get a picture of how much abuse they have endured in their lives. Child abuse, bullying, domestic violence, emotional abuse – you don't have to go very far in mental health work before you come across an example of one or more of these things.

Jordan, a community psychiatric nurse

Ageism

Ageism is also a consideration worthy of our attention when it comes to exploring the relationship between abuse and inequality. This is partly because many older people are vulnerable to abuse as a result of age and infirmity in certain circumstances. For example, older people can be abused in a variety of ways: physically, emotionally, financially and even sexually. It takes little imagination to make links between the way in which older people can be abused in these ways and the second-class citizen status assigned to older people through ageist assumptions and practices.

Disablism

A similar argument can be made in relation to disablism. Discrimination against disabled people is sadly not uncommon (Oliver and Barnes, 2012), and this negative attitude towards people with disabilities can be a basic factor in terms of leaving them open to various kinds of abuse. Unfortunately, there is a long history of people with disabilities being exploited, victimized and abused in a variety of ways.

Overall, then, there are several ways in which issues of abuse can be linked with the significance of inequality in modern societies.

How abuse affects, and is affected by, other social problems

Abuse is another social problem that forms part of a complex web of inter-connections. It is therefore not too difficult to find examples of how abuse relates to various other social problems.

Poverty

I have already commented on the relationship between poverty and abuse, as there are significant linkages at a number of levels. However, it is worth reaffirming this important relationship because the inequalities associated with poverty can be significant factors in relation to the development of abuse in any of the three types of abuse we have outlined. As Stepney and Popple point out, there is evidence that: 'variations in rates of child maltreatment are associated with the strength of social support networks and general poverty levels' (2012, p. 194).

As we have noted in Chapter 4, poverty can generate considerable strain on individuals, families and, indeed, whole communities. These tensions associated with poverty can then be a significant factor contributing to the experience of abuse. When people feel that they have little to lose, then their sense of what is and what is not acceptable may in certain circumstances be challenged.

However, we have to be careful not to make two errors. First we should not assume that abuse takes place only in areas of poverty. We need to be clear that abuse occurs across all sectors of society (although the wealthy and powerful may be much better placed and more fully resourced when it comes to hiding such abuse – social workers investigating allegations or suspicions of abuse in affluent families will often find that the inquiry into the child's circumstances provokes a response from the family's solicitor). Second, we should not overgeneralize and see poverty-stricken areas as 'breeding grounds' for abuse. The vast majority of parents wrestling with poverty do not in any way abuse their children. Jones, in his important study of how people from areas of deprivation are stigmatized and demonized, reflects on how media coverage can fuel unhelpful and misleading stereotypes:

> That's not to pretend that there aren't people out there with deeply problematic lives, including callous individuals who inflict barbaric abuse on vulnerable children. The point is that they are a very small number of people, and far from representative. 'Freakish exceptions – such as people with ten children who have never had a job – are eagerly sought out [by journalists] and presented as typical,' believes *Independent* journalist Johann Hari. 'There is a tiny proportion of highly problematic families who live chaotically and can't look after their children because they weren't cared for themselves. The number is hugely inflated to present them as paradigmatic of people from poor backgrounds.'
>
> (2012, p. 24)

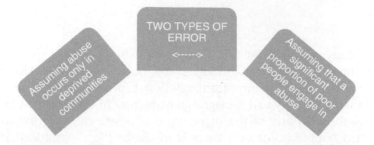

Figure 8.2   Two types of error

Problematic alcohol and drug use

We can also identify links between various forms of abuse and problematic alcohol or drug use. Alcohol and drugs can be both a cause and a consequence of abuse. For example, much abuse takes place when the perpetrator is under the influence of alcohol. On the other side of the coin, it is sadly the case that many people who have experienced abuse will then turn to drink or drugs as a way of finding solace and an escape from their unpleasant and distressing circumstances.

Practice focus 8.3

Alice was a support worker in a multidisciplinary alcohol and drugs team. A significant part of her role was working with parents – mainly mothers, as it turned out – to support them in trying to be effective parents while trying to sort out their drink or drugs problems. She saw the extremes in her work. On the one hand she saw some incredible resilience shown by some parents who seemed to cope superbly well in their parenting roles, despite having huge adversity to deal with as a result of their problematic drug use challenges. On the other hand, she saw some parents who were so 'blown away' that their ability to parent to an acceptable level – even with support – was just not anywhere to be seen. She had seen situations where it had been necessary for a child or children to be removed on a court order and placed with foster carers for their own safety and welfare. It always broke her heart when that happened, but, thankfully, the positive experiences outweighed the negative ones and she felt that she was able to do a lot of good in her role.

Mental health problems

As Jordan, in Voice of experience 8.2 highlights, mental health problems can also be associated with abuse. I have already noted the increasing recognition of the role of childhood trauma, particularly in relation to adult mental health issues (Bracken, 2002). It is not surprising, of course, to find that people who have been abused in one or more ways are more likely to be anxious and/or depressed. A person's mental well-being can easily be disrupted by the experience of abuse.

In some circumstances, mental health problems are also important factors underpinning the development of abusive situations. This can apply in one of two ways. Having a mental health problem may make somebody vulnerable to being abused. They may be seen as an easy target, for example (encompassed within the term, 'vulnerable adult'). Also, it can work in the opposite direction, in the sense that the perpetrator of abuse may have mental health problems. However, it is important not to overgeneralize and to come to rely on stereotypes here. It would certainly not be correct to say that anyone who perpetrates abuse is suffering from a mental health problem, since the situation is far more complex than that. Nor should we jump to the false conclusion that people with mental health problems are more likely to perpetrate abuse. Such discriminatory oversimplifications have the effect of making difficult situations even harder to deal with.

Responses to the problem

As far as child abuse is concerned, there have been huge investments of time and resources in efforts to protect children from abuse. There are well-established child protection procedures in place, and these are dealt with in very firm ways, in the sense that these are taken very seriously (Corby et al., 2012). This was not always the case, and nor has it been the case that vulnerable adults have experienced the same level of protection (Mandelstam, 2013). Increasingly, however, vulnerable adults are being given a similar level of protection through procedures that were initially referred to as POVA (Protection of Vulnerable Adults). The term 'safeguarding' is now generally used as a generic term to apply to protecting both children and vulnerable adults from harm. There are some significant differences between the circumstances relating to child abuse and the abuse of vulnerable adults, but there are sufficient similarities for the issues to be given a shared approach in many respects.

However, one of the consequences of the emphasis on safeguarding has been the development of a risk-averse approach. Ironically, there are now situations where efforts to address, for example, child abuse have proven to put children at even greater risk. Sadly, there are now examples of children removed from their family where there was suspicion of abuse who have subsequently been placed in foster care placements or in residential care where they have then been abused. This is an example of the counter-finality theme that was discussed earlier.

> ➤ CHOICES *Counterfinality* Taking children from one risky situation to another.

The greater awareness of abuse issues among the general public (because of media coverage presenting abuse as a moral panic) has produced a much higher level of referral to protection agencies, leading to an extremely high level of pressure on practitioners and managers in those services. This, combined with a risk-averse culture has led to a major emphasis on 'proceduralization' – that is, dealing with such matters in a rigid, standardized way (Parton, 2014). This leads Munro to argue that bureaucratic processes are no substitute for professionalism:

> trained, experienced professionals cannot be replaced with bureaucrats with sets of forms, but they can be trained to develop their intuitive reasoning skills, understand their limitations, and use more analytic skills to test and augment them.

> (2008, p. 1)

We are now seeing a much greater understanding of how abuse can lead to a traumatic reaction. There are now in place in various settings trauma recovery programmes for children (Tomlinson and Philpot, 2008).

This recognition of the significance of trauma is a welcome development, although there are dangers of trauma being medicalized. This is a point to which we shall return later, specifically in Chapter 9.

In response to the problems associated with domestic abuse, there is a well-developed network of Women's Aid refuges for women who are on the receiving end of domestic violence. Voluntary bodies in various countries are able to provide this type of support through hostel accommodation and other ways of trying to help women deal with the challenges they face as a result of domestic violence. However, such facilities for men who are victims of abuse are less well in evidence. This is a matter that has created problems in a number of places where men who have been victims of abuse have had little or nothing to rely on by way of support.

> ### Voice of experience 8.3
>
> I have often had to refer women to Women's Aid refuges, either clients or the partners of clients, but we don't have an equivalent service – well, not in this area anyway – for men who are subject to domestic abuse of any description. I suppose it is a serious issue for any man who has been abused, but for my work with offenders it is particularly tricky. On more than one occasion I have been working with someone who has been making great progress, then an abusive incident occurs, they react strongly to it, and we are back to square one with our plans to stop their offending behaviour. We need to do more about this.
>
> **Ashley, a probation officer**

There are also extensive education and therapy programmes for, on the one hand, perpetrators of abuse (so that they can be helped to tackle any abusive tendencies they may have) and, on the other, for victims of abuse to try to ensure that they recover from the traumatic experiences involved as far as possible.

Once again we find that there have been various responses to the problem, but each of these responses by and large is premised on a fairly narrow basis. Once again we find that a holistic understanding is lacking. What is more, public service cutbacks in the name of austerity have significantly reduced the resources available to address problems associated with abuse. We therefore have a long way to go before we reach a situation in which our response to abuse could be described as adequate.

Conclusion

However harmful and devastating abuse can be, we need to remember that it is none the less a socially constructed entity. As Barnshaw illustrates in relation to child abuse:

> Stephen Pfohl (1977, p. 318) demonstrated how the problem of child abuse was first identified during the nineteenth-century "house of refuge" movement, but it wasn't until nearly a century later, when pediatric radiologists took ownership over the issue and "discovered" child abuse, that social norms toward mistreating children began to change.
>
> (2013, p. 153)

In this regard we can also see the significant role of the media. For example, Ray Jones, in his important study, highlights how the media distorted their reporting of the death, at the hands of his mother and her boyfriend, of baby Peter Connelly in ways that vilified the social workers involved (Jones, 2014). In this way, it was not just the perpetrators who were depicted as 'folk devils', but the social workers involved even more so than the guilty parties. This process of persecution of the social workers went on for over a year. This is therefore a very powerful example of how what strikes a chord with the general public is not so much the immense hardships, distress and adversity brought about by social problems, but a highly distorted and discriminatory picture painted by – in this case at least – a highly unfair, unethical and grossly distorted representation of some very complex issues.

Abuse, then, needs to be understood as a multifaceted phenomenon rooted in a range of highly complex processes. Our understanding of it, and our responses to it, therefore need to be at quite a sophisticated level – far removed from the gross oversimplifications constantly fed to the general public.

Points to ponder

> Can you identify any ways in which definitions of abuse have changed over time or are different from society to another?

> How might you explain the notion of a 'cycle of abuse'?

> In what ways can the concepts of moral panic and folk devils be applied to media reporting of abuse?

Exercise 8

Why is there a tendency for media representations of professional efforts to safeguard vulnerable people from abuse to be distorted? What factors might explain this? Also, what effect do you think such distortions have on (i) the professionals concerned; and (ii) the people who are on the receiving end of abuse?

9

Mental Health Problems

Introduction

Where someone experiences a mental health problem it can be quite a challenge not only for that particular individual, but also for their family and friends and possibly colleagues. At times, they can also be perceived as a threat to society at large. Hence their status as a social problem, rather than simply an individual problem for the individuals concerned.

Mental health problems can range from relatively minor to extremely distressing and devastating. They are therefore worthy of careful consideration. However, the subject matter is not as clear cut as it might originally appear. This is because the dominant ideology relating to mental health problems is an atomistic and pathologizing one, reducing complex, multilevel phenomena to simple matters of individual illness. To understand mental health challenges as a social problem, and to examine their relationship to social justice, we need to look critically at this dominant thinking and question its hegemony.

Understanding mental health problems

Traditionally mental health problems are seen as examples of an illness or set of illnesses, but it is important, from a sociological perspective, to examine this assumption carefully. This is because to define something as an illness has major consequences in terms of not only whether or not it is perceived as a problem (and indeed whether it is seen as a personal or a social problem), but also how any such responses to it are framed. As we noted in Chapter 2, James is one of many people to have questioned the validity of describing mental health problems as symptoms of an underlying illness when there is little or no firm evidence to support the view that what is happening when somebody experiences mental health difficulties is in some way a form of disease entity. As Stepney puts it:

Historically, UK mental health policy has been dominated by notions of care, control and cost, rather than prevention, with discourses of deviance, madness and segregation underpinning the medical model of psychiatry.

(2014, p. 308)

However, there is now a growing literature base that is highly critical of a biomedical model approach to mental distress (Bentall, 2004; 2010; Crossley, 2006; Cohen and Timimi, 2008; Tummey, and Turner, 2008; Tew, 2011; Thompson, 2011a; Cromby et al., 2013; Davies, 2013; Kirk et al., 2015). What we are encountering, then, is hegemony, the dominance of certain ideas that favour powerful groups (the pharmaceutical industry, for example) are presented as being in everybody' interests (good mental health for the nation).

> ➤ CHOICES *Hegemony* Ideas that favour particular interest groups presented as being in everybody's interest.

The social construction of mental health problems

The socially constructed nature of mental health problems can be evidenced by the way in which understandings of 'mad behaviour' have varied over time. For example, at one point what we would today call mental health problems were interpreted as evidence of demonic possession. Witchcraft has also been seen as an explanation of mental health problems in its time.

> ➤ CHOICES *Social construction* Conceptions of mental disorder vary from society to society and over time.

To many people moving away from such explanations of mental health problems and developing a medical model of 'mental illness' has been seen as a more sophisticated, scientific and humane understanding of mental health concerns. However, for many years now there has been a growing set of critical perspectives on such a medical model. Voice after voice is now questioning how wise it is to assume that the difficulties associated with mental health are directly and closely comparable to the difficulties associated with physical health.

Practice focus 9.1

Jon was a psychologist in a psychiatric clinic. Understandably, his training had helped him to focus on the psychological aspects of mental health, but he was now working in a setting where the focus was almost exclusively on biomedical issues – the talk was generally about diagnoses, treatments, symptoms and medications. This caused him some difficulties as he was more interested in psychological processes that contributed to patients' distress. What he found with some patients was that their medication made them drowsy and unresponsive, something that acted as a significant barrier to the progress he was trying to make. He felt a little bit like a fish out of water in such a strongly medicalized context. However, he was determined to do the best he could in difficult circumstances. He took every opportunity to get support from fellow psychologists elsewhere and also had a good rapport with one of the social workers in the team who was also uncomfortable with the biomedical emphasis.

Biomedical bias

In particular, a medical model focuses narrowly on biological aspects of the experience of mental disorder. A more holistic approach would also incorporate issues relating to psychological, social and spiritual factors. One of the main problems with a narrow, medicalized approach is that it rests mainly on the assumption that we can understand mental health and its associated difficulties by reference to biomedical causes alone. This can then block off our development of a more sophisticated understanding of the complex issues that a holistic perspective on mental health can encourage us to explore.

Moloney's views reflect this concern with the limitations of the dominant biomedical perspective:

> Certainly, the harmful nature of social circumstances rarely appears in the writings of psychological therapists. By contrast, surveys in the UK and elsewhere suggest that lay people from all backgrounds are more willing to place the blame for mental disturbance on worklessness, loneliness, abusive relationships, poor general wealth and material and financial hardship – in short, upon a cruel world.

> (2013, p. 59)

In a nutshell, therefore, a medical model of mental health problems confuses an explanation with an explanandum. An explanandum is something that needs to be explained. To say that a person demonstrating psychotic behaviour, for example, is ill is not to present an explanation so much as to provide something that requires explanation. This links with the oft-quoted argument that the biomedical model is based on circular logic: Why is this person hearing voices? Because they are schizophrenic. How do you know they are schizophrenic? Because they are hearing voices.

Stigma and stereotypes

What has accompanied the various explanations of mental health from demonic possession through witchcraft to illness is a strong element of stigmatization (Thronicroft, 2006). The stereotype of the 'mad axeman' is just one example of this. By and large, people who have experienced mental health problems are perceived as being untrustworthy, not to be relied upon, or unsafe – particularly around children. These stereotypical assumptions fuelled by distorted media coverage can do considerable harm to people's well-being – for example, in relation to their ability to obtain employment.

Medication and its side effects

But, it is not just the stigma associated with mental health problems that can lead to detrimental consequences. The medication used can have significant side effects and, at best, will help to contain the problems, rather than to solve them in any way. It is also important to consider how having the label of 'mentally ill' attached can result in problems associated with self-esteem and confidence, our spiritual sense of identity and such matters as housing, employment and so on.

> ➤ CHOICES *Interconnectedness* A medical model neglects the influence of wider social factors and social problems

Moloney's work can again be useful in developing our understanding. He is critical of the tendency to reduce the complexity of mental distress to a simple illness model:

> There is nothing like tablets and injections for conferring a spurious reality to the 'mental illnesses' that they are ostensibly designed to tackle. If the science of psychiatry is shaky, then this has not stopped hordes of its practitioners,

with a few psychologists for company, from stepping forward to create new forms of deviance. For the shy and the socially awkward, for the restless and the disruptive, or for those who are merely 'odd' – a host of stigmatising diagnostic labels await.

(2013, p. 1)

Davies (2013) is also critical of the tendency to apply diagnostic labels to what Szasz (2010) called 'problems of living' and what Bentall (2010) describes as 'complaints'. He relates how he interviewed key people who were involved in developing the Diagnostic and Statistical Manual of Mental Disorders (DSM – the definitive text used by psychiatric professionals to make a diagnosis), some of whom admitted that the decisions made as to what to include and what to leave out were based on subjective consensus, rather than objective fact. That is, a particular psychiatric condition is officially defined as an illness because a group of influential (biomedically trained) psychiatrists say it is!

Similarly, Kirk et al. (2015) are highly critical of the nature of the scientific research used to justify a biomedical approach. They identify significant methodological flaws, biased interpretation of data and large-scale inconsistencies in the psychiatric research and its presentation. For example, they point out that studies into the effects of pharmaceutical products tend to be presented in a biased way, with studies that show no positive effects not being published, thereby giving an unbalanced picture of the research evidence (see also Goldacre, 2013, who raises similar concerns).

Voice of experience 9.1

The mental health component on my social work degree was quite confusing. We had a guest lecturer from the Psychiatry Department who was telling us all about symptoms and diagnoses and stuff like that, while we had a social work tutor encouraging us to see mental distress (she refused to use the term, 'mental illness') in much broader terms. Now that I have a couple of years' experience under my belt I can understand it better. I can see that the psychiatry lecturer was representing the mainstream view and our tutor was urging us to look at the issues more holistically as social workers always should do.

Ally, a mental health social worker

Disempowerment

One of the other significant consequences of a medical model of mental health is disempowerment – that is, an undermining of people's sense of control over their own lives and circumstances. Tew comments on the significance of power:

> It is being increasingly recognised that the power issues are closely implicated in the onset of mental distress. Experiences of humiliation, social defeat and entrapment are often seen as precursors of mental distress (Gilbert and Allen, 1998; Selten and Cantor-Graae, 2007). People who have come to see their relationship with the world in terms of an external locus of control – seeing their lives as being largely controlled by the actions of others – are more likely to develop psychosis in adulthood (Bentall et al., 2001; Frenkel et al., 1995). Research into voice-hearing experiences suggests that it is not so much the content of voices that can be problematic, but one's perceptions of the power relations between oneself and one's voices (Birchwood et al., 2000).
>
> (2011, p. 47)

Power and control are therefore important issues when it comes to trying to make sense of mental health problems, even though they rarely feature in the mainstream psychiatric literature.

One particular consequence of the biomedical model is that it disempowers people by giving them a message that control of their circumstances lies in the hands of others – hence Tew's reference to the 'locus of control'. This refers to our perception of where control lies. Having an internal locus of control means having a strong sense of what you can control in your life. Having an external locus of control, by contrast, is to have a very weak sense of our own ability to influence our circumstances. It encourages a defeatist attitude and/or an expectation that it is up to others to address our concerns for us.

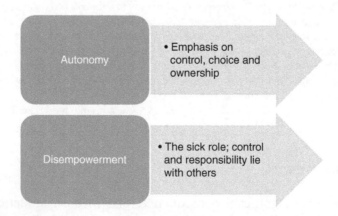

Figure 9.1 Autonomy vs disempowerment

This is very significant for people experiencing mental health difficulties. To be told that you are ill is to be informed that you are not responsible for your circumstances and to give you an expectation that it is up to other people to help you to 'get better'. The problem with this approach is that it gives a misleading message that can, in many circumstances, discourage people who are facing mental health challenges from doing anything actively about the difficulties they experience. This is not to blame people for their own difficulties, but, rather, to recognize the key role of a sense of control, agency and autonomy in addressing mental health challenges.

How mental health problems affect, and are affected by, inequality

Dorling, whose work we have already encountered, argues that inequality and social injustices can have major negative effects on a person's mental health. As he comments: 'If any reason were needed as to why injustice is harmful it is the effects that we now know the resulting inequalities have on our general mental health' (2011, p. 306).

Similarly, Moloney (2013) argues that social problems, such as poverty, economic insecurity and child abuse have come to be seen in medical terms, another example of atomism and the construction of pathology.

> ➤ **C**HOICES *Construction of pathology* Social problems come to be seen as individual frailties.

Racism

There is also a significant body of research relating mental health problems to racism. The diagnosis of schizophrenia, for example, is far more likely for people from minority ethnic groups than it is for others (Fernando, 2010). There are also many examples on record of how culturally appropriate behaviour can be misunderstood by somebody not familiar with that culture and assumed to be symptoms of a mental disorder.

Sexism

Sexism and gender-related discrimination are also significant factors in relation to mental health. For example, women are much more likely than

---

Practice focus 9.2

Rajeev was a race relations adviser in a health authority. Part of his role was to investigate complaints of racial discrimination. Each case was unique and had to be judged on its own merits, but there were also patterns that Rajeev could discern across the range of cases he had to deal with. One pattern he began to notice was that mental health issues tended to feature quite a lot. He decided to look into this further and began researching what he could find out about the relationship between mental health problems and racism. He soon found that there was a wealth of literature on the subject and clearly quite considerable concern about racial discrimination in mental health services. Consequently, he decided to speak to his manager about the possibility of setting up a working group to explore what could be done to address the issues in their authority.

---

men to report being depressed (Keyes, 2006). There are clearly, therefore, significant implications in terms of the relationship between gender and mental health problems.

James highlights the significance of gender when he explains that:

> Two of the strongest predictors of who gets depressed in a developed nation are being of low income and being a woman – the poor and females are twice as likely as the rich and males to be depressed.
>
> (2008, p. 24)

Linking depression to oppression potentially raises a number of significant issues worthy of fuller treatment than we can give them here.

Mentalism

The term 'mentalism' has not really caught on to the same extent as terms like racism, sexism or ageism. However, discrimination against people because of their mental health status is quite common and highly problematic (Thornicroft, 2006). It can affect housing, employment and public services, and leave people with mental health problems open to harassment and anti-social behaviour. Much of it stems from stereotypical portrayals of people with mental health problems that once again bear little resemblance to the reality. This relates to the stigma that was mentioned earlier and the associated stereotypes of fear.

This also links to the tendency to perceive the social problem of mental disorder in individualistic terms. Davies makes the important point that:

> Of course, the danger of underestimating the social roots of discontent is that many normal and natural human responses to social problems will be misdiagnosed as stemming from mental disorders. Once this mistake is made, suffering is then mistreated as a product of some internal pathology, while the real social problem is left intact.
>
> (2013, p. 36)

This means that a wide range of behaviours that are understandable responses to social circumstances can become constructed as symptoms of a mental illness. One example of this would be grief. Despite common misconceptions about presumed standardized ways of grieving, different people grieve in different ways (Thompson, 2012b). Some people's expression of grief can therefore be seen as 'pathological' – indeed, for many years complications in grieving were referred to as 'pathological grief'. Grief and depression are very different processes, but superficially can appear similar (Schneider, 2012). Consequently, grief can often be mistaken for depression and therefore be construed as a sign of mental illness. Similarly, behaviour that would be considered harmlessly eccentric in some circumstances can be labelled as a symptom of mental illness in another set of circumstances.

Trust and security

I have already commented on more than one occasion in this work on the significance of a sense of trust and security in relation to social justice. A society that prevents its citizens from feeling that they can be secure and can generally be trusted is problematic if that does not apply to all citizens.

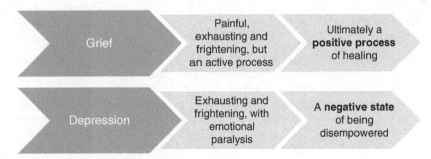

Figure 9.2   Grief vs depression

Wilkinson and Pickett make apt comment when they argue that:

Given the importance of social relationships for mental health, it is not surprising that societies with low levels of trust and weaker community life are also those with worse mental health.

(2009, p. 70)

> ➤ CHOICES *Existential/spiritual issues* Trust and security are important elements of mental well-being.

We also need to come back to the important theme of power and power relations. The term 'mental illness' implies that the emphasis will be on care, the suggestion being that people with mental health problems will be cared for by the appropriate professionals. However, a growing body of literature argues that there is a much stronger emphasis on professional control, rather than care, when it comes to the lives of people with mental health problems. For example, Pilgrim and McCranie make the important comment that:

In our case of madness, an entire state apparatus of surveillance and control is constructed to regulate its actual or imagined threat to social order. Those who are mad are picked upon when others are not. Thus we cannot address the matter of recovery from madness unless it is placed in a wider context of social justice.

(2013, p. 28)

This further encourages us to think more holistically about mental health problems, and to see them as part of a wider social canvas, rather than simply matters of individual health need.

Voice of experience 9.2

I've been involved in training a wide range of mental health professionals and volunteers over the years. I have emphasized the need to tune in to discrimination and social justice issues, because I think they are at the heart of so much of the struggles people with mental health problems face. The response to me putting forward these issues has been mainly positive, but not always so. Most people have been very open to thinking more broadly about what is involved, but some have made it clear that they are not interested in looking at mental health work in any other way than as providing help and care for sick people.

Stevie, an independent trainer

How mental health problems affect, and are affected by, other social problems

As in previous chapters, our focus now is on how mental health problems interrelate with other social problems. Once again there is no shortage of linkages to be explored, but our emphasis will be on three in particular.

Poverty

Poverty can be seen as a social problem, not only in its own right, but also as a major factor in relation to other social problems, and the issue of mental health problems is no exception. What can be seen as particularly significant is the ideological emphasis on materialism in a neoliberal society. As Barry points out:

> Tim Kasser in his book *The High Price of Materialism* does suggest that attaching happiness and self-esteem to the possession of material goods for their own sake is liable to endanger mental health: 'Contemporary American culture leads many people to work overtime and go into debt [and] ... the price of overwork and debt is stress'. [Kasser, 2002] Those who place a high value on wealth are also found, not very surprisingly, to place a low 'emphasis on personal relationships', while their 'contributions to their community decline'. [ibid p. 64] This kind of social isolation has been shown in study after study to create psychological problems.
>
> (2005, p. 183)

Emphasizing material gain in a society where many people are prevented from achieving positive material standing can be seen in many respects as a significant challenge to mental well-being.

Unemployment

There are also significant links between mental health problems and unemployment. Indeed, there is a strong argument that positive social factors, such as employment, housing and relationships are likely to make much more of a positive difference to people with mental health problems than medication can (Tew, 2011). There can be a vicious circle in which people who are unemployed can be under considerable strain that can subsequently trigger off mental health problems. Those mental health problems can, in turn, make it more likely that they will remain unemployed.

Practice focus 9.3

Serena was a social worker in a multidisciplinary mental health team. She was also a trained counsellor and was able to put her knowledge and skills to good use. However, her social work training had also taught her to think more holistically about the circumstances of clients who are facing mental distress. She had found it really useful to focus more broadly on housing, employment, finances, relationships, activities and so on, rather than just on medication. She found that this combination of a holistic, sociologically informed perspective combined well with her counselling ethos which had a strong emphasis on active listening and trying to fully understand each person's unique circumstances and their feelings about them. She saw this as a good example of what she had been taught about the need for a 'psychosocial' approach – that is, one that combines psychological and sociological insights. This avoided focusing narrowly on individual matters and losing sight of important wider issues, but also avoided losing sight of the real human being within those social circumstances.

Crime and anti-social behaviour

Another important link is with crime and anti-social behaviour. In some circumstances people with mental health problems can be the perpetrators of crime. However, there are two sets of factors to consider here. One is the point that we have already touched on, namely that stereotypes around mental health can mean that the danger of a person with mental health problems committing criminal acts will generally be exaggerated. We also need to recognize that people with mental health problems are actually more likely to be the victims than the perpetrators of criminal acts. People with mental health problems can be vulnerable in a number of ways and they can be prone to being exploited and/ or the victims of violence. Targeting the 'looney' is sadly a common enterprise in some sectors of society. The stress and potential trauma associated with being the victim of crime can then provoke further mental health problems. We are then faced with yet another vicious circle.

Responses to the problem

Since we left behind the days of witchcraft and demons, the major emphasis on mental health and its problems has been of a medical dimension. It is largely biomedical, but with some psychotherapeutic input as well, largely but not exclusively, due to the historic influence of Freud and his work on psychodynamic problems. Furedi relates this to the development of a 'therapeutic culture':

> Through the language of psychology, therapeutic culture frames the way that problems are perceived. 'The result is that social problems are increasingly perceived in terms of psychological dispositions: as personal inadequacies, guilt feelings, anxieties, conflicts and neuroses', concludes Beck [2002] ... Of course, understanding the self and the internal life of the individual is important for comprehending individual behaviour and the wider life of the community. However, a one-dimensional preoccupation with the self often leads to overlooking the social and cultural foundations of individual identity. This approach leads to a novel and specific representation of the self – one that the American sociologist John Rice has characterised as an 'asocial self' [Rice, 1996]. From the standpoint of the asocial self what matters is its internal life. The significance of social and cultural influence is discounted in favour of a narrow psychological deliberation of personal emotions.
>
> (2004, p. 25)

In terms of PCS analysis, this amounts to focusing primarily, if not exclusively, on the **P** level, while neglecting the important roles of the **C** and **S** levels.

In a similar vein, Moloney (2013) argues that a therapeutic outlook allows the power elite to place responsibility for social problems on the people who experience them – poverty, for example, is seen as the responsibility of poor people, resulting in interventions like parenting training, rather than strategies for poverty alleviation.

Voice of experience 9.3

My work basically revolves around helping communities to tackle their problems and to build on their strengths. In some ways this involves going against public opinion and the assumption that people are responsible for their own problems. People are unemployed because they are lazy, not because there aren't enough jobs to go round; people are homeless because they spent their money on booze and fags instead of paying the rent; that sort of stuff – pure prejudice about situations they really know nothing about. It's the same with mental health. It's all about pumping people full of tablets instead of looking at what life is like for people in grinding poverty who have to put up with abuse and stigma, people who have had really distressing experiences that no one has really helped them get over. I know I am biased because community work is my bread and butter, but we really do need to look more closely at what life is like in our most disadvantaged communities and pay less attention to the next wonder cure that the pharmaceutical industry will come up with.

Wynn, a community worker

In recent years we have seen a development which in some ways moves away from a medical model, but is still firmly rooted in it in some ways. I am referring to what has come to be known as the recovery model. One of the assumptions traditionally associated with, for example, a diagnosis of schizophrenia was that it was a lifelong condition. People who appeared to get better were said to be 'in remission', the assumption being that they could return to their psychotic state at any time. However, as more and more cases came to be noticed of people having psychotic episodes, but then having none further provoked an exploration of the idea of recovery. Consequently, there is now a school of thought that emphasizes that, where people have mental health problems, we should not write them off and assume that they will be lifelong conditions. There are steps that can be taken to encourage a recovery from those difficulties (Pilgrim and McCranie, 2013).

While this is in some ways a positive development, it is still located primarily in an apparent medical model, strongly implying that it is a matter of recovering from an illness. What is needed, then, is a more holistic understanding of recovery (Stepney, 2014).

I have already commented on the growing awareness of trauma as a factor and while this remains a far from mainstream approach to mental health issues, it is certainly gaining ground in terms of its credibility as a partial explanation of how and why mental health problems develop for some individuals. It will be interesting to see how this develops, as the emphasis on trauma can remain within a biomedical approach (trauma is what causes, or at least contributes to, the 'illness') or it could be used as a means of challenging a biomedical model. Much will depend on whether trauma is conceptualized in narrow, atomistic terms or viewed more holistically as a multidimensional phenomenon (Bracken, 2002, Thompson et al., 2016).

There is also the growing critique of current understandings I mentioned earlier which is steadily developing ground in terms of a large number of publications. The idea of 'anti-psychiatry' has been around since at least the 1960s and had largely been discounted by the mainstream mental health field. However, what is different today is that critiques of a biomedical approach are coming from various angles – from psychologists who are critical of the neglect of psychological factors (Cromby et al., 2013), from sociologists who bemoan the failure to take account of important socio-political factors (Rogers and Pilgrim, 2014), from within psychiatry itself (Bracken and Thomas, 2007), from ex-patient groups (who tellingly refer to themselves as 'survivors), from social work (Tew, 2011), and from the research methodology community (Kirk et al., 2015).

The medical model continues to have a highly dominant place in terms of the mental health field and, although criticisms of it have been coming thick and fast for quite some time, it is likely to be some considerable time before that hegemonic position is changed.

Conclusion

Once again, what we are seeing in terms of response to a particular social problem is a fairly narrowly circumscribed one, and one that is far from holistic in its scope. Moloney captures this point well when he reminds us that:

> Psychiatric diagnoses and treatments persist as the keystone for the medicalization of social problems. In claiming to identify and treat objective bodily disease, mental health professionals have been able to reframe social ills such as poverty, economic insecurity and the widespread abuse of children and adults as medical issues, requiring expert management.
>
> (2013, p. 50)

Describing the huge distress, disruption and immense fear associated with mental health problems as an illness may well be an improvement on witchcraft and demonic possession, but it remains highly problematic in terms of our efforts to understand the issues more fully, to address the difficulties caused and to promote social justice for those involved.

Points to ponder

> ➤ Why do you think the media are prone to offering distorted portrayals of people with mental health problems?
> ➤ Why is it important to distinguish between grief and depression?
> ➤ How might social factors contribute to a person experiencing mental health problems?

Exercise 9

What are the implications of applying the label 'mentally ill' for (i) the individual concerned; (ii) their immediate family and friends; (iii) their work setting; and (iv) the wider community?

10

Problematic Drug Use

Introduction

Problems associated with drug use are many and varied. If we include alcohol as a drug that commonly creates problems, then the picture becomes even more complex. As we have found with other social problems explored in Part 2, public perceptions as fuelled by media representations are often different from the reality in our communities.

As we shall see, problematic drug use is a major concern because of: (i) the harm it does to the individuals so affected, to the people close to them and beyond; and (ii) its negative impact on other social problems. Once again we will see that there are important links between problematic drug use as a social problem and social justice (or the lack thereof).

Understanding problematic drug use

Underpinning many of the difficulties in contemporary society is a reliance on drugs and alcohol, particularly alcohol. As we shall explore in more detail below, drugs issues are closely linked to a number of social problems. This means that progress in addressing problematic drug use could have a positive knock-on effect in relation to other social problems. Although there is a social disapproval of drugs because they are illegal and perceived to be very harmful, the approach to alcohol is more mixed. While the problems associated with alcohol are certainly frowned upon, its role as a social lubricant of interaction is generally viewed in relatively positive terms. These differences are reflected in both media representations of illicit drugs and of alcohol and in policy responses to the problems involved.

The role of alienation

The causes and consequences of the problems associated with drugs and alcohol are many and varied. However, one important factor is the significance of alienation, a feeling of not belonging, of not fitting in and of not being valued. This is especially the case with illegal drugs where there will tend to be subcultures associated with the use of those drugs. The 1960s notion of 'dropping out' and belonging to an 'alternative society' is strongly associated with the development of drug cultures and associated problems.

As well as these issues, what we need to understand are matters associated with existential uncertainty and the role of escapism as a form of relief from pressure. Whether we are talking about illegal drugs or alcohol, the point is the same. A key factor is the role of such substances in providing a relief from pressures and tensions. The more pressurized modern life becomes, the greater the risk that certain groups of people will take to escapism through drugs or alcohol as a means of coping with their concerns.

The appeal of drugs

However, it is not just pressure or escape from pressure that can lead to the use of such substances. What we have to recognize is that a key factor is that drugs bring a certain degree of enjoyment, in the form of a sense of adventure and feelings of euphoria. Drug use can be exciting, stimulating and highly pleasurable. They can also help people feel part of a group, community or subculture. Of course, whether those positives are worth the negatives is a very significant point. People who have never experienced problematic drug use may struggle to understand the appeal of such

---

Practice focus 10.1

Jan was a youth worker in an outreach project. She was aware that many of the young people she worked with faced a wide range of challenges. Just the challenges and uncertainties of adolescence were enough to create difficulties. But, when you add to that problems like poverty, family tensions, possibly abuse, poor-quality housing and other such concerns that many young people face, you start to appreciate why drugs can be an appealing prospect. She was also aware of how drugs can wreck young lives and place huge strain on families. She knew that just telling young people to steer clear of drugs would only work with a small proportion of people – much more than that was needed. So, what she decided to do was to launch a project to get young people involved in learning about three things: (i) the parts played by drugs in modern life; (ii) the harm that drugs can do; and (iii) other ways of relieving their pressures. It was clear to her that giving a 'no drugs' message, while not offering alternative ways of handling pressures was not going to be effective.

substances. However, people who have either experienced it or researched the evidence relating to the positive effects, can have a much fuller understanding of the appeal of drugs.

The effects of drugs

Drug problems can be seen to apply at biological, social and psychological levels. At a biological level there is what is known as physiological toxicity. This refers to the harm to the body that can be brought about by such substances as heroin. Overdoses can also be physically harmful, of course, leading to fatality in some cases. Linked to this is the idea of behavioural toxicity. That is, being under the influence of drugs or alcohol can lead to people behaving in socially unacceptable or even criminal ways (we shall return to this topic below when we consider the links between problematic drug use and other social problems). Psychological effects can include people behaving at times in self-destructive ways, placing themselves and/or other people at significant risk. Furthermore, there is also the problem of addiction whereby the reliance upon the use of a particular drug has far-reaching consequences in terms of the detrimental effects involved (Kleiman et al., 2011).

The social context of drugs use

Our understanding of problematic drug use can also be enhanced by taking account of the implications of different social attitudes and contexts. The legal use of alcohol can lead to significantly high levels of consumption, while the illegal status of, for example, cannabis can have the effect of discouraging use for many people (although clearly not all). Interestingly, though, closer inspection will show that the problems associated with alcohol can be of far greater proportions than those associated with cannabis. This has led many people to argue the case for the legalization of cannabis, although the arguments for and against are quite complex and not clear cut either way (see Nutt, 2012, for an interesting discussion of these issues).

Voice of experience 10.1

There's a certain irony about people making a song and dance about drug use and then getting roaring drunk at the weekend! Whether you are talking about alcohol as a legal drug or any of the illegal drugs, there are risks involved and benefits to be

▶

◄

gained, in some ways at least. Our drugs policy is confused, contradictory and generally unhelpful. It's driven more by prejudice and misunderstanding than by a genuine
appreciation of what is involved. And I am not too optimistic that it is going to change
for the better any time soon.

Chris, a drugs education worker

Much will depend on the extent to which the particular drug is used and
the context in which the use takes place. Kleiman et al. explain some of
the complexities involved:

> The effect of a drug on a person is determined, in the classic formulation of
> Harvard psychiatrist Norman Zinberg, by "drug, set, and setting." Of course the
> drug itself matters; so does the quantity consumed and the route of adminis-
> tration (oral, inhaled, or injected). The "set" refers to the user's psychological
> makeup, previous experience with that and other drugs, expectations, and
> intentions. And the "setting" is the entire social surround: the price of the
> drug; conventions about times, places, quantities, and circumstances of use; the
> presence or absence of others who will provide support if things go wrong or,
> alternatively, take advantage of an intoxicated individual; and the social cachet
> or stigma attached to the use of that drug in its social context.
>
> (2011, p. 12)

Some people may use certain drugs on an occasional basis and have little
harm as a result of that. Consider, for example, people who drink alcohol
socially without presenting themselves or others without any significant
problems. Next can come the problematic use of the drug. This involves
more than occasional use and does begin to cause problems of some
description. This can then lead to problematic and dependent use which
involves a degree of reliance on the drug. This could be a psychological reliance, whereby the person concerned cannot concentrate or relax
because they are, to a certain extent, preoccupied with the drug and wanting it more and more. In some circumstances addiction can arise which
also has a physiological element, in the sense that withdrawal from the
drug can produce significant, painful and disorientating consequences –
what is often referred to as cold turkey (or 'detoxification' to give it its
technical term). Where problematic drug use or dependency arises, a
common problem is that of craving. This involves persistent intrusive
thoughts where the person concerned struggles to do without the drug,
not necessarily because of a physiological addiction, but because they are
psychologically so keen on having the benefits of the drug that it is acting
as a barrier to their leading their life in more socially effective ways.

Cultural pathways

What is also important to consider in terms of the causes of problematic drug use are what are known as 'cultural pathways'. This can include peer pressure where people are under pressure to take drugs because that's what the people who are part of their world do. For example, if somebody is a member of a group or an association of people, formal or informal, and problematic drug use is common within that circle, then the pressure for them to conform can be immense. This is especially the case with alcohol where, as I mentioned earlier, there is considerable approval of the disinhibiting effects of alcohol in terms of helping people to relax and to socialize more easily. For example being a teetotaller in modern society can be quite difficult because of the constant pressures to consume alcohol. Similar pressures apply in much the same way for some people in some cultural contexts when it comes to the use of illegal drugs.

Inappropriate use of prescription drugs

Another important factor to consider is that there are problems associated with not only illegal drugs or alcohol, but also with the inappropriate use of prescription medication. It is possible for people to become addicted to, for example, pain killers, and the consequences can be similar, in the sense that people's lives can be ruined by the way in which the need for the drug dominates their life. It can have adverse effects on their ability to maintain employment, to sustain relationships, to parent effectively and to find enjoyment and fulfilment in anything but the particular drug. This is an aspect of problematic drug use that attracts relatively little attention, due in no small part to the fact that it does not fit with media stereotypes of lower-class 'druggies'. It is, none the less, a source of considerable distress and social disruption.

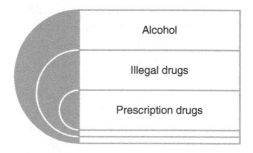

Figure 10.1   Types of problematic drug use

Medicalization

In Chapter 9 I outlined the problems arising from medicalization that has reduced the complex, multilevel phenomenon of mental distress to a simple disease process. A similar analysis can be applied to problematic drug use. For example, alcoholism is commonly construed as a disease. People wrestling with alcohol dependence issues are generally described as having an 'illness'. The same logic has also come to be applied to other problematic drug use issues.

Terms like 'treatment' and 'rehabilitation' are widely used. As with the medicalization of mental distress, this has had the effect of removing an emphasis on ownership. It is assumed that people with drink or drugs problems cannot be held responsible for their actions (without first being 'rehabilitated'). This can be seen to place considerable obstacles in the way of progress by placing the responsibility for advancement in the hands of the professionals.

> ➤ CHOICES *Constructing pathology* Reducing complex, multilevel problems to a 'disorder' in the individual.

Emphasizing ownership is not the same as blaming people for their problems, but, rather, a matter of promoting empowerment – helping people to re-establish control, agency and autonomy. This needs to be understood in the context of the wider social factors that contribute to the problematic use of drugs in the first place. Unfortunately, a medicalized approach to problematic drug use also distracts attention from such wider concerns. Orcutt and Rudy capture this point well when they argue that:

> We do not use a language of personal deficiencies to talk about economic concerns or to describe recession as the problem of sick businessmen, nor do we describe investment counsellors as "market therapists." The income of the client affects the language of the profession. Subsidies to the auto industry are not called "aid to dependent factories."
>
> (2003, p. 12)

The challenge, then, is to be able to address the social problems associated with drug use without oversimplifying the complexities involved by adopting an individualistic medical model that conveniently sidesteps the psychological, sociopolitical and spiritual issues involved.

Schweingruber and Horstmeier point out that even the notion of addiction is a phenomenon that has become medicalized:

> The modern idea of addiction is an example of medicalization, the tendency to frame troubling conditions as medical problems. However, "addiction" was not originally a medical term: rather, the concept of addiction itself became medicalized. The English word is derived from a Roman legal term that "refers to the judicial action of legally sentencing a person to be a bond slave"; the English meaning involves "a similar state of servitude, not to a slave-master but to a 'habit of pursuit'" (Alexander, 2008, p. 28)
>
> (2013, pp. 197–8)

We can see, then, that there are strong parallels between how mental health problems have become medicalized and the way that drug- and alcohol-related problems are commonly understood and handled.

How problematic drug use affects, and is affected by, inequality

As with the other social problems we have explored in Part 2, there are various links between problematic drug use and social injustices.

Class differences

Perhaps the first point to emphasize is that there are recognized significant class differences in terms of the use of drugs, and there will also be class differences in terms of the response to drugs. For example, the use of certain illegal substances by working-class youth is generally criminalized, whereas their use by more affluent young people may be seen as youthful hijinks and experimentation. This reflects discrimination within the criminal justice system in terms of stereotypical expectations related to class differences (Thompson, 2009).

Gender differences

There are also significant gender differences in terms of what drugs are used by men or women and how problems associated with those drugs are subsequently dealt with. There is now a growing level of awareness of

> **Practice focus 10.2**
>
> Mari was a family support worker assigned to a number of families who were in danger of having their children removed from them. When she first started she did not know what to expect. What, she wondered, could cause parents to get to the point that there was sufficient concern for the authorities to consider taking their children into care? Before too long two things stood out for her, two common themes. One was depression. She saw parents living in fairly dire circumstances and, understandably to her mind, wrestling with depression and despair as a result. She could also see that this just made the problem worse. She could see them, in a sense, digging themselves into a deeper hole, and she wondered what she could do to help with this, to help break this cycle. The other common themes she noted was alcohol. Quite a few of the parents she worked with were struggling with alcohol, either openly or behind closed doors. What was also apparent to her was that the two things were related. The depression and the drinking were both about coping with immense pressures and huge insecurities – they were not helpful ways of coping, but they were none the less attempts to cope. Mari felt out of her depth with these problems and this made her think about whether she should take steps to become a qualified social worker so that she would feel better equipped to handle the difficulties she could see each day.

the significance of this, particularly in relation to alcohol (Staddon, 2015). What is also relevant here, whether we are talking about class differences or gender differences, is that underlying tensions and a sense of insecurity can once again lead to the need for escapism as a relief from everyday pressures.

The drugs economy

Hari (2015) also links drug problems to inequality by commenting on the significance of the drugs economy. What he means by this is that there is significant funding at stake in terms of the huge profits that can be made from the production and sale of illegal drugs:

> When we hear about drug-related violence, we picture somebody getting high and killing people. We think the violence is the product of the drugs. But in fact, it turns out this is only a tiny sliver of the violence. The vast majority is … to establish, protect, and defend drug territory in an illegal market, and to build a name for being consistently terrifying so nobody tries to take your property or turf.
>
> (2015, p. 66)

The illicit market feeds the profits of the wealthy groups who benefit from the human misery of drugs, while it is the less powerful groups who face the consequences of the violence, the destruction and the despair. This insight enables us to broaden our perspective considerably and to recognize how narrow a disease approach to problematic drug use is and how much it leaves unsaid.

Added to this is the significant economy underpinning the pharmaceuticals industry and the potential abuses in that are, especially in relation to psychiatric medication (Davies, 2013; Kirk et al., 2015).

Racism

There are also important considerations related to race and racism, in so far as there is evidence to suggest that the criminal justice system will respond more harshly to members of minority ethnic communities who are involved in drugs-related offences (Hari, 2015).

By moving away from a medicalized approach to drug and alcohol problems and trying to understand them more holistically we can begin to appreciate the significance of social deprivations, discrimination and disadvantage. It therefore takes very little imagination to see how those members of minority ethnic groups who face those challenges are also going to be targets for unscrupulous drug dealers seeking to capitalize in human misery by selling their devastating wares.

Overall, then, there are significant linkages to be drawn between the social problems associated with problematic drug use and the prevalence of inequality in modern societies.

How problematic drug use affects, and is affected by, other social problems

One of the strongest links is between problematic drug use and crime. Much crime is rooted in drug use. For example, the need to steal or embezzle money or to steal goods to sell to produce money is a major underlying factor in terms of the need to pay for the drug habit. As Kleiman et al. explain, there are (at least) three dimensions to this:

> In general, the relationship between drugs and crime tends to follow three paths. Drugs lead people to commit crimes because: (1) drug use makes them act irrationally, (2) they need money to buy drugs, or (3) they get involved in the violence that surrounds the business of producing and dealing in drugs.

(2011, p. 119)

Hari offers further insights into the relationship between problematic drug use and crime by highlighting the significance of drugs in the context of the criminal justice system and the prevalence of people with drug-related offences in prison:

> In 1993, in the death throes of apartheid, South Africa imprisoned 853 black men per hundred thousand in the population. The United States imprisons 4,919 black men per hundred thousand (versus only 943 white men). So because of the drug war and the way it is enforced, a black man was far more likely to be jailed in the Land of the Free than in the most notorious white supremacist society in the world.
>
> Indeed, at any given time [in the USA], 40 to 50 percent of black men between the ages of fifteen and thirty-five are in jail, on probation, or have a warrant out for their arrest, overwhelmingly for drug offences.
>
> (2015, p. 93)

This illustrates the 'knock-on effect', the interconnectedness of social problems. Various social problems and various forms of social injustice combine in a multitude of ways to produce a multidimensional reality far removed from ideologically driven, media-fuelled 'common sense' understandings.

Practice focus 10.3

Robin was a prison chaplain with many years' experience. He was only too aware of how tackling drugs problems was one of the most significant features of his work. He could see what he thought of as a domino effect. Problems of poverty, unemployment, poor housing and so on fuelled a sense of low self-worth for very many people. For some of these people the next step was to become involved in the drugs world, partly for cultural reasons (drugs being part of their everyday reality in their community), partly for reasons of escapism and partly for a whole host of other reasons specific to each and every one of them. What all this had in common, as Robin saw it, was a degree of spiritual impoverishment, a struggle to feel like a worthwhile and valued human being. Drugs would then lead to crime – to feed the habit, for example, or as a result of being immersed in the criminal underworld associated with acquiring drugs. Crime would then lead to prison and all the deprivations associated with incarceration. Those deprivations would then lead to a craving for the escapism and positive feelings offered by drugs. Imprisonment and a drugs habit then reduced employment opportunities considerably and thereby created a choice between poverty or further criminal activity. Robin did his best to help with spiritual guidance but he was well aware that what was needed was a much more radical way of preventing this devastating domino effect.

> ➤ CHOICES *Interconnectedness* We need to appreciate how different problems relate to one another.

Problematic drug use can also be related to mental health in a number of ways. For example, the excessive use of alcohol and other problematic drug use can exacerbate mental health problems. Somebody who is already wrestling with mental health challenges, when faced with the powerful effects of alcohol or other drugs can find that they are experiencing major difficulties in terms of maintaining a sense of mental well-being.

Alcohol and illegal drugs can also be used by people with mental health problems as a form of self-medication. In general, mental health-related medication has no curative basis; its role is largely to contain the problem by sedating the individual concerned or by supressing the symptoms through chemical means (Kirk et al., 2015). These drugs often have significant side effects that can be highly problematic and disruptive. Some people with mental health problems therefore prefer to find other ways of sedating themselves through alcohol or other substances and of course that can then lead to significant problems in their own right.

Similarly there can be the inappropriate of prescription-based medication. People who are taking antipsychotic medication, for example, may abuse that medication possibly because of their mental health condition or other reasons.

Problematic drug use is also associated with the social problem of terrorism, in so far as the drugs economy of which Hari speaks can be understood as a major source of funding for illegal pressure groups who use terrorist methods to promote their political viewpoint or worldview. The existence, then, of a global economy around drug production, distribution and sale is a key factor in the maintenance of terrorist regimes. As Kleiman et al. put it:

> Dependent users commit enormous amounts of crime under influence or to finance drug purchases, while dealers' violence strikes innocent bystanders and devastates neighbourhoods. International drug trafficking supports corruption, insurgency, and terrorism.
>
> (2011, p. xviii)

What we are seeing, then, is a very complex picture in which problematic drug use is a focal point in an intricate web of difficulties. So, how are these issues tackled? It is that question that we now turn.

Responses to the problem

One of the most common responses to drugs problems is what has gained the term the 'war on drugs'. However, this approach can be severely criticized for oversimplifying a complex picture. The notion of a war implies that there is an enemy. In the drugs field there is no direct enemy. There are various complex, interrelated factors that need to be taken into consideration to make sense of drugs and the associated problems. The idea that there is some sort of enemy that we can wage war on therefore adds little to our understanding of how we can tackle the problems associated with drugs use. Another approach along similar lines has been the criminalization of drugs. This was tried in relation to alcohol in the United States in terms of the era of prohibition. However, the prohibition approach was abandoned when it was found that what it was doing was creating criminally based underground markets for alcohol that were being run by organized crime cartels, something that produced counterfinality. That is, the attempt to address the problem actually invoked other problems that were in some ways of a more serious nature.

> ➤ CHOICES *Counterfinality* Some attempts to tackle a problem can create new problems.

Kleiman et al. argue that a similar process has occurred as a result of the criminalization of problematic drug use:

> Making a highly desired commodity illegal creates an opportunity that some illicit entrepreneur is certain to seize on, and black-market business methods can be as devastating as the drugs themselves.
>
> (2011, p. xx)

However, there are signs that things are beginning to change. In March 2016 President Obama spoke at a summit in Atlanta, Georgia and put forward a view that many social policy commentators had aired before him:

> For too long we've viewed drug addiction through the lens of criminal justice ... The most important thing to do is to reduce demand. And the only way to do that is to provide treatment – to see it as a public health problem and not a criminal problem.
>
> (www.theguardian.com/us-news/2016/mar/29/
> barack-obama-drug-addiction-health-problem-not-criminal-problem)

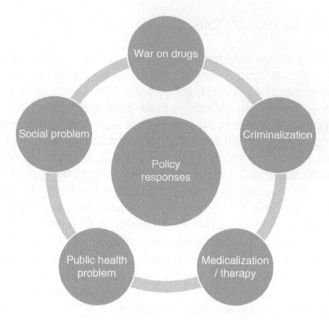

Figure 10.2 Policy responses to problematic drug use

Perhaps we could go a step further and see it as a *social* problem that needs a holistic response, rather than revert to a medical model that calls for 'treatment'.

This brings us back to the medically based approaches to problematic drug use discussed earlier. Within a biomedical approach the focus on addressing the problem has understandably had a strong emphasis on treatment. 'Treatment' is a term that we use in relation to pathology – we treat a pathology. This approach therefore takes us back to the problem of a lack of a holistic perspective whereby one aspect (the biomedical) is prioritized at the expense of trying to understand the other issues involved in terms of psychological, social and spiritual factors that can contribute to drugs-related problems and/or alcohol use.

When we discussed the limitations of a narrow biomedical approach to mental health problems, we noted that dominant official definitions of mental disorder have no basis in objective fact; they arise from a subjective consensus of experts schooled in a particular perspective on the problems involved. There is a strong parallel with drug and alcohol problems, as Orcutt and Rudy demonstrate. They refer to the work of Jellinek, a pioneer in the medical approach to alcohol dependency:

> Jellinek's (1960: 12) comments on whether his Gamma and Delta types are "really" diseases are instructive:

> Physicians know what belongs in their realm ... a disease is what the medical profession recognizes as such ... the medical profession has officially accepted alcoholism as an illness, whether a part of the public likes it or not, and even if a minority of the medical profession is disinclined to accept the idea.
>
> Almost impatiently, the concept's leading proponent argues that diseases are what physicians say they are and since physicians, as represented by their major professional organization, have said so, alcoholism is a disease and that should settle the matter!
>
> (p. 28)

The flimsiness of the basis of this rationale should, then, be perfectly clear.

As a development from the simplistic medical model, what is beginning to emerge now is a much stronger emphasis on a public health approach – that is, to understand the problems more holistically in terms of issues in society that need to be addressed more broadly. Therefore, instead of focusing narrowly on individuals and the individual causes and consequences of problems, the emphasis is on trying to understand the fuller picture of such factors as social concerns that can lead to pressures and insecurities, social expectations in terms of peer pressures, and important matters relating to access to drugs and alcohol and to what extent these are controlled.

This public health approach takes us some way towards developing a more holistic perspective and is therefore something to be welcomed. However, the fact that it is still within the health field means that there can still be the predominance of a medical model within it. To understand social problems from a public health perspective has its advantages, but it also means that some aspects that are not directly related to health, public or otherwise, will be excluded – hence my comments above in relation to Barack Obama's speech.

Linked to the public health approach is the emphasis on 'recovery', and this too involves a degree of movement away from a medicalized approach to the problem towards a focus on self-help and personal growth (Best, 2012).

Voice of experience 10.2

I have seen it all now. I've seen the men in white coats try to 'cure' addiction, I've heard all the rhetoric about this so-called war on drugs. I've seen people talk things through with their various 'therapies', as if that's magically going to take all the pain away and make it all better. But what I haven't seen in all my years is anyone actually looking at what is going on underneath, what's going on in society to create the problems in the first place. It's all sticking plaster stuff at best.

Kelly, an ex-addict now working as a drugs worker

Conclusion

Humans have been using mind-altering substances for a very long time. Such usage can bring certain advantages and positive results, but also major risks and highly destructive consequences for significant numbers of people – leading to family breakdown, extensive and severe health problems, violence, lost opportunities, lives ruined in various ways and, of course death. What is more, alcohol- and drug-related problems are also, as we have seen, significantly implicated in a range of other serious social problems. There is therefore much that we need to take notice of.

However, as Kleiman et al. comment: 'Our current drug policies allow avoidable harm by their ineffectiveness and create needless suffering by their excesses. Deference to myth in place of fact helps hold bad policies in place' (2011, p. xxi). So, on this basis, we still have a long way to go in making an impact on these hugely important problems.

Points to ponder

➤ In what way is alienation associated with problematic drug use?

➤ In what ways might the 'drugs economy' fuel other problems?

➤ Why is a 'war on drugs' approach likely to prove ineffective?

Exercise 10

What might a holistic approach to the problems associated with alcohol and drug use look like? What factors would need to be taken into consideration? What steps would need to be taken? What obstacles might there be and what could be done about it?

11

Terrorism

Introduction

The subject of terrorism is one that is not traditionally included in discussions of social problems. However, it has come to feature so strongly in so many people's lives that it is now being recognized as quite a significant social problem worthy of close attention. This chapter therefore provides an introductory overview of some of the key issues involved.

As we shall see, terrorism is a complex topic, but it is also one that fits with the pattern of being closely related to; (i) inequality; and (ii) other social problems.

Understanding terrorism

Terrorism, like the other social problems discussed in Part 2, is a topic that merits far more attention than I am able to give it here, but what follows should give at least a basic framework of understanding.

Competing worldviews

I earlier explained the significance of globalization, the process whereby modern communications technology has played an important role in bringing nations together in ways that were previously impossible. We now have much more of a global economy, in the sense that the movement of goods and resources across the world is facilitated. Markets are now generally international, and there are implications of that at a number of levels. We are now more aware, for example, of the significance of different cultures and different worldviews. One of the consequences of that is that there can be significant ideological and worldview differences across nations, cultures and communities. These differences are often dealt with in a positive and cooperative way – for example, the modern emphasis on the importance of valuing diversity and appreciating one another's point of view (Thompson, 2011a).

However, this is not always the case and competing ideologies can result in considerable conflict (Andrews, 2016). The history of warfare over the decades, and indeed centuries, gives us ample evidence of how different worldviews can result in devastating human and financial costs. We are now in a situation in which we are increasingly recognizing how such differences can also lead to conflicts that are not necessarily wars in the traditional sense of the word, but which are none the less of major proportions. This is where certain groups of people adopt a guerrilla-based approach to conflict. Where this involves the use of terror as a weapon or political tactic we tend to adopt the term 'terrorism'.

However, this is not a straightforward matter. As Heiner explains, the use of the word terrorism is quite problematic:

> The word has little or no social scientific value, and like so many other phenomena … it is socially constructed. It has different meanings to different audiences in different contexts. The term describes a class of phenomena of which we do not approve, but it does not distinguish the objective reality of such phenomena from very similar phenomena of which we do approve. The word terrorism is a politically loaded one. It usually, but not always, is used in reference to violence; but if a group happens to approve of the violence in question, then it is not likely to be considered "terrorism."
>
> (2006, p. 142)

We can see already, then, that we are exploring territory where the ideas put forward in the media represent a considerable oversimplification compared with the actual complexities that lie below the surface of the superficial portrayals featured.

Terrorism in action

Examples of terrorism would include the conflicts in Northern Ireland known as 'the Troubles' whereby opposing factions in terms of both religious affiliation and national identity have resulted in years of fear, death and great pain for significant numbers of people across a range of communities (McKittrick and McVea, 2012).

Another example of terrorism would be the events of 9/11 which were rooted in a conflict between two different ideologies around social expectations (2002b). So, while the destruction of life and property by means of the 9/11 attacks produced no direct gain for al-Qaeda, what it did was to

Practice focus 11.1

Callum was a community worker who was involved in 'peace and reconcilia-tion' efforts. He had lost several relatives in the Troubles and was well aware of the immense grief, distress, fear, anger and insecurity the conflict had generated year after year. He could see that the two factions were poles apart in terms of not just religion, but also national identity. His community work training had taught him about the importance of identity and how far people would be prepared to go to protect their sense of individual, community, religious and national identity. So, he could under-stand why there was so much conflict, but what he couldn't understand was why that conflict had to be fought out in such destructive ways. It does not bode well for our future, he thought, if we can't learn to live with our differences, however significant those differences may be. It was this that was the driving force for him to get involved in peace and reconciliation work. He recognized that it would be hugely challenging and that there were easier ways of making a living, but he felt that the stakes were so high that this would be the best career direction for him.

create an atmosphere of terror. This development of fear as a tactic to try and achieve political goals is what is commonly associated with terrorism.

Similar comments could be made about the activities of ISIS, Boko Haram and other groups. Cockburn describes ISIS as 'experts in fear' and goes on to argue that:

> ISIS is the child of war. Its members seek to reshape the world around them by acts of violence. The movement's toxic but potent mix of extreme religious beliefs and military skill is the outcome of the war in Iraq since the US invasion of 2003 and the war in Syria since 2011.
>
> (2015, p. 80)

Terrorism can therefore be seen to have complex political roots, and that is partly why there can be no easy answers or straightforward solutions.

Terrorism, as the name indicates, involves deploying terror as a strat-egy for pursuing the political goals of the perpetrators. Its potency lies in its ability to disrupt everyday activities by suffusing them with fear. One of the dangers associated with this is that a vicious circle can be created. As the old cliché has it, two wrongs do not make a right, but the intense antipathy towards the terrorists serves to intensify the conflicts and, in the longer term, makes a resolution less likely. As Scraton comments:

> Terror is a strategy which ostentatiously denies the conventions of 'acceptable' conflict. Its purpose is to demonstrate as widely as possible a disregard for the

boundaries or limits to formal combat. To strike terror into the heart of an identifiable community is to frighten people so deeply that they lose trust and confidence in all aspects of routine daily life. Yet, to demonise perpetrators, to represent their humaneness as monstrousness, creates a climate within which a deeper understanding of historical, political and cultural contexts is inhibited and is replaced by an all-consuming will to vengeance.

(Scraton, 2002, pp. 2–3)

Even where conflicts are legitimate and there are significant grievances to be addressed, the use of terror as an illegitimate strategy is likely to result in less general support for the perpetrators' case (but perhaps more support from within their own group), thereby intensifying and sustaining the conflict. Terrorism, as a tactic, is therefore very effective, in the sense that it can be very successful in generating great fear and thereby cause huge disruption and expense (in both human and financial costs). However, as a tactic in bringing about political change in the perpetrators' favour, its effectiveness is far more limited.

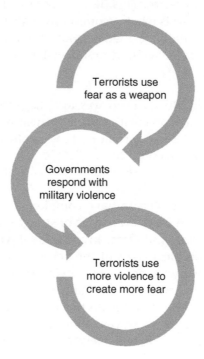

Figure 11.1   The vicious circle of terrorism

State terrorism

Jackson et al. (2011) are critical of what they call orthodox approaches to the understanding of terrorism that restrict the analysis to non-state political groups. They point out that governments can, and often do, engage in the use of terror as a political strategy. The work of the American political commentator, Noam Chomsky has consistently and persistently criticized his own government for such actions – and, of course, the USA is not alone in doing this (Chomsky, 2003; 2012). This is illustrative of the socially constructed nature of social problems; it is rare, for example, for state terrorism to be presented in the mainstream media.

> ➤ CHOICES *Social construction* Who defines what is a legitimate or illegitimate strategy for pursuing political ends?

The role of fear

There are many other examples of terrorism that I could quote, but the important point to establish without getting bogged down in too much detail is that what characterizes terrorism as a social problem is the fear it generates. In reality, the vast majority of people are unlikely to be directly affected by a terrorist attack. Those people who, unfortunately, have been injured or lost their lives, loved ones or important property as a result of terrorist attacks are very much in the minority in terms of the total population. But, it is important to appreciate that the vast majority of people have none the less been affected by the fear that was instilled by those attacks. Consider, for example, the increased airport security measures and the significant delays, inconvenience, tension and expense that have been brought about by that – no doubt something that pleases the terrorists in their efforts to destabilize their political opponents.

> ➤ CHOICES *Existential/spiritual issues* Insecurity can be both cause and consequence of social problems.

Disproportionate consequences

One of the implications of terrorism is that the effects of having a higher level of fear are experienced disproportionately by certain members of the community. It takes us back to the idea that it is the least powerful groups who are more prone to difficulties as a result of social problems, and terrorism is no exception. For example, the emphasis on anti-terrorist efforts has had the result of reducing civil liberties, and once again we can see that it is the poorest and/or least powerful groups that are most affected.

Unfortunately, one of the consequences of terrorist activities that are claimed to be in the name of Islam has been an increase in discriminatory actions and attitudes towards Muslims. We shall return to this point below.

Risk aversion

One of the other consequences of terrorism is an increase in risk aversion – that is, a greater prevalence of overly cautious approaches to risk rooted in a distorted perspective of the hazards involved. There are now many examples on record of people who have adopted fairly extreme approaches to risk as a result of the heightened sense of anxiety associated with terrorist threats. For example, I am aware of situations where extreme measures have been taken to respond to minor threats, such as people being arrested for making jokes with airport security staff.

Voice of experience 11.1

I spend a lot of my time trying to convince people of the need for a more balanced approach to risk, like we used to have. I use a lot of examples on courses of how extreme some people can get when it comes to risk aversion, verging on paranoia. I'm sure some people think I am making them up, but they are all real examples I have come across. It's not all down to terrorism, but all this 'war on terror' talk has just made a bad situation worse. The irony is that getting so het up about risk is actually dangerous, because it means we have a distorted picture of the risks we are facing.

Avery, a training officer in a local authority

Furedi relates this overemphasis on risk to a sense of vulnerability, something that terrorism is intended to exploit:

Many of the beliefs that shape the current response to terrorism – the idea that humanity faces unprecedented threats, that we inhabit a new era of terror, that we are confronted by a new species of terrorist threat, that what we must really

fear is the unknown – are the product of a cultural imagination that is dominated by a sense of vulnerability.

(2007, p. 127)

Fear, threat, panic, vulnerability: these are the basic components of terrorism.

How terrorism affects, and is affected by, inequality

There are various ways in which terrorism intersects with inequality. We
begin by considering prejudice against Muslims.

Islamophobia

The problem of Islamophobia (that is, a negative, discriminatory attitude
towards Muslims) was in existence long before the 9/11 attacks or the
more recent problems associated with ISIS. However, as noted earlier, one
of the consequences of terrorism has been an increased level of negativity towards Muslims. Sadly, there are many cases on record of people confusing terrorists who claim to be following Islam with the wider Muslim
community (Gilliat-Ray, 2010). This has tended to exacerbate racism and
difficulties associated with race relations.

Practice focus 11.2

Rachel was a chaplain in a hospice. Although she was a Christian herself, she and the
rest of the hospice staff were committed to offering spiritual support to any faith or
none. They therefore replaced their original chapel room with a 'Prayer and Reflection
Room' that could be used by anyone, regardless of their religious beliefs. This proved
to be a positive move as there was a large Muslim population in the area who had not
really engaged with the hospice up to now. Rachel did her best to reach out to them
and had quite a lot of success. However, she was quite distressed at a staff meeting
when one of the support workers voiced concerns about letting 'people like that' into
the building. Instead of embarrassing the member of staff by saying something there
and then, Rachel arranged to speak to her afterwards. What emerged from that conversation was that the member of staff concerned had not previously harboured any
racist views, but, in light of various terrorist attacks and threats, she had developed a
negative attitude rooted in fear. Rachel tried to reassure her and to convince her that
the vast majority of Muslims were decent, law-abiding citizens and nothing to worry
about. But Rachel was not convinced the message had been taken on board and she
wondered how many other people had developed this sort of prejudice because of the
way some sectors of the media reported terrorism.

Sectarianism

Discrimination and inequality can also be seen to be relevant in other ways. For example, sectarianism can be seen as a key factor in both the Northern Ireland Troubles (McKittrick and McVea, 2012) and in the problems associated with the terrorist activities of ISIS (for example, in terms of ideological differences between Sunni and Shia Muslims – Cockburn, 2015).

Sects are subsections of a particular religion. The members of different sects will have much in common in terms of their religious beliefs, but there will key differences that set the groups apart. At times differing sects can live and work alongside each other without difficulty, each tolerating and accepting the other. However, this is not always the case. The conflicts can form the basis of open warfare or can materialize in the form of terrorism. Discrimination against the other sect is then closely linked with terrorism – indeed, the terrorism can be seen as an expression of that discrimination.

Health inequalities

We can also draw links between neoliberalist ideology and health inequalities, in so far as these are linked to terrorism. What I mean by this is that the austerity and cutbacks associated with neoliberalism have resulted in greater difficulties for less powerful groups in terms of having access to decent levels of health and associated support services. Terrorist attacks and threats have resulted in greater time and resources being devoted to security matters, and this takes away money and other resources from important facilities like the health service, So, while terrorism has a direct impact on those people affected by attacks, we should not underestimate the more indirect effect on a much broader population as a result of the consequences of being aware of, and responsive to, the potential for further attacks. The overall costs of tackling terrorism are of major proportions, and the bulk of these costs come from the public purse, leaving far less money available for those who need support from public services. This is highly significant in terms of social justice, in so far as the poorest, least powerful groups are more likely to rely on public services. For example, they are less likely to be able to pay for

> ➤ CHOICES *Over-reliance on the market* Neoliberalism seeks to reduce public services by minimizing the role of the state.

private health care, but are more likely to face significant health problems (Davidson, 2014).

How terrorism affects, and is affected by, other social problems

Terrorism, as we have seen, is rooted in fear, and the insecurity associated with such fear is something we have already identified as a significant feature of social problems. There is therefore a strong 'amplification' effect associated with terrorism – a heightening of tension, mistrust and insecurity. There are also more specific links, and we shall explore three of them here.

Crime

There are clear links between terrorism and crime, not least because terrorism, to a large extent, is a crime in itself. However, the levels of threat and fear that are generated by terrorism then present opportunities for unscrupulous people to exploit others – for example, through scams that are related to claimed efforts to protect people from terrorist attack. There is also the issue of terrorism being funded through organized crime. I have already mentioned the significance of the drugs economy in this regard.

Mental health

There are also links between terrorism and mental health. The increased level of anxiety and threat can be seen to be a significant factor in term of such challenges as depression and anxiety. There is also the question of whether some terrorists are behaving in the way they do because of their own mental health problems. However, we would have to be wary of the stereotype that assumes that terrorists are, by the very nature of what they do, insane. Their actions in everyday common-sense terms may appear to be insane, but this would be to misunderstand and oversimplify how terrorism works. What we need to be aware of is that perpetrators of terrorism are by and large fervent believers that what they are doing is right and for good. None the less, it would be unwise to fail to recognize that, in some circumstances, mental health problems may be implicated in the development of terrorist activities.

Voice of experience 11.2

With some of my patients there is a tendency to get distressed by what is happening in the wider world. It's as if they can't distinguish between what is likely to affect them and what is not. So, all this terrorism stuff is not only a problem for the people directly affected, but also a really nasty complicating factor for a lot of people who are struggling with mental health issues.

Taylor, a mental health nurse

Destruction of habitat

Terrorism is also associated with the destruction of habitat. This may be, for example, in terms of the terrorist destruction of important environmental features, such as the al-Qaeda destruction of Buddha statues. There are also habitat implications directly in terms of the effects of bombings, whether these are the direct terrorist attacks or the response to terrorist attacks in the form of military activity. Terrorism also has the effect of increasing the production of arms and military resources, and this increase in the production of weapons has significant implications in terms of natural resources.

The anxiety and insecurity associated with terrorism can also be seen to have the effect, at times, of distracting attention from efforts to conserve energy and adopt 'greener' lifestyles. Even though the threat to our collective well-being posed by the destruction of habitat, is, arguably, much greater than the threat posed by terrorism, it is likely in the present political and media climate that the latter will receive far more attention and potentially sideline efforts to recue energy consumption, minimize pollution and tackle overpopulation issues.

Practice focus 11.3

Shahid was an environmental services manager in a large multinational corporation. His job was twofold. First, he needed to make sure that the company was complying with the various environmental protection laws and their own environmental policies. Second, he was paid to try to make sure that their activities were as 'green' as possible without adversely affecting the profit levels. The former role was fairly straightforward most of the time, but the latter was much more challenging. None the less,

▶

◄

he had made some good progress in getting green issues on the agenda and getting people to tune into environmental issues more fully. However, after a major terrorist attack took place what he found was that several steps backwards were taken. People seemed to be preoccupied with the idea that some horrific incident was about to happen and that then took their eye off the ball when it came to taking care to minimize energy usage. The risk of a terrorist attack was, of course, once that had to be taken seriously, but what was happening was that this risk was being exaggerated, while the risk of harm to our very habitat was being downplayed.

We also have to bear in mind that there is the potential use of nuclear weapons in terms of terrorism, whether on the part of terrorists ('dirty bombs') or in response to their activities. This would clearly have profound and far-reaching implications in terms of the environment.

Responses to the problem

The main response has been, parallel with the war on drugs, to have a 'war on terror'. Once again, this can be seen as an oversimplification of a complex set of issues. While there may, in some respects, be an identified enemy, the issues involved are more complex than a simple idea of a war. The idea of a war justifies military intervention, sanctions against certain nations or sections of population, and a concern with preventing 'radicalization'. All these can be seen as problematic in various ways.

Given that terrorism represents a strategy for promoting political objectives in a context of a conflict of worldviews, military intervention as an automatic knee-jerk response rooted in anger and a thirst for vengeance is hardly likely to move anyone towards a resolution of the conflict or a more peaceful way of handling the differences. This is not to say that military interventions are never justified, but the rhetoric of a 'war on terror' sets a military response as the default setting.

Similarly, economic sanctions against certain countries can have the effect of creating greater hardship (among largely innocent populations), thereby generating greater resentment and antipathy. Attempts to prevent 'radicalization', while potentially worthwhile in themselves, will often come at the expense of a reduction in civil liberties – for example, in terms of the monitoring of electronic communications.

Indeed, the war on terror has also had the effect of restricting civil liberties in a number of ways. Part of the ideology of a war on terror has been the acceptance that a reduction in civil liberties is a small price to pay for our safety. However, there is a significant danger here that this could be used as a means of increasing control over citizens, and could represent a worrying move towards totalitarian regime tactics.

In addition, radicalization is a problematic term in itself, as so called radicals are rarely so – they are not tackling the problems 'at the roots' ('radical' comes from the Latin word 'radix' which means root).

Scraton (2002) argues that, from its inception the 'war on terror' ethos that arose in the Bush/Blair era was fundamentally flawed. Fuelled by a sense of moral outrage, it had, he contends, neither sufficient intellectual understanding nor political capacity to wage such a war, let alone win it. Part of this war on terror strategy was to promote an ideology of demonizing 'the enemy'. As he puts it: 'In the "monstering" of Osama bin Laden, the Taliban and al-Qaida and their use of terror as a strategy, there was a serious failure to come to terms with the origins, definitions and manifestations of terrorism' (2002, p. 8). In other words, the response was a simplistic one that did not take account of the complexities involved or consider the wider and longer-term ramifications. For example, as we noted earlier, Cockburn (2015) argues that the rise of ISIS as a terrorist organization was a direct result of the war on terror mentality

There is also the question of risk amplification to consider. Although the loss of life involved in the 9/11 attacks was clearly a tragic turn of events, it is important to put these losses in context in terms of the level of risk posed. Furedi highlights a comparison between the losses involved with those in the Second World War:

One American journalist writes:

> Imagine that on 9/11, six hours after the assault on the twin towers and the pentagon, terrorists had carried out a second wave of attacks on the United States, taking an additional 3,000 lives. Imagine that six hours after that, there had been yet another wave. Now imagine that the attacks had continued, every six hours, for another four years, until nearly 20 million Americans were dead. This is roughly what the Soviet Union suffered during World War II, and contemplating these numbers may help put in perspective what the United States has so far experienced during the war against terrorism. [Bell, 2007]
>
> (Furedi, 2007, p. 82)

While again emphasizing that this is by no means to downplay the major tragedy and devastation of the 9/11 attacks (or other, subsequent atrocities), it is important to see these in context and perspective if we are to develop an adequate understanding of terrorism as a social problem.

Although the war on terror approach has been the primary one, there have also been elements of a therapeutic response. What I mean by a therapeutic response is to presume that the actions taken by terrorists are psychologically based and can therefore be best addressed by some form of psychotherapeutic approach. Once again Furedi, writing from a sociological perspective, has an important contribution to make to our understanding:

> One consequence of the representation of the impact of 9/11 through the medium of psychology was to one-sidedly exaggerate the vulnerability of the public. Through conceptualising the problem as that of the impact of terror on the public, the role assigned to people becomes a passive one. 'What will happen to the national psyche if the country is attacked again', asks one report [Booth, 2002]. The therapeutic world view dictates that the answer will be a psychological one – 34 per cent will develop PTSD, etc. However, such a narrow focus on mental health overlooks the possibility that through a sense of common purpose, unity or a commitment to fight, the so-called national psyche may alter and gain purpose and definition. Experience suggests that the impact on the national psyche of sudden military attacks, such as the bombing of Pearl Harbor, the Blitz, terrorist attacks in London and suicide bombers in Jerusalem are mediated through cultural and political influences and institutions. Such violence need not simply traumatise its targets. It can provoke a determination to fight or stimulate the construction of a community around a common cause.
>
> (2004, p. 16)

Bracken (2002) echoes this view by arguing that there is a danger of perceiving trauma in individualistic (atomistic) terms and not taking account of the wider sociopolitical context (the C and S levels of PCS analysis), thereby distorting the picture of the situations professional staff are called upon to deal with. Situations that have the potential to lead to trauma can also bring personal empowerment (as captured in the notion of post-traumatic growth – Calhoun and Tedeschi, 2006) for individuals and community strengthening and enrichment for whole groups of people – what is often referred to as 'community resilience' (Jerard and Mohamed, 2015).

> ➤ CHOICES *Constructing pathology* Neglecting the wider context risks 'blaming the victim' by not appreciating the significance of wider factors.

Voice of experience 11.3

I was involved in the aftermath of a terrorist incident. The psychological harm caused was quite significant for a lot of people. But, on the positive side, what it did very visibly was to pull the community together. There were people who had never spoken to their neighbours before who were now supporting one another with a strong sense of community spirit – it was what some people called 'Dunkirk spirit'. It was amazing to see, and really good too.

Lou, an emergency response coordinator

What has made huge progress in the Northern Ireland Troubles situation is the use of negotiated settlements and reconciliation. Huge efforts have been made by both sides in the Troubles conflict to find constructive ways of working and living together. This has not proven to be, in any sense, a sinecure or magic answer, but we do need to acknowledge that huge progress has been made in a number of respects. Whether this approach can be adopted in other terrorist situations remains to be seen, but, while the simplistic war mentality continues to be the dominant approach, it is highly unlikely that we would be able to move in such a positive direction.

As we have noted, terrorism, by design, strikes fear in the heart of large numbers of people. This additional strain and tension can then have a knock-on effect in a number of ways, each of which can add to the impact and seriousness of social problems. There is therefore much to be gained from addressing terrorism in terms of not only the problems presented

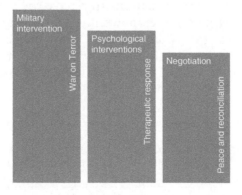

Figure 11.2   Responses to terrorism

directly by terror, but also its impact in raising tensions that can in some ways add to other social problems.

Points to ponder

> In what way(s) is terrorism socially constructed?
> What do you understand by the term 'state terrorism'?
> What dangers are involved in trying to respond to terrorism by focusing on an individual level only?

Exercise 11

Search online for one or more media accounts of terrorism (an account of either a specific terrorist incident or of terrorism as an entity more broadly). How balanced do you feel the reporting is in terms of the level of risk? What assumptions does the reporting seem to be relying on in terms of the nature of terrorism? How might the presentation of risk and the apparent assumptions being made about terrorism affect how people reading, watching or listening to the coverage perceive terrorism?

12

Destruction of Habitat

Introduction

In some respects, the destruction of habitat can be seen as the most important social problem of all, in so far as it has the potential to lead to the end of the human race. If we continue to abuse our environment and its resources at the current rate, we will inflict greater and greater harm on both present and future generations. This chapter follows the same patterns as its predecessors in Part 2 in highlighting some of the key issues involved.

While this destruction affects literally everyone on the planet, what we will see is that it affects some people more than others, and so inequality is also a factor here, as with the other social problems highlighted. The interconnectedness of the problem being focused on in this chapter with other social problems will also surface as an important issue once again.

Understanding the destruction of habitat

First of all, it is important to clarify why I am using the term 'destruction of habitat'. People commonly refer to 'environmental problems' destroying our planet, but, in reality, the planet will continue to exist in its own right, despite the harm that we are currently doing to it, long after humans have ceased to occupy it. What is being destroyed, therefore, is not the planet itself, but the conditions on the planet that allow human life, and indeed wildlife, to continue. The patterns of work, production and consumption that we have adopted have hastened the end of a viable habitat for us. We are already seeing the destruction of habitat for many forms of wildlife, with many species becoming extinct each year. Our own human habitat is also being shaped in a negative direction. Some people fail to recognize the significance of the harm that we are doing and the term 'destruction of the planet' may seem unrealistic to them, whereas it is easier to believe and accept that we are, in very real terms, destroying our habitat. The planet will still be there, but we will not if we continue to pollute the environment at the current rate.

While the destruction of habitat for wildlife is an important considera-tion in its own right, we also have to bear in mind that human existence is premised in various ways on the existence of other life forms. Consider, for example, the concerns arising from the dwindling numbers of bees surviving and the potentially disastrous knock-on effects of that for agri-culture and food supplies. As Scandrett explains:

> we ignore the interrelationships between human societies and the diversity of biological species, genetic resources and ecosystems at our peril. The global destruction of biodiversity, which has accelerated in the past 200 years, has led to an ecosystem far more vulnerable to disruption and catastrophe, which inevitably has a disproportionate impact on the poorest sections of society. Environmental injustice therefore constitutes a social relation that nevertheless occurs within a complex ecological context.
>
> (2012, p. 241)

We shall return to the notion of environmental injustice below, but, for now, we should note that, at the root of the problem is our arrogant atti-tude to nature: assuming that it is simply a set of resources for us to use and exploit as we see fit, with little consideration of the consequences – for ourselves and other species – of regarding natural resources as infinite. Increasingly now there are calls for us to change our attitude towards our environment, to think of the relationship with nature as one of symbiosis – a form of partnership, as it were – rather than one of dominance and submission rooted in an attitude of exploitation.

Pickering captures the situation well we he argues that:

> What seems to be going wrong is that our relationship with the environment is increasingly violent and destructive. We are beginning to realize that the effects of our technologized lifestyles are leading to damage on a global scale that we may not be able to repair. The unease that this creates is fundamentally detri-mental to well-being.
>
> (2012, p. 153)

Practice focus 12.1

Bikkhu was an environmental adviser in a local authority. A key part of his job was to make sure that energy use was kept to a minimum and pollution was reduced as far as possible. When he first started the job he was confident that, with proper

▶

◀

'environmental husbandry', as he liked to call it, we should be able to save the day. However, to make sure he was up to date with the latest thinking on ecological matters, he read widely. The more he read, the more he felt that what we were doing as a society was just not enough. The better informed he became, the more convinced he was that we needed a more radical approach. This view was reinforced when he attended an environmental protection conference and heard about the latest projections. At first he felt quite depressed by it all, but after a while, he realized he needed to be more proactive. So, this spurred him on to press for a rethink of his council's environmental policies and to become more actively involved in green issues in his private life. He knew he couldn't change the world singlehandedly, but he was determined to play his part in whatever reasonable way he could.

Excessive energy consumption

One of the main causes of the destruction of habitat is global warming. This is due to the greenhouse gases that are being produced and rapidly increased through industrial processes and our excessive use of energy resources. The effect on the ecosphere can be quite profound, and we are facing potential long-term massive destruction as a result of this. By affecting the chemical composition of the earth's atmosphere we are allowing health-harming rays to penetrate more easily, with highly detrimental results.

While mass destruction may not come within the lifetime of those people who are currently alive, there are significant issues in terms of the negative legacy we are leaving for future generations. We are already seeing, as I have mentioned, significant threat to wildlife that will continue to accelerate if our current patterns of energy consumption continue at the same rate. Also, because of global warming and rising sea levels, there are precarious human populations. For example, there are some islands and coastal areas where a rise in sea level could potentially wipe out a viable habitat for significant numbers of people.

Over time we have become complacent in our energy usage patterns. Although, for example, it is now quite common to see signs in public buildings next to light switches that say 'Please switch off the lights when not in use', it is equally common to find room after room not in use, but with all the lights on. However, this is but one small part of the energy problem. Industry uses (and often wastes) energy at such high levels that it dwarfs the domestic or public building usage. Efforts to reduce energy consumption therefore need to be more far reaching than is currently the case, incorporating domestic, civic, commercial and industrial sectors.

While many people have got the message, and take pride in their green credentials, there are many who have yet to take it on board – especially in industry where environmental concerns may be seen as an unnecessary expense or an obstacle to profit maximization.

Another aspect of excessive energy consumption is the reliance on carbon fuels (coal and petrol, for example). Relative affluence has produced much higher levels of consumption, adding further to the problems. Higher consumption also means higher levels of industrial activity in the production and distribution of goods, adding to both energy consumption and pollution levels. As Klein comments:

> We know that if we continue on our current path of allowing emissions to rise year after year, climate change will change everything about our world. Major cities will very likely drown, ancient cultures will be swallowed by the seas, and there is a very high change that our children will spend a great deal of their lives fleeing and recovering from vicious storms and extreme droughts. And we don't have to do anything to bring about this future. All we have to do is nothing. Just continue to do what we are doing now, whether it's counting on a techno-fix or tending to our gardens or telling ourselves we're unfortunately too busy to deal with it.
>
> (2014, p. 4)

Klein's book is entitled *This Changes Everything*, and this is a very apt title. We shall return to this point below.

Overpopulation

Another aspect of the destruction of habitat comes through patterns of overpopulation. The population of the earth is increasing at a relatively rapid pace. How much further the expansion of population can be tolerated without significant depletion of natural resources remains to be seen. There is, of course, only a finite number of people who can be safely and adequately housed on the planet without destruction of certain aspects of that habitat.

Each new child that is born will, on average, be beginning a pattern of resource consumption that will last several decades. This is not to argue, of course, that no one should give birth. But, what it does mean is that efforts to reduce energy use and pollution will be counteracted by a steadily increasing world population. Significantly, overpopulation is an aspect of the destruction of habitat that receives relatively little attention.

Voice of experience 12.1

We cover ecological issues in our science syllabus. We have to get the balance right. On the one hand we don't want to frighten the children and send them home distressed and fearful about the end of the world, but we do want them to get the message about the challenges we face and the big changes we all have to make.

Wynn, a secondary school teacher

Productivism

Much of what has been written and said about the threat to the environment is pitched at the level of individuals and families, focusing on how each of us can save energy, use less fuel, pollute less, recycle more and so on. However, what this fails to take account of is that consumption by individuals is just one part of the problem. Even if all individuals and all families were to follow green guidelines, there would still remain a major problem because of the overconsumption at a more macro level in terms of industry, commerce, the military and so on. This overconsumption is driven by an ideology of consumerism and materialism, or what Fitzpatrick calls 'productivism'. He links this to the role of the state in relation to social policy and welfare provision:

> By perpetuating the ideologies of productivism, welfare systems help to fuel more unsustainable growth. One implication is that welfare reforms tend only to address what environmentalists regard as the surface symptoms of social problems and miss the fact that the roots of many problems lie in ecological degradation and injustice. For instance, environmentalists note the extent to which poor health is caused by economics that place profits ahead of physical and mental well-being. 'Productivism' is therefore the assumption that economic growth is infinite and should take priority in all our economic, social and public policies (Fitzpatrick, 2003b, 2007a; Jackson, 2009; Paehlke, 2010: 246–7).

(2011a, p. 62)

This is an important passage, but one point in particular is especially significant, namely the idea that productivism rests on: 'the assumption that economic growth is infinite and should take priority.' This is a dangerous assumption as it does not fit with what environmental science is telling us about the harm we are doing to our habitat.

Our consumerist and materialist lifestyle driven by neoliberal ideology has accelerated the problems that we face. As noted earlier, part of the problem is our relative affluence resulting in higher fuel consumption. In turn, this increased use of fuel and energy in general results in significant pollution of rivers, streams and the sea, increasing levels of toxicity in the air and other related problems.

> ➤ CHOICES *Over-reliance on the market* Neoliberal thinking encourages consumerism, which, in turn, has environmental costs

Underpinning these difficulties is an ideological conflict between an emphasis on economic growth and viable sustainability. Sustainability refers to the ability for the human race to be able to have lifestyles that are not threatening to the environment – that is, that sustain our habitat rather than undermine or destroy it. The dominant thinking in the economics sphere is that economic growth is a good thing; the more the better, but, of course, it is important to recognize that economic growth comes at an environmental cost – and quite a significant one at that.

Philosophically this boils down to a difference between what is sometimes referred to as 'anthropocentrism' (which refers to the way in which human issues are prioritized at the expense of environmental factors), as opposed to Spinoza's philosophy which emphasizes the significance of nature and the role of humanity as just one part of that wider, natural environment (Spinoza, 1996). It is all a matter, therefore, of whether we see the earth as simply a set of resources to be exploited as we see fit or a wider biosphere that we are part of and which essentially is part of our survival.

Practice focus 12.2

Megan was a county councillor in a rural area. She had never given much thought to environmental matters as her authority was facing major cutbacks, and so her priority was to try and balance the books without creating problems through cuts to services provision. She and her colleagues were under great pressure to make efficiency services, but there is only so much that can be done to make operations more efficient and cost-effective. In this pressurized atmosphere, environmental concerns seemed to her to be fairly low priority. However, her daughter was at university and had just started a module on environmental science. When she came home for the weekend she put her mother under a lot of pressure to place more emphasis on environmental

▶

◀

issues. It didn't take Megan long to realize that her daughter was right, so what she had to do now was to add a new challenge to her (already very long) list. She now wanted to look at whether she could reduce costs and be environmentally friendly at the same time – a big ask in some ways, but not impossible.

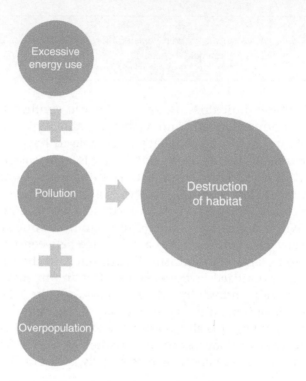

Figure 12.1   Contributions to the destruction of habitat

These, then, are some of the key causes of the destruction of habitat problems that we face. In terms of the consequences of our ecological problems, we need to recognize the need for changes above and beyond the individual level. We shall return to this point below.

How the destruction of habitat affects, and is affected by, inequality

While the ultimate consequence of the destruction of habitat will, if its present trajectory is allowed to continue, will affect everyone equally, in the meantime the effects are far from equal.

Power protects

Perhaps the most significant thing to note in regard to inequality is the disproportionate effect on poorer and less powerful people and nations as a result of destructive lifestyle practices and processes. It would be naïve to think that, in a situation of major environmental challenge, the power elite will take their fair share of the detrimental consequences. Of course, the most powerful groups will have the resources to do whatever they reasonably can to minimize the impact, whereas those at the other end of the social power hierarchy will bear the brunt of the greater proportion of the negative consequences.

The logic of inequality and social injustice is very apparent in these circumstances. The most powerful play a greater role in creating the ecological crisis, but are in the strongest position to be cushioned, as far as possible from the harm done. Meanwhile, the least powerful groups contribute less to the destruction of habitat, but are in the frontline for taking the full hit of the ensuing problems. As Sprintzen comments:

> Consider some preconditions of market relations. Capital and labor must be free to move wherever the profit is greater. This free mobility of capital and labor must inevitably result in the systematic destruction of settled community life, as jobs follow investments and communities are left to fend for themselves. Meanwhile, nature is treated as but a collection of raw materials for production and a repository for waste. With an unprecedented drive for growth and development, this free enterprise system has literally "created a world after its own image", radically transforming the conditions of life of people across the planet.
>
> (2009, p. 21)

Gender inequalities

There are also gender implications to consider. There is a school of thought that goes by the name of 'ecofeminism' that argues that women are experiencing greater problems as a result of our environmental mismanagement (Mies and Shiva, 2014). This is because women are more associated with the home and the private sphere and face greater difficulties relating to their lifestyles. This is part of the 'deep ecology movement' (Sessions, 1995) which emphasizes that we need to recognize humanity as part of this wider environment, echoing Spinoza's thoughts on this matter. A key part of deep ecology is the idea that we are not simply resident on the planet. Rather, we are part and parcel of a set of complex biological processes and the disruption of those processes is harmful, not only to ourselves but also to all forms of life on the planet.

Environmental injustices

There are also what are known as 'environmental injustices' to take into account. This term refers to situations in which certain groups lose out as a result of environmental mismanagement – for example, in terms of housing. The development of slum dwellings in some parts of the world is because of the shortage of land as a result of land masses being used for mining, quarrying and other money-making endeavours.

Sprintzen again offers a helpful insight consistent with the deep ecology approach:

> we are currently in the midst of a global cultural and metaphysical transformation at least equal in scope to that which began to transform the planetary culture four centuries ago. Our fundamental modes of thought and action, institutional structure, personal identity, economic development, and relation to nature, all require radical revision if human life on the planet (and beyond) is to survive and prosper. We are thus confronted with a world whose structure of meaning and corresponding institutional foundations are being undermined, thus presaging a revolutionary transformation the import of which, however unclear at present, cannot fail to be radical and comprehensive.
>
> (2009, p. 9)

In a similar vein, Beck (2016) argues that what we are witnessing is not just social change, but a more or less complete world metamorphosis. Central to this is the way in which the threat to the environment is changing social relations, adding new dimensions of inequality (for example, between those whose homelands are threatened by rising sea levels and those that are not). We shall consider this idea further in Part 3.

A positive reaction?

The picture of environmental threat is a very negative and disconcerting one. However, this is not to say that there are no positives to draw on. For example, Klein has argued that our current precarious position has the potential to bring people together:

> through conversation with others in the growing climate justice movement, I began to see all kinds of ways that climate change could become a catalysing force for positive change – how it could be the best argument progressives have ever had to demand the rebuilding and reviving of local economies; to reclaim our democracies from corrosive corporate influence; to block harmful

new free trade deals and rewrite old ones; to invest in starving public infrastructure like mass transit and affordable housing; to take back ownership of essential services like energy and water; to remake our sick agricultural system into
something much healthier; to open borders to migrants whose displacement
is linked to climate impacts; to finally respect Indigenous land rights – all of
which would help to end grotesque levels of inequality within out nations and
between them.

(2014, p. 7)

Of course, this does not lessen the seriousness or severity of the challenges
we face, but it does offer some degree of a silver lining.

Reduced public spending

Another significant issue is the reduced public services expenditure
brought about by the need to address the harmful effects of our current
environmental practices. The significant level of funding that needs to be
invested in addressing environmental concerns reduces the level of financial resources available for tackling other social problems. This will then
have an effect on those who rely most on public services, this being generally the least affluent and least powerful members of our communities.

The neoliberal project of minimizing the role of the state on the misguided assumption that a free economy will benefit everyone results in a
lower level of investment in public services under the heading of 'austerity
measures'. The financial costs of the harm done to the environment will
therefore have a greater impact on those who are least well-resourced to
respond to the problems encountered.

> ➢ *Hegemony and universalized interests* The idea that a free economy will benefit all
> masks the discrepancy between the profit benefits for the wealthy and the austerity-
> related hardship for the least powerful groups.

Pickering makes an important point when he reports that:

Gandhi remarked that 'The world has enough for everyone's needs, but not for
some people's greed'. Someone who experiences the world from this viewpoint
will feel fundamentally secure. Corporate greed, acquired second-hand via
the advertising industry, makes people feel insecure. The world cannot seem
ever to provide enough. It has been clear for decades that the natural needs of
the world's peoples can be met, and met sustainably, given the technological

resources we now possess (e.g. Seabrook 1985). Artificial needs created through media stimulation, by contrast, are designed specifically not to be met. Unmet needs create violence.

(2012, p. 161)

This takes us back to Merton's (1996) argument that society generates consumerist expectations that many people cannot achieve.

Voice of experience 12.2

We find ourselves in a difficult situation a lot of the time at the centre I work at. People are constantly exposed to advertising and other media messages that tell them that they must have the latest and greatest this and the super-wonderful that. They get a strong, consistent message that you are nobody unless you have an impressive range of consumer goods. Many people accept that they can't afford these things and they do their best to get round the problem in whatever ways they can. But some people, for whatever reason, don't seem able to do that. And, of course, there is then a huge debt creation industry happy to lend people money they will struggle to pay back at high levels of interest. Now that's where I come in, trying to help people find a way out of the mess. And, believe me, it is not an easy job, because even if they can clear the debt, the pressure to spend more is still there. That means that some people have serial debt problems. It's like a roller coaster: they're in debt, they get out of debt, they get into debt again, and so on. Not a great way to live a life, but some people just can't resist those consumer messages.

Jess, a debt counsellor in an advice centre

However, it needs to be remembered, as Klein has pointed out, that climate change can be seen as a galvanizing force for social justice claims. That is, as we do more damage to our environment, and, as this becomes more and more apparent, then the critique and protest in relation to current organizational and corporate practices will grow stronger.

How the destruction of habitat affects, and is affected by, other social problems

Scandrett helps us to understand the importance of not seeing environmental issues in isolation. We need to appreciate the links with other problems and other social policy challenges:

Environmental policy is only one contributor to socio-environmental change. Other factors include ecological changes, ideological shifts and other policies in the context of global and local economic trends. This is not to underplay the significance of policy in relation to the environment, but to locate it in relation to these other factors.

(2012, p. 239)

One significant factor to recognize in terms of social problems generally is that the greater pressure and stress brought about by environmental problems can have the effect of upping the ante in terms of a wide range of such problems. For example, the tensions brought about by poorer living conditions linked to environmental mismanagement can be seen to be quite detrimental to significant numbers of people.

Arguably, there is a link between the use of drugs and alcohol as a form of escapism in relation to the problems that we face. Instead of facing up to the reality of the situation and challenging current practices, alcohol and drugs provide an easy way out of the difficulties we face – or so it would seem to those who are misguidedly relying on such means of not facing up to the environmental crisis that we face.

Similarly, mental health issues have already been linked earlier in this book to the increasing pressures of a modern consumerist life. Part of this is concern about the harm done to the environment so again there are issues that arise from increased tensions and a sense of insecurity brought

Practice focus 12.3

Gavin was a drugs worker in a multidisciplinary team. He was aware that there was no single reason why people got themselves into difficulties with alcohol or other drugs. However, he realized that escapism was a common theme. One woman he was asked to work with was fully committed to tackling environmental problems. She was very much into the idea of Gaia, of the earth as a totality of which humans were a part – very different from the dominant thinking about humanity vs nature. For many years she had been a heavy cannabis user, to the point where her thought processes were very slow and laboured. She was an interim user of Gavin's service, as she would go for a while and be totally free of drugs. Then, after a while, things would start to get on top of her and she would start smoking cannabis and drinking heavily as a means of escape. What triggered these bouts of drug use was an increase in anxiety. Concerns about 'destroying nature' as she put it were not the whole story, but they were certainly a key part of it. Gavin was trying to help her find ways of coping that did not involve drugs, but so far he had had very limited success.

about by the knowledge that our ways of living and working are highly detrimental to our habitat and therefore to our future survival.

We can also draw links with abuse in terms of greater tensions that as we develop a more consumerist lifestyle with higher demands on people to purchase goods (which in themselves have environmental costs) and as the pressure for people to be able to 'keep up with the Jones's' continues, then many people are going to feel that they are excluded from their society. Feeling excluded, feeling less powerful, feeling undervalued, can be a significant contributory factor towards processes of abusing power and therefore processes of child abuse, abuse of vulnerable adults and domestic abuse.

Responses to the problem

The dominant way of approaching environmental concerns is to work towards sustainability – that is, to look at ways in which carbon reduction can be achieved through increased or improved technology, how fuel use can be limited by various measures and how, in general, a more energy efficient approach can be developed. However, the deep ecology movement I mentioned earlier, adopts a different approach. This is why it is referred to as 'deep' because it regards such a sustainability approach as superficial and untenable. A basic premise of deep ecology is the need to look more fundamentally at the relationship between humanity and our environment, to have a much more thoroughgoing understanding of the holistic nature of the relationship between humanity and nature.

In a related vein, Lister helpfully distinguishes between 'technocentrism' and 'ecocentrism':

> 'Technocentrism' is typified by a belief that environmental problems can be sorted out by technocratic means, for example taxes that make polluters pay. It is a reformist position, which does not represent a challenge to the dominant economic or political order. It can therefore be incorporated easily within capitalism ... 'Ecocentrism' represents, in contrast, a fundamental challenge to the economic order premised on economic growth and consumption. It therefore rejects both capitalism and socialism.
>
> (2010, p. 85)

This is parallel with the distinction we mentioned earlier between an anthropocentric view (that is, one that puts humanity at centre stage and nature as simply a set of resources to be exploited at will) and a more holistic view that presents humanity as part of a wider biosphere that we need to learn to live in harmony with.

Voice of experience 12.3

Things have improved enormously in the recycling world. We are doing so much better now. But, we mustn't be complacent. We have to bear in mind that recycling is just one part of what we need to do to safeguard our environment for future generations. Unfortunately, a lot of people seem to think that recycling is saving the Earth, but in reality it's just slowing down the rate that we are harming it. Of course, recycling is really important, but it's certainly not enough on its own.

Charlie, a recycling manager

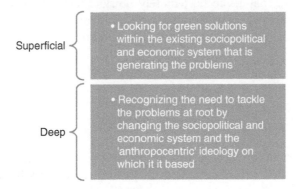

Figure 12.2   Surface vs deep responses

Unfortunately, one approach to the problem of destruction of habitat is to make it worse by trying to capitalize on the potential profits to be made. Klein, in her important study of the exploitation of disaster situations, looks at how the Chicago School of Economics has focused on the way in which crises can be used to generate revenue (Klein, 2007). She describes how this group of academics has developed a method for generating considerable sums of money by using crisis situations to bring about economic changes that involve moving in a neoliberal, free-market direction. Their primary concern is not environmental protection, but, rather, using climate change-related catastrophes (the New Orleans floods, for example) as a springboard for promoting and instituting free-market systems.

➤ CHOICES *Over-reliance on the market* Free marketeers are capitalizing on environmental catastrophes to promote their ideology.

There are already clear examples of how the environmental crisis is being used by certain corporations to generate increased profits. This then feeds the consumerism and materialism that are at the heart of the problem in the first place. So while at a theoretical level we have important contributions that can guide us from the deep ecology movement, we also have to recognise that at a pragmatic level, existing dominant ideologies can be seen to be taking us in precisely the opposite direction to the one we need to go in.

Klein sums up succinctly the situation we now face:

> The challenge, then, is not simply that we need to spend a lot of money and change a lot of policies; it's that we need to think differently, radically differently, for those changes to be remotely possible. Right now, the triumph of market logic, with its ethos of domination and fierce competition, is paralyzing almost all serious efforts to respond to climate change.
>
> (2014, p. 23)

Conclusion

For a variety of reasons, patterns of behaviour (P), dominant ideas (C) and structural power relations (S) and economic systems have developed that put our very living space at risk, steadily destroying our habitat. The long-term consequences of continuing with our current levels of energy use, pollution and population growth are nothing short of lethal. In the short to medium term such problems are reinforcing existing patterns of inequality and social injustice and forming part of a complex web of other social problems. The challenges we face are therefore of major proportions.

Fitzpatrick captures the point well:

> What we face, in other words, are circumstances that challenge us to revise our social administrations and our social imaginations. The former is crucial and we always need social policy engineers to build, maintain, repair and tell us how things work within their specialities. But without vision, idealism, ambition and utopianism, social policy can be a very dull affair, dedicated to intervening in people's lives without much idea of why or with what purpose in mind.
>
> (2011b, p. 316)

We therefore need the vision and the commitment to take forward, in whatever ways we can, the exploration of what needs to be done to address these very serious problems.

Points to ponder

> In what ways is human behaviour contributing to the destruction of habitat?

> What is meant by the term 'productivism'?

> What is the difference between surface and deep approaches to the environment?

Exercise 12

What changes will be necessary to halt the pace of the destruction of habitat? Who has the power to make those changes? What are the obstacles to such changes being made?

PART 3

Addressing Social Problems and Social Justice

13
Efforts to Date

Introduction

In this chapter I offer a review of the main political, policy and professional responses to social problems. My aim is not to provide a comprehensive analysis, but simply to offer a critical review of some of the key issues that have characterized efforts to date. What this chapter should achieve is an overview of the range of responses commonly developed as a result of particular social problems and the challenges they present.

Political tensions

What has been apparent throughout the various chapters of this book is a tension between neoliberalism, with its emphasis on the free-market economy and the restriction of the role of the state, and a commitment to a public service ethos that emphasizes an important role for the state in supporting the well-being of its citizens. This is a long-standing tension and it is not likely to disappear very soon. It is important to be aware of it, and its implications, because it informs and influences how social problems are defined in the first place and what policy responses are developed as potential solutions.

Three models of the state

It can be helpful to try and understand the role of the state in terms of three different models or levels. Neoliberalism focuses on what is known as a *residual* model of the state – that is, a governmental level that is the minimum required to oversee the workings of the economy and wider society. According to neoliberalism, the state should play the minimum role that it needs to and nothing more, hence the term residual. Everything else should be left to the free market to encourage enterprise and economic growth. Lister captures this point well in the following passage:

Neo-liberalism represents a reaction against the social liberalism that dominated in the 20th century and a return to classical forms of liberalism. It is thus
distinguished by hostility to the state in the field of welfare and by the lauding
of the private market sector and private domestic sphere over the public sector
as a source of welfare. The market is regarded as the most efficient producer and
allocator of resources and the state's role should be confined to providing the
necessary framework for the market and private property and to protecting the
liberty and security of the individual.

(2010, p. 32)

> ➤ CHOICES *Over-reliance on the market* Within neoliberalism the market is given a
> primary role and the role of the state is minimized.

Contrary to a neoliberal residual model, since the 1940s the UK has
been characterized by a *welfare state*. Following the disastrous consequences of the Second World War where it was recognized that such
issues as poverty, poor education and poor health were clearly visible
among people who had been involved in the conflict. We saw the development of various Acts of Parliament that were based on the philosophy
that the state should take some degree of responsibility for its citizens.
This included the development of the National Health Service, free at
the point of delivery, 'national assistance' benefits for those who had no
other source of income, free universal education and so on. The basic
idea was the government of the day should offer a safety net and thus
ensure that all citizens had a sound foundation of citizenship and social
inclusion. This was, of course, in stark contrast to the neoliberal idea of
a residual, minimalist state.

However, one of the criticisms of the notion of a welfare state is that it
involves doing things for people that they are capable of doing for themselves. The argument is that it makes people dependent and discourages
them from being self-sufficient. This type of state is often referred to as a
'nanny' state whereby the state is expected to play some sort of parental
role in relation to its citizens. Proponents of a residual state often use this
term 'nanny state' as a way of disparaging the achievements of the welfare
state. It is, of course, entirely possible to have a welfare state that in no way
resembles the criticisms that go under the heading of a nanny state. By contrast, a neoliberal state leaves little room for an emphasis on citizen well-
being. As we have seen at various junctures in the present analysis, there
are various ways in which neoliberal thinking increases inequality, creating

greater problems for the poorest and least powerful groups in our society – the very people who are most likely to need what the welfare state offers as a safety net. There is, then, a 'double whammy', as far as the impact of neoliberalism is concerned, in that it creates greater problems for the most disadvantaged groups, while seeking to reduce the level of support available to address those disadvantages. This problem associated with neoliberalism and the residual state creates a vicious circle not just for the individuals directly affected. As a result of the emphasis on the state having a minimal role, there is a reduced level of investment in public services (what has come to be known as 'austerity', as we noted earlier). As a result of that lower level of investment, we encounter greater social problems. For example, early in 2016 it was announced that the number of people sleeping rough in England had doubled since the Conservative government, with its neoliberal approach, had come into power (www.theguardian.com/society/2016/mar/09/rough-sleeping-rise-london-homelessness-every-day-struggle). What happens when investment in public services is reduced and problems subsequently increase is that there are then greater costs in terms of dealing with those problems. There are the human costs for the people concerned and those close to them, but there are also costs for wider society in terms of, for example, increased levels of criminal activity, increased social tensions and all the attendant problems from that. Neoliberalism can therefore be seen to offer an unhelpful approach in relation to social problems because of the vicious circle that it tends to provoke.

Practice focus 13.1

Val was a social worker in a 'Gateway' team – that is, she was involved in responding to all the new referrals that came into the Department. She had been in the team for over four years and had seen referral rates vary over time. However, she was aware that the variations were within a fairly narrowly circumscribed range. She had learned that if the referral rate went up, it wouldn't be long before it came back down again. However, what had struck her was that, since 'austerity' had become a key word in response to public spending difficulties brought about by the banking crisis some years before, what she noticed was that the referral rate was not only going up and up, with no sign of it coming down, but also the severity of problems people were bringing to the Department had increased. At one point the referral rate did start to go down again and she began to think the really busy patch was over, but, no, very soon it started to rise – the decrease had just been a blip. Sadly, what Val was also aware of was that, while the referral rate was going up, council cutbacks meant that the resources available to respond to those referrals were now at a much lower level.

Atomism

Another problem with neoliberalism is that one of its features is atomism – that is, the tendency to focus on individuals in isolation. This is because this type of thinking suits the ideology behind the idea of the free market. A welfare state ideology, by contrast, is based on the idea of collectivism, of people supporting one another and addressing problems collectively. One of the consequences of neoliberalism, therefore, is that social problems (that is, problems that affect significant proportions of our society) are not defined as social problems, unless and until they become a threat to the social order and the interests of the power elite. Otherwise, they are simply defined as a large number of cases of individual problems. This takes us back to the 'blaming the victim' mentality where there will then be a tendency, for example, to blame poor people for being poor, and thereby fail to recognize the wider cultural and structural factors that are operating.

Prilleltensky and Prilleltensky argue the case for collective solutions and thus, by extension, a role for a welfare state:

> If you work in the helping professions, you know the experience of working with clients on a strategy, only to see it diminished by overwhelming social forces. How far can you go in helping a teenager feel safer when he goes back to a crime-infested neighbourhood? How effectively can we curb violence against women when the media and the culture are full of it? Collective problems require collective solutions.
>
> (2012, p. 64)

Leaving individuals to wrestle with problems that are actually social problems in their nature and consequences is a poor basis for developing social policy responses to current challenges.

Voice of experience 13.1

I enjoy my job, but especially the training aspect of it. New volunteers come in all shapes and sizes, and with all sorts of different experiences and attitudes. We try to set our project in the context of the welfare state, but emphasize that that's very different from a nanny state. We are there to help people make a positive contribution to their local community – that's the 'welfare' bit – but what we won't do is do things for people that they are able to do themselves, so no one can say we are part of some 'nanny' state.

Pat, a volunteer coordinator in a community development project

Misrepresenting the welfare state

As we have seen, part of neoliberal ideology is the tendency to present a (positive compassionate) welfare state as if it were a (negative, disempowering) nanny state. In an important study of the welfare state, Hills warns of the common misunderstandings of the welfare state fuelled by politically biased representations of it:

> Public perceptions (and misconceptions) are dominated by two linked notions, often tapped into by politicians and then further fed by their own rhetoric and parts of the media. First, the beneficiaries of the 'welfare' system are largely unchanging and are different from the rest of us who pay for them through our taxes. Second, the bulk of this huge amount of spending goes on hand-outs to a group of people who are out of work, often claiming fraudulently.
>
> (2015, p. 249)

It is worth examining each of these two assumptions in more detail:

1. *Welfare benefit recipients form a fixed underclass.* Hills's detailed analysis shows that there is considerable variation in terms of who receives benefits and when. It is a constantly shifting picture of many people moving out of the benefits safety net while others move in.

2. *The majority of payments are to unemployed people,* with fraud a common feature. In reality, pension payments and support to individuals in work far exceed the total amount paid to unemployed claimants. Also, benefits fraud accounts for 0.7 per cent of social security spending and is a drop in the ocean compared with the amounts involved in tax evasion (estimated to be about £25 billion per year), according to Jones (2015).

It is also important to recognize that the welfare state is much, much broader than the benefits system. Indeed benefits (or 'income maintenance' to use the technical term) is only one of the five traditional 'pillars' of the welfare state.

Figure 13.1   The five pillars of the welfare state

Hills goes on to point out how significant these misrepresentations can be:

> Misconceptions about the welfare state and the way it is abused is not just a matter of harmless misunderstanding. They create serious problems in how the welfare state is run, affecting both those in or on the margins of poverty at any one time, and all of us through the choices we are making for the whole of the welfare state. Actual fraud of jobseeker's allowance may be less than one thousandth of all spending on social security, according to official analysis, but if we believe it to be over a tenth of the total, we will demand that our politicians react accordingly.
>
> (2015, pp. 264–5)

Presenting benefits fraud as being a much greater problem than it is, while also glossing over the much bigger problem of tax evasion reflects neoliberal thinking in terms of maximizing the role of the market for thFigure 13.1   The five pillars of the welfare state e benefit of the wealthiest echelons, and minimizing the role of the (welfare) state that seeks to protect the interests of the most disadvantaged groups in our communities. 'Clamping down' on scroungers and seeing benefit fraud as a serious social problem is an example of the universalizing of interests – a benefit to the power elite is presented as a benefit for everyone. By contrast, a stronger emphasis on tax evasion would benefit the wider populace, but will be a problem for at least some elements of the power elite.

➤ *Hegemony and universalized interests* It is important to question who benefits from what is defined as a social problem (and from what is not defined as a social problem).

Practice focus 13.2

Carol was a welfare rights adviser. She had been unemployed herself for a while, so she knew how difficult and demoralizing it could be. She appreciated that this experience had helped her in her current job to know where people were coming from. She was not naïve enough to think that there were no people who had no intention of working and were happy to live on benefits, but she was aware that this was certainly not the case for all the people she had been involved in helping for the past three years. It struck her that the notion of 'scrounger' is a stereotype that overgeneralizes from a tiny few to the vast majority. 'It's not fair and it's not helpful', she thought. 'People who have to rely on benefits have enough to contend with'. She wished that people who were so judgemental would find out more about what they were talking about before jumping to negative conclusions about people.

Social problems

To date, efforts to address social problems have tended to have a limited consideration of social justice issues. Problems have been addressed in their own right. That is, poverty has been addressed as an issue affecting a certain proportion of the population without any fuller consideration of how this reflects the wider structure of society and the cultural norms and ideological explanations that encourage an individualistic or atomistic approach to the problem. One of the things we can learn from this analysis, therefore, is that there is a need to link together social problems issues and social justice issues.

Voice of experience 13.2

One of the most challenging aspects of my job is getting people to think holistically. I have teachers who, understandably, focus on education, health care staff who focus on health, housing officers who focus on housing, and so on. Sticking to your own turf may work well most of the time, but when we're looking at abuse and safeguarding issues, we have to think beyond our normal boundaries. If we don't, there is a danger that abuse issues slip through the net. We all have to try and get into the child's shoes and think what life is like for them. Then, if there is any abuse going on, we are in a better position to realize that and act accordingly.

Nic, a child protection development officer

Interconnectedness

What we have tended to see to date is a fragmented approach with little consideration of interconnectedness. For example, there will be different professional groups operating within different social policy contexts focusing on their own concerns in terms of one or more social problems. However, a more holistic approach to the very nature of social problems and the common processes (inequality and social exclusion for example) has tended to be lacking.

➤ CHOICES *Interconnectedness* For the most part social problems are connected with one another in various ways.

In some areas as well there have been problems in terms of a simplistic approach to social problems, something that in my earlier work I have characterized as 'dogmatic reductionism' (Thompson, 2011a). This refers to the tendency to oversimplify complex issues (reductionism) and to address the issues concerned in a rigid and dogmatic way. For example, the 'war' mentality, whether it be in relation to drugs or terrorism, illustrates how an oversimplified, rigid approach is far from helpful in tackling some very complex, multilayered sets of issues. The notion of 'interconnectedness' therefore helps us to appreciate the complexities involved and warns us against too simplistic an approach.

Social justice

Just as the literature on social problems has had relatively little to say about social justice, we can see that the literature relating to social justice has likewise had relatively little to say about social problems. However, what should be very clear from the discussions in earlier parts of the book is that we need to acknowledge inequality as a source and exacerbation of social problems at a number of levels. In addition to the examples that have been explored in this book, there are plenty more instances besides that could be brought to bear. The analysis here is far from comprehensive or exhaustive. There is therefore considerable scope for developing a much fuller understanding of the links between inequality and other aspects of social justice and the social problems that we face in modern-day society.

Dogmatic reductionism

In terms of social justice, the dogmatic reductionism I refer to earlier has had the effect of putting issues of inequality and discrimination higher on the social agenda than was previously the case, but this is done so at the cost of alienating many people and presenting oversimplified understandings that have led to a number of policies that have proven to be highly problematic. For example, the handling of circumstances relating to black children being received into care proved to be quite counterproductive. The criticism that black children were being placed with white foster carers who had little understanding of their ethnic needs or no experience of dealing with the challenges of racism, was met with a dogmatic reductionist policy of not placing black children with white foster carers. Given the absence relatively of black foster carers in our care system, the net result was that the vast majority of black children being received into care were placed in children's homes with predominantly white staff. The situation was therefore exacerbated, rather than alleviated, by a knee-jerk defensive reaction to criticism.

The more recent emphasis on equality and diversity is more likely to be effective in managing the complexities involved because it adopts a more nuanced approach to the issues involved. However, there is a danger that the commitment to tackling social injustices becomes diluted by this approach. This is a complex matter that requires fuller attention than I can give it here, but for present purposes it is important to recognize that we need to avoid the extremes of, on the one hand, dogmatic reductionism and, on the other, an approach that fails to recognize the serious impact of social injustice on a significant number of people.

Sadly, at times dogmatic reductionism has been particularly to the fore in areas relating to inequality. For example, some approaches to tackling racism have been characterized by oversimplified and dogmatic approaches, what have been referred to as 'the excesses of anti-racism' (Penketh, 2000). This is highly problematic because a commitment to challenging racism is very important, but the key issues tend to be over-simplified in such an approach, with the dogmatic tendencies being likely to alienate people from such matters. For example, I am aware that the habit of rejecting issues around language equality as 'political correctness gone mad' has often been triggered by dissatisfaction with the hectoring approach associated with dogmatic reductionism (Thompson, 2011b). The issues of anti-racism deserve a much fuller and more nuanced consideration; a much more sophisticated level of understanding is called for.

Practice focus 13.3

Afiya had been appointed as a race relations development worker in a large company. She had had a long-standing interest in anti-racism so this seemed to be an ideal job for her in many ways. However, it soon proved to be no bed of roses, as she encountered considerable difficulties. This was because there were two different factions, with two different schools of thought. Despite having shared interests and sharing the same ultimate goal of getting as close to eradicating racism as possible, the two groups were quite antagonistic towards one another. One group saw anti-racism as part of a wider agenda of equality and diversity and the need to challenge discrimination and oppression in all its forms. The other saw this as a watering down of the anti-racism struggle and wanted to focus primarily on anti-racism, leaving others to fight the battles around other forms of discrimination. Afiya could see that she faced a tough time trying to unite the two factions in an anti-oppressive alliance, but she was determined to do that, as she felt that racial equality was far too important to allow this sort of in-fighting to get in the way of progress.

PCS analysis revisited

At various points in the book I have mention PCS analysis as a multilevel framework of understanding. It can be useful now in terms of
reviewing how efforts to tackle social problems have fared to date.
At a **P** level, Davies (2012) argues that aggression arises as a result of
problems we encounter. However, he claims that secondary problems,
such as addiction, anxiety and obsessions come to the fore when
that aggression is not used to address our primary problems. It then
becomes misdirected against ourselves in destructive ways. We may
go on to create problems for ourselves at a personal level as a result
of how we are reacting to wider issues and external forces. This means
that there is a personal element to social problems but this is not to
pathologize individuals, but to recognize that there is always a personal, subjective dimension to social phenomena and life experiences,
and social problems are no exception to this.

At a cultural level (**C**) we can see that there are significant issues
to consider in terms of how ideas about social problems and indeed
about social justice shape the way social problems are defined and
responded to. Illouz highlights the significance of culture when she
argues that:

> culture matters a great deal for who we are. By "who we are" I do not refer
> to our objectives, interests, or material resources. Rather, I refer to the
> way we make sense of who we are through actions shaped by values, key
> images and scenarios, ideals, and habits of thought: through the stories we
> use to frame our own and others' failures and successes; through what we
> feel entitled to; and through the moral categories we use to hierarchize our
> social world. Our actions, narratives, accounts, and moral categories not
> only help us make sense of who we are but are central to the way we com-
> municate ourselves to others, the way we mobilize their support, what we
> are ready to defend and fight for, and how we orient ourselves in the face of
> ambiguous choices.
>
> (2008, p. 8)

Policy approaches to social problems often have little to say about the
cultural level and how pre-established frameworks of meaning (discourses
and ideologies) can play a significant part in deciding what constitutes a
social problem and what the response to any such problem should be.

At a structural level (**S**), what we need to recognize is that to date there
has been limited consideration of the disproportionate effects of social
problems. That is, while certain issues such as crime can affect the whole

population in a number of ways and at a number of levels, to date inadequate attention has been paid to the fact that it is the poorer and less powerful groups (the lower levels of the social hierarchy at a structural level) that experience the brunt of the difficulties involved. For example, consider burglary. If somebody who is financially comfortable experiences a burglary and has items stolen, their ability to replace those items is likely to be much greater than someone who is, for example, living on benefits or on a low income who may then not be in a position to replace the items stolen. Given, as mentioned earlier, the fact that burglaries are ironically more likely to occur in low-income areas than high-income ones, this adds to the severity and extent of the problem. Linked to this as well is the significance of insurance. People who are trying to survive on a low income are less likely to have insurance that would cover any such losses, and, if they do, have insurance, that insurance is likely to be more expensive if they are living in a high-crime area than for someone living in a more affluent area where there are fewer chances of a burglary taking place.

As we have seen, social problems can be understood as problems *for* society, but this idea is often put forward without recognizing that society is not a level playing field. Who will experience what consequences from social problems varies considerably. However, that variance is not at random; it follows the structural fault lines of society. To date, this is an issue that has not been given the full attention it deserves.

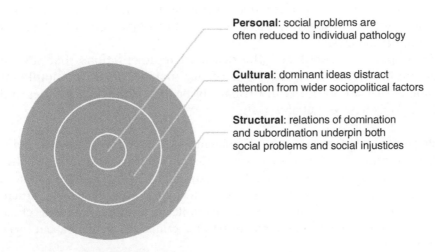

Personal: social problems are often reduced to individual pathology

Cultural: dominant ideas distract attention from wider sociopolitical factors

Structural: relations of domination and subordination underpin both social problems and social injustices

Figure 13.2   PCS analysis revisited

Voice of experience 13.3

My course has really opened my eyes to social problems. I can see now that there is a world of difference between how the media and politicians talk about problems and what it is really like. My placement showed me a different side to it all, and boy, what a difference it was. When I started the course there was a lot of emphasis on discrimination and, to be honest, I thought they were overdoing it, giving it more attention than it deserved. But now, looking back at that, I can see why they did and realize they were right to do so.

                                                     Ira, a social work student

Conclusion

What this chapter has shown is that efforts to tackle social problems to date have not been able to take sufficient notice of key issues relating to social justice. There is therefore a clear message that future efforts to address social problems need to be rooted in a much more thorough and more extensive understanding of the significance of social justice and the impact of social injustices.

Dominant neoliberal thinking presents an atomistic model of social problems that pays little or no attention to cultural and structural aspects. In doing so, it distracts attention from the key role of inequality and social injustices, thereby presenting a distorted picture. That picture reinforces the social hierarchy, with members of dominant groups benefitting, while ordinary citizens – especially those from disadvantaged groups – lose out in a number of ways.

These power relations and the distorted representations that sustain them are firmly rooted in the fabric of our society and in the dominant ideologies that are so powerful in shaping people's thoughts, feelings and actions. As DeKeseredy et al. put it:

Progressive solutions to ... [social problems] are easy to find. The problem is implementing them because they challenge conventional wisdom (Chambliss, 2001), and because neoconservative politicians oppose progressive solutions because they fear losing financial gains they have made under the current system (Barak, 1986). Thus, ideological hurdles rather than economic obstacles account for the failure to mount rational campaigns to bring about social justice.

                                                            (2003, p. 125)

It is clear, then, that the situation is not going to change overnight. However, as we noted in Chapter 1, it is not the case that 'there is no alternative'. There is certainly no *easy* alternative, but there are steps we can take and an exploration of some of these will be our focus in Chapter 14.

Points to ponder

➤ What are the main differences between residual, welfare and nanny models of the state?

➤ What problems might arise from adopting an attitude of dogmatic reductionism?

➤ What influence on the C level are the media likely to have?

Exercise 13

In Exercise 1 you were asked to identify what you thought were the three most important social problems. After reaching this point in the book, have you changed your view? If so, how and why? If not, have any of your views about social problems changed at all?

14
Future Avenues

Introduction

In this final chapter I present an exploration of alternative political, policy and professional responses to social problems. It is important to emphasize from the beginning that this chapter does not constitute a set of predictions or simplistic answers. It is to be hoped that my comments thus far will have illustrated the lack of wisdom involved in any such approach. Taleb (2010), in an impressive study of improbability, emphasizes the uncertainty of the future and thereby warns against being too confident in making predictions. There are just too many variables to create a realistic picture of what the future holds.

Rather, what this chapter is intended to offer is food for thought to inform future policy development and professional practices in responding to the challenges presented by such a wide range of social problems. It is an exercise in considering how the future *could be* different, depending on the choices we make, individually and collectively.

The themes revisited

Much of this chapter will be taken up by revisiting the themes highlighted in the introduction to the book and considering each in turn in terms of possible ways of moving forward to produce a more adequate approach to social problems and social justice – one that begins to do justice to the complexities involved.

Constructing pathology

It should be clear from the discussions to date that we need to move away from a 'blaming the victim' mentality that falls foul of the logical

error of atomism – that is, the tendency to see things in purely individual terms (the **P** level of PCS analysis) without also considering the
wider implications (the **C** and **S** levels). Blaming the victim is not only
logically or intellectually unsound, it is also highly problematic in
terms of the unfair consequences for people who are blamed for their
own misfortune. This can be seen as a sort of double whammy. Not only
are they the victims of certain wider social processes that produce problematic outcomes, but they are then stigmatized and disadvantaged by
being blamed for the fact that they are on the receiving end of such difficulties. Hedges helps us to appreciate the significance of this when he
argues that:

> For those who run into the hard walls of reality, the ideology has the pernicious
> effect of forcing the victim to blame him or herself for his or her pain or suffer-
> ing. Abused and battered wives or children, the unemployed, the depressed, the
> mentally ill, the illiterate, the lonely, those grieving for lost loved ones, those
> crushed by poverty, the terminally ill, those fighting with addictions, those suf-
> fering from trauma, those trapped in menial and poorly paid jobs, those facing
> foreclosure or bankruptcy because they cannot pay their medical bills, need
> only overcome their negativity.
>
> (2009, p. 119)

Practice focus 14.1

Carl was a psychologist in a general hospital. He specialized in cognitive behavioural work which involves identifying how current (problematic) behaviours are
rooted in particular thoughts or beliefs. To change the behaviour, you need to
change the underlying belief that spurs that behaviour. Consequently, much of
Carl's time was spent helping people identify what those underlying beliefs were.
Over time he came to realize more and more that, while everyone is a unique
individual, with their own specific beliefs, for the most part the beliefs that were
proving problematic generally reflected 'messages' from wider society. Beliefs
that led to low self-esteem were common and Carl could see that many of his
clients had been given the message that they were of little or no value – they
had little status or value in society's eyes, due to their class, ethnic group, drug
problem or whatever. He could do little about the way these messages are fed to
certain groups of people, but he tried to make sure that he helped his clients realize that it was important for them to challenge these unfair, prejudicial labels that
had been attached to them.

One example of how we can move away from a pathologizing approach is what is now referred to as 'co-production'. This refers to the process whereby groups of professionals work with people who are wrestling with the consequences of social problems (what are often referred to as 'experts by experience') to try and develop schemes, programmes and strategies for addressing the problems concerned. For example, there may be such professionals as social workers, community workers, police officers, youth workers and probation officers working with parents of young people whose lives have been wrecked by illegal drug use. Instead of it simply falling to the professional services to tackle the problem, a partnership develops between the people who are paid to address social problems and people whose lives are adversely affected by such problems. This form of partnership makes it clear that this is not a question of blaming people for their own misfortunes, but, rather, trying to work together in a more holistic way to explore the wider circumstances that have given rise to such problems, and thereby exploring potential solutions that can be developed.

Witcher provides a helpful explanation of co-production:

Co-production can be defined as 'a partnership between citizens and public services to achieve a valued outcome' (Horne and Shirley, 2009, p 3). According to Boyle and Harris 'Co-production means delivering public services in an equal and reciprocal relationship between professionals, people using services, their families and their neighbours. Where activities are co-produced in this way, both services and neighbourhoods become far more effective agents of change.' (2009, p. 11). It can be a means of developing policy and strategy, a method of community development and an approach to formulating personalised services, such as care packages.

(2015, p. 195)

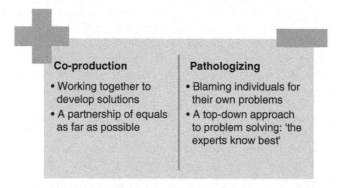

Co-production	Pathologizing
• Working together to develop solutions • A partnership of equals as far as possible	• Blaming individuals for their own problems • A top-down approach to problem solving: 'the experts know best'

Figure 14.1   Co-production vs pathologizing

Voice of experience 14.1

I was a bit sceptical about co-production at first – just another buzzword, I thought. But, to be honest, I am really into it now. We have traditionally worked with individual families, but we are now exploring ways of working more collaboratively with groups of families across communities. It's still early days, but it's already showing signs of making a really positive difference.

Glen, a social worker in a family support team

The existentialist writer, Jean-Paul Sartre is well known for making the point that hell is other people (Sartre, 1989). What he meant by that was other people's plans and circumstances can get in the way of our own. They can be an obstacle to progress because other people may want different things from ourselves. But what Sartre did not point out is that other people can be heaven too, in the sense that working together in cooperative collaborative ways has much to commend it. The tendency to pathologize individuals has acted as a break on the development of collective collaborative approaches despite the fact there is much to be gained from such a community based collective approach to the difficulties that people encounter. Wilkinson and Pickett echo this point:

> As well as the potential for conflict, human beings have a unique potential to be each other's best source of co-operation, learning, love and assistance of every kind. While there's not much that ostriches or otters can do for an injured member of their own species, among humans there is. But it's not just that we are able to give each other care and protection. Because most of our abilities are learned, we depend on others for the acquisition of our life skills. Similarly, our unique capacity for specialization and division of labour means that human beings have an unrivalled potential to benefit from co-operation. So as well as the potential to be each other's worst rivals, we also have the potential to be each other's greatest source of comfort and security.
>
> (2009, p. 198)

In terms of this theme of constructing pathology, therefore, what we need to work towards is the rejection of atomistic understandings and approaches, to be replaced by holistic ones, enabling us to see the bigger picture – the cultural and the structural as well as the personal. This would amount to not falling foul of the common tendency to oversimplify complex issues relating to social problems and social justice.

Hegemony and universalized interests

As we noted in Chapter 1, hegemony is a process of dominance mainly through ideas or ideologies, rather than through force or threat. To understand hegemony, we need to ask the question: Whose interests are being served by a particular way of working or a particular way of thinking? Jones (2015), in his important analysis, has shown a clear Establishment bias in a number of ways and at a number of different levels. One way in which this manifests itself is the idea of 'universalized interests'. What this refers to is the common tendency for the media and other powerful institutions to put across the idea that what is in fact in the interests of the dominant few (the power elite) is actually in the interests of the many, the general populace. This mythology is a very common feature of many aspects of modern life. What Jones illustrates in his important work is a systematic bias in the channels of communication. In each way that information about society is communicated there is a consistent bias in favour of the dominant thinking which, of course, is currently neoliberal thinking.

Communication is an important dimension of power (Thompson, 2011b). Bernstein helps us to appreciate the significance of this:

> at the most basic level, the words "politics" and "communication" are nearly synonymous; all politics, after all, is nothing more and nothing less than communication applied in the service of power. Only by understanding the relative access to and control over information and communications technology, which has grown ever more complex over the centuries, can we understand the ebb and flow of politics, of culture, and of the human condition itself.

> (2013, p. 14)

The bias in systems of communication is therefore of considerable significance. More and more, people are recognizing the potential role of social media as a way of getting round this consistent systematic bias. Bernstein reminds us that in Ancient Greece the alphabet proved mightier than the sword and, in the medieval era, the printing press proved to be mightier than the Roman Catholic Church. Perhaps today, he argues, the ubiquitous mobile phone camera can prove to be mightier than the surveillance camera.

Of course, information and communication technology is neither liberating nor oppressive in itself, but can be used to take us in either direction. This is just as true of social media. Bernstein makes the point that key to its use is who is allowed to have access to it. It is no coincidence, for example, that repressive political regimes will have a tendency to try

Practice focus 14.2

Liz was a teacher in a further education college. She was aware that her students generally had very little political awareness, but they did have a strong grasp of social media and lots of experience of using the various channels of communication. So, what she did was to set her students a project of comparing how politically signifi-cant events were reported in the conventional mass media and how they featured in the social media world. Some of the students struggled to get any meaningful sense of the differences, but there were enough students in the class who produced some really useful comparisons to have made it a very worthwhile learning experience. This enabled Liz to draw out a wide range of learning points about communication and power and how the conventional media are quite restricted in what and how they report. She decided that this was an exercise she would repeat with other classes in future, as she felt it had given the group some important insights that she hoped would encourage them to develop more interest in politics.

and suppress the use of social media. This is because social media enable ideas to be promulgated outside of the dominant patterns of thinking – that is, beyond the biases.

There is therefore considerable scope for exploiting the potential of digital technology to circumvent the workings of ideology and to there-fore break down the hegemony of the one per cent who are able to control various aspects of social life through the dominance of the thinking that supports their approach.

This is not to present social media as some sort of panacea, but as a foothold in terms of trying to find ways round the consistent bias that presents social problems as matters of individual failing, rather than as phenomena that have wider cultural and structural dimensions.

Over-reliance on the market

There are now many writers who have begun challenging the myth of the free market and the dominant assumption that the market if left to its own devices will produce the best outcomes (see, for example, Chomsky, 1999; Chang, 2010). The New Economics Foundation (NEF) has strongly challenged this thinking and is offering an alternative way of approach-ing economic matters that is more consistent with the holistic approach to social problems and social justice presented in this book.

The idea of corporate social responsibility which has grown in stature and emphasis in recent years, goes some way in a positive direction, but it is not enough on its own. The idea of corporate social responsibility is that large organizations that are primarily profit-making machines should not focus exclusively on maximizing their profit if that then has negative consequences for communities and for the environment. The notion of corporate social responsibility is therefore a valuable one. However, how it is practised in reality is often in a tokenistic way and, although the concept is a positive one, it needs to be taken much, much further if it is to make a significant difference to the problems that we currently face. It remains within an ideology of an over-reliance on the market, with just some limited softening of the blow of such a profit-driven approach at the expense of individuals, families, communities and, indeed, our habitat.

Bauman strongly rejects this neoliberal commitment to allowing the market to dominate:

> We can no longer trust in the unseen forces and the invisible hand of the market. Growth in justice requires more than economic growth ... it requires decisions, programmes, mechanisms and processes specifically geared to a better distribution of income, the creation of sources of employment and an integral promotion of the poor which goes beyond simple welfare mentality ... the economy can no longer turn to remedies that are a new poison, such as attempting to increase profits by reducing the work force and thereby adding to the ranks of the excluded.
>
> (Bauman and Donskis, 2016, p. 43)

While it is positive to have such a strong rejection of neoliberalism from such a leading sociologist, we should not expect too many of the people in positions of power to pay much attention.

We have seen that the communications bias already discussed stands in the way of moving forward. To challenge market dominance, we need to recognize that the challenge of bypassing neoliberal ideology is something that deserves considered attention. Part of this consideration needs to be how political processes can be influenced. Academic research can be part of this but, as Witcher points out, we should be careful not to overestimate the contribution the academic world can be expected to make:

> It may persuasively be argued that social policy development is not driven by theory – or empirical evidence for that matter – but by political imperatives to reduce public expenditure, enable tax cuts, promote economic growth and, of course, win elections. Policy may be made reactively in response to unforeseen events, or used opportunistically to lend credence to pre-existing ideologically derived intentions or assumptions. In such cases, it may appear that theory has no role to play. Nevertheless, whether or not those responsible are conscious of it, whether or not *post hoc,* some form of theoretical underpinning is always

discernible, even if just at a level of broad assumption. The more considered and substantial that underpinning is, the greater the chance should be that policy will achieve its goal.

(2015, p. 25)

Voice of experience 14.2

I am very conscious that a huge amount of time, money and effort goes into social research, but the impact it makes is often not great. That's partly because research is often not clear cut or results are ambivalent, but mainly because research findings that go against certain taken-for-granted ways of seeing the world generally fall on stony ground when it comes to policy development.

Robbie, a university-based researcher

Interconnectedness

At various points in the book I have highlighted the way social problems can be seen to interconnect. However, this is not something that is being widely recognized in terms of social policy responses. For example, a common way of tackling social problems at a governmental level is for a particular social problem to be the responsibility of an individual government minister and his or her department. This tends to mean that different ministers and different departments are tackling their own priority areas, but without any overall consistent holistic approach. There is therefore scope for efforts to become counterproductive, where progress in relation to one social problem can actually make it more difficult for other government efforts to tackle their own priority areas.

What is needed, then, is the idea of a helicopter vision – the ability to look holistically at a situation – that is, to rise above it like a helicopter does, but also have the ability to descend back into that problem and be able to deal with it in a pragmatic way. That helicopter vision needs to incorporate an understanding of the interconnectedness of not only social problems, but also how those social problems connect with issues of social justice.

Counterfinality

As we noted in Chapter 1, the idea that some attempts to tackle one or more social problems can either make them worse, create new problems or exacerbate other problems is what is known as 'counterfinality'. This is another reason for why we need a holistic approach. We need to look at the big picture, and this involves thinking through changes that are made, thinking of the wider consequences of acting in a particular way. If there is no joined-up thinking on these issues, then there is a danger that scarce public sector resources for tackling social problems will be wasted through ineffective, misdirected efforts.

This need to think things through and look holistically at situations is therefore a strong basis for advocating reflective practice and evidence-enriched practice (Thompson and Thompson, 2008). We need to be able to use our professional knowledge to make sense of the difficulties that are encountered. This takes us back to the ministerial approach mentioned earlier, whereby decisions about social problems are often made on the basis of political expediency and ideological attractiveness, rather than on social science research or professional knowledge and experience that can offer better understanding of the complexities involved.

In an earlier work (Thompson, 2016c) I drew a distinction between different types of reflection: immanent, transitive and transformational. Immanent reflection is the type of reflection that produces no concrete results. Immanent is a philosophical term that refers to something that is internal or self-contained – that is, something that does not have an external effect. Immanent reflection therefore refers to time spent thinking, mulling something over, but without bringing about any change as a result of that thinking.

Transitive reflection, by contrast, is something that has a distinct outcome; it makes a pragmatic difference. The thought leads to positive action. Clearly, transitive reflection is of more value than immanent reflection. However, what is better still, where it is possible, is transformational reflection. This involves being able not only to improve the situation, but also to transform it, so that it is no longer a problem. For example, where there is an underlying conflict that is causing problems, immanent reflection would involve reflecting on that, but doing nothing about it. Transitive reflection would lead to doing something about the problems caused by the conflict. Transformational reflection would involve addressing the underlying conflict and thereby transforming the situation, rather than just improving it.

Sadly, to date much of the thinking on social problems and social justice has been at best transitive. How we can move towards a transformational approach is a huge question and one to which there are no easy answers.

Existential/spiritual implications

We have touched on the importance of phenomenology and the significant role of the frameworks of meaning. As Bauman puts it: 'All societies
are factories of meanings. They are more than that, in fact: nothing less
than the nurseries of *meaningful* life' (2001, p. 2). Focusing on meaning is
important, because the very notion of what is a social problem, as we have
seen, is socially constructed. It is not something that is written in stone. It
is part of a wider framework of (ideological) meaning.

Another important existential dimension is that of ontology (the study
of being). We have seen at various points that the existential suffering
associated with a lack of trust and security can make a huge difference in
terms of people's well-being or quality of life. The existentialist concept of
ontological security is therefore an important one. People will struggle to
tackle their life challenges positively, to deal with their problems and difficulties if their lives are held back by the anxieties associated with ontological insecurity.

So, while I have emphasized at various point the tendency to neglect
the wider cultural and structural aspects of social problems and social
justice, it is important to emphasize that such understandings need to be
in addition to the understanding of personal, psychological or spiritual
matters. These are important elements of our multidisciplinary multilevel
understanding of social problems and social justice.

Practice focus 14.3

Susheela was a counsellor in private practice. She worked mainly with people who
could afford to pay her fees. However, she was approached by a fellow counsellor
and friend who asked her to undertake some pro bono work at a voluntary sector
project. Her value base had led her to respond to each individual and their unique
needs. However, working in her new context she very quickly recognized some strong
patterns. She was used to dealing with anxiety and various insecurities, but somehow
what she was encountering now was different. There were what she was used to – the
'human frailties', as she called them – but there were also some things she wasn't
used to. She didn't understand what it was at first, but after a while she started to
realize that what she was witnessing was additional anxieties linked to social circumstances. So, she thought, there are the existential insecurities we all face, regardless
of our circumstances, but for some people from disadvantaged groups, there were
also the social anxieties that come from poverty, housing problems and so on and all
the negative messages that come with them.

Social construction

We have seen the role of powerful institutions, such as the media, in not only defining what constitutes a problem, but also determining how such problems should be addressed. The process of social construction – that is, of developing frameworks of meaning – is therefore at the heart of our understanding of social problems. In order to appreciate the significance of social construction, we need to think about how some people have the privilege of having more of a say in what happens, compared with others. Consider, for example, the way in which certain problems, such as corporate manslaughter through employer negligence, receive minimal attention compared with, say, manslaughter perpetrated by an individual.

One of the implications of social construction is positive, though, in the sense that it does not have to be this way. We have choices. If social processes have defined and constructed our existing social problems and our existing patterns of (in)equality, then steps can be taken to change that. Of course, this is where hegemony plays its part in terms of the dominance of certain ideas that stand in the way of making positive changes.

That hegemony – dominance maintained by ideas that become accepted as normal, natural and unquestionable – is maintained through powerful institutions, especially the media. Chomsky explains:

> So what the media do, in effect, is to take the set of assumptions which express the basic ideas of the propaganda system, whether about the Cold War or the economic system or the "national interest" and so on, and then present a range of debate within that framework – so the debate only enhances the strength of the assumptions, ingraining them in people's minds as the entire possible spectrum of opinion that there is. So you see, in our system what you might call "state propaganda" isn't expressed as such, as it would be in a totalitarian society – rather it's implicit, it's presupposed, it provides the framework for debate among the people who are admitted into mainstream discussion.
>
> (Mitchell and Schoeffel, 2002, p. 13)

What this illustrates is that the media create a framework of boundaries that constrains debate, discussion and, to a certain extent, thought. This relates back to our discussion in Chapter 1 of the 'there is no alternative' mentality that constrains consideration of a wider range of understanding and action.

Although the mass media are a primary source of information, we should not forget that they are not educational bodies. They are, for the most part, businesses seeking to make a profit. Chomsky's comment reflects this well:

Well, I once asked another editor I know at the Boston Globe why their coverage of the Israeli/Palestinian conflict is so awful – and it is. He just laughed and said, "How many Arab advertisers do you think we have?" That was the end of that conversation.

(Mitchell and Schoeffel, 2002, p. 22)

Information drawn from the media therefore needs to be received critically and understood in context.

Metamorphosis or more of the same?

In Chapter 1 I mentioned the significance of existentialism as a philosophy that can help us cast light on social problems and social justice. One of its tenets is that change is a constant feature of existence. If things stay the same it is because something is happening (actions or processes) to reproduce them ('autopoiesis' is the technical term for this – Thompson, 2011a). On this basis, we can see that social problems and associated social injustices are not written in stone. What has been socially constructed can, in principle, at least, be socially reconstructed.

Renowned sociologist, Ulrich Beck, has argued that what we are currently witnessing is more than social change; it is what he calls: the 'metamorphosis of the world'. By this he means not just a new chapter in social history, but a radically different world order:

> the agent of the metamorphosis of the world is the endless story of failure. To put it bluntly, global poverty is on the rise, the poisoning of the planet is on the rise, so too is global illiteracy, while global economic growth leaves much to be desired, the world's population is growing ominously, global famine relief is inadequate, and the global market – especially the global market – is driving us all to ruin.
>
> (2016, p. 17)

Beck argues that the challenges facing the world, including the global ecological threat, create new forms of inequality (for example, in terms of which communities are at risk because of rising sea levels). He also contends that the nature of this global threat may actually bring nations together in the search for solutions – collaboration in the face of a shared threat of extinction instead of at war. Whether this will indeed be the case remains to be seen. We should not lose sight of the warning from Taleb (2010 of the hazards of making predictions in such an unpredictable world.

One of the features of metamorphosis that Beck discusses is the recognition that things that were previously deemed unthinkable are now seen as normal and natural. This reflects the success of ideology – particularly neoliberal ideology – in shaping our cultural assumptions at the **C** level.

In political terms this represents a shift to what is traditionally seen as the right. As Jones (2015) argues, what were previously seen as extreme right-wing views are now accepted as part of the centre ground. Similarly, moderate left-of-centre ideas are readily dismissed as 'hard left' or 'extremist'. Future developments will depend on whether that shift continues, stabilizes or reverses.

Voice of experience 14.3

I think of myself as a realist. I know people who buy into all this 'positive psychology' optimism stuff and I reckon they are only seeing one side of the story. There again, I know people who are dyed in the wool pessimists, always just one step away from defeatism. Shouldn't people be able to see that there are positives and negatives in life, pluses and minuses? Why the need to focus on just one side of the story? It's the same when I look to the future. I can't imagine that won't be a mixture of positives and negatives too.

Mel, a voluntary sector manager

So, at one extreme we have Beck's notion of metamorphosis, the emergence of a new world order prompted by the global challenges we face. At the other extreme we have 'more of the same', the continued neoliberal hegemony, with its increasing inequality, the continuing oppression of a significant proportion of the population and the ongoing destruction of our very habitat. Where we go between those two extremes depends on a number of complex, interacting variables and at each point of these interactions, at each 'nodal point', to use the technical term, there will be choices. We need to make sure that we choose wisely.

Conclusion

Social problems are complex. Social justice is complex. The relationship between social problems and social justice is complex. We should not, therefore, expect simple or straightforward 'answers'. However, it is to be

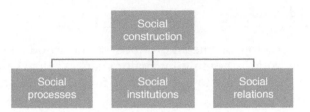

Figure 14.2 Social construction

hoped that the analysis presented here will act as a foundation for taking our understanding further and for helping to make us better equipped for addressing the problems.

We have seen that social problems are not just individual problems writ large. They reflect social processes, institutions and relations. They are defined, as are the policy responses designed to address them, through processes of 'social construction'. Who has the power to contribute to these processes is linked to the structure of society, the complex web of power hierarchies (the **S** level). Those definitional processes shape our shared understandings of problems, their causes and their consequences (the **C** level) and our views about how best to respond to the challenges involved. Our actions and attitudes at the **P** level are in part shaped by the influences of the **C** and **S** levels (and our reactions to those influences). To understand social problems and social justice we need to appreciate the interactions of these three levels.

We also need to appreciate the interactions across social problems (the 'interconnectedness') and the intricate ways in which social problems and social injustices reinforce one another. Continuing to address social problems in isolation will do us no favours in our efforts to solve or alleviate the problems. Neglecting the links between social problems and social justice will similarly hold us back in our endeavours to develop a fairer, more humane and more compassionate society.

Points to ponder

➤ Who benefits from individuals being blamed for their own problems?

➤ Why is it important to see the connections between social problems?

➤ What is the role of the media in shaping our understanding of social problems?

Exercise 14

Consider Beck's notion of 'metamorphosis of the world'. In what ways do you feel the world is heading for major changes? How can concerned citizens play a part in trying to influence the future direction and shape of any such changes?

Guide to Further Learning

Introduction

This guide has been developed to help you take your learning forward. I have emphasized that this is not intended to be a comprehensive book and that there is much more to be said about social problems and social justice. You are therefore encouraged to use this guide to start to see what literature is available (books and journals) and what online resources you can begin to explore. I very much hope that what we have covered in this book together will have sparked your interest and given you an appetite to take your knowledge further and deeper.

Social problems

Best, J. and Harris, S. R. (eds) (2013) *Making Sense of Social Problems*, London, Lynne Rienner Publishers.
Heiner, R. (2006) *Social Problems*, Oxford, Oxford University Press.
Isaacs, S., Blundell, D., Foley, A., Ginsburg, B., McDonough, B., Silverstone, D. and Mooney, G. and Scott, G. (eds) (2012) *Social Justice and Social Policy in Scotland*, Bristol, The Policy Press.
Young, T. (2015) *Social Problems in the UK: An Introduction*, London, Routledge.
Zavala, A. G. D. and Cichocka, A. (eds) (2013) *Social Psychology of Social Problems*, Basingstoke, Palgrave Macmillan.

Social justice

Atkinson, A. B. (2015) *Inequality: What Can Be Done?*, Cambridge, MA, Harvard University Press.
Barry, B. (2005) *Why Social Justice Matters*, Cambridge, Polity Press.
Chang, H-J. (2010) *23 Things They Don't Tell You About Capitalism*, London, Penguin.
Dorling, D. (2014) *Inequality and the 1%*, London, Verso.
Dorling, D. (2015) *Injustice: Why Social Inequality Persists*, 2nd edn, Bristol, The Policy Press.

Gilliat-Ray, S. (2010) *Muslims in Britain: An Introduction*, Cambridge, Cambridge University Press.

Jansen, S. C., Pooley, J. and Taub-Pervizpour, L. (eds) (2011) *Media and Social Justice*, Basingstoke, Palgrave Macmillan.

Jivraj, S. and Simpson, L. (eds) (2015) *Ethnic Identity and Inequalities in Britain*, Bristol, The Policy Press.

Jones, O. (2015) *The Establishment and How They Get Away with It*, London, Penguin.

Mendoza, K-A. (2015) *Austerity: The Demolition of the Welfare State and the Rise of the Zombie Economy*, London, New Internationalist.

Mooney, G. and Scott, G. (eds) (2012) *Social Justice and Social Policy in Scotland*, Bristol, The Policy Press.

Sayer, A. (2015) *Why We Can't Afford the Rich*, Bristol, The Policy Press.

Stiglitz, J. (2016) *The Great Divide*, London, Penguin.

Thompson, N. (2007) *Power and Empowerment*, Lyme Regis, Russell House Publishing.

Thompson, N. (2011) *Promoting Equality: Working with Diversity and Difference*, 3rd edn, Basingstoke, Palgrave Macmillan.

Thompson, N. (2016) *Anti-Discriminatory Practice*, 6th edn, London, Palgrave Macmillan.

Wilkinson, R. G. and Pickett, K. (2009) *The Spirit Level: Why More Equal Societies Almost Always Do Better*, London, Allen Lane.

Witcher, S. (2015) *Inclusive Equality*, Bristol, The Policy Press.

Poverty

Alcock, P. (2006) *Understanding Poverty*, 3rd edn, Basingstoke, Palgrave Macmillan.

Hills, J. (2015) *Good Times, Bad Times: The Welfare State Myth of Them and Us*, Bristol, The Policy Press.

Jones, O. (2012) *Chavs: The Demonization of the Working Class*, London, Verso.

Lansley, M. and Mack, J. (2015) *Breadline Britain: The Rise of Mass Poverty*, Oxford, Oneworld.

Lister, R. (2004) *Poverty*, Cambridge, Polity.

Ridge, T. and Wright, S. (eds) (2008) *Understanding Inequality, Poverty and Wealth: Policies and Prospects*, Bristol, The Policy Press.

Unemployment

Ford, M. (2015) *The Rise of the Robots: Technology and the Threat of Mass Unemployment*, Oxford, Oneworld.

Gorz, A. (1999) *Reclaiming Work: Beyond the Wage-based Society*, Cambridge, Polity Press.

Grint, K. and Nixon, D. (2015) *The Sociology of Work*, 4th edn, Cambridge Polity Press.

Jahoda, M. (2009) *Employment and Unemployment: A Social-Psychological Analysis*, Cambridge, Cambridge University Press.

Housing problems

Barker, K. (2014) *Housing: Where's the Plan?*, London, London Publishing Partnership.

DeKeseredy, W. S., Alvi, S., Schwartz, M. D. and Tomaszewski, E. A. (2003) *Under Siege: Poverty and Crime in a Public Housing Community*, Lanham, MD, Lexington Books.

Dorling, D. (2015) *All That Is Solid: How the Great Housing Disaster Defines Our Times, and What We Can Do About It*, London, Penguin.

Garnett, D. (2015) *A-Z of Housing*, London, Palgrave Macmillan.

Lund, P. (2011) *Understanding Housing Policy*, Bristol, The Policy Press.

Crime and anti-social behaviour

Davies, M., Croall, H. and Tyrer, J. (2009) *Criminal Justice*, 4th edn, London, Longman.

Maguire, M., Morgan, R. and Reiner, R. (eds) (2012) *The Oxford Handbook of Criminology*, 5th edn, Oxford, Clarendon Press.

Muncie, J. (2015) *Youth and Crime*, 4th edn, London, Sage.

Pickard, S. (ed.) (2014) *Anti-social Behaviour in Britain: Victorian and Contemporary Perspectives*, Basingstoke, Palgrave Macmillan.

Roberts, J. V. (2015) *Criminal Justice: A Very Short Introduction*, Oxford, Oxford University Press.

Abuse

Corby, B., Shemmings, D. and Wilkins, D. (2012) *Child Abuse: An Evidence Base for Confident Practice*, 4th edn, Maidenhead, Open University Press.

Groves, N. and Thomas, T. (2014) *Domestic Violence and Criminal Justice*, London, Routledge.

Mandelstam, M. (2013) *Safeguarding Adults and the Law*, 2nd edn, London, Jessica Kingsley.

Munro, E. (2008) *Effective Child Protection*, London, Sage.

Parton, N. (2014) *The Politics of Child Protection: Contemporary Developments and Future Directions*, London, Palgrave Macmillan.

Pickard, S. (ed.) (2014) *Anti-social Behaviour in Britain: Victorian and Contemporary Perspectives*, Basingstoke, Palgrave Macmillan.

Silvers, A. (2014) *Abuse OF Men BY Women*, Gig Harbor, WA, Silvers Publishing.

Mental health

Bentall, R. (2004) *Madness Explained: Psychosis and Human Nature*, London, Penguin.
Bentall, R. (2010) *Doctoring the Mind: Why Psychiatric Treatments Fail*, London, Penguin.
Cohen, C. I. and Timimi, S. (eds) (2008) *Liberatory Psychiatry: Philosophy, Politics and Mental Health*, Cambridge, Cambridge University Press.
Cromby, J, Harper, D. and Reavey, P. (2013) *Psychology, Mental Health and Distress*, Basingstoke, Palgrave Macmillan.
Kirk, S. A., Gomory, T. and Cohen, D. (2015) *Mad Science: Psychiatric Coercion, Diagnosis and Drugs*, New Brunswick, NJ, Transaction Publishers.
Tew, J. (2011) *Social Approaches to Mental Distress*, Basingstoke, Palgrave Macmillan.

Problematic drug use

Ghodse, H. (ed.) (2005) *Addiction at Work: Tackling Drug Use and Misuse in the Workplace*, Aldershot, Gower.
Hari, J. (2015) *Chasing the Scream*, London, Bloomsbury.
Kleiman, M. A. R, Caulkins, J. P, Hawken, A. (2011) *Drugs and Drug Policy*, New York, Oxford University Press.
Staddon, P. (ed.) (2015) *Women and Alcohol: Social Perspectives*, Bristol, The Policy Press.

Terrorism

Andrews, J. (2016) *The World in Conflict: Understanding the World's Troublespots*, London, Economist Books.
Cockburn, P. (2015) *The Rise of Islamic State: ISIS and the New Sunni Revolution*, London, Verso.
Furedi, F. (2007) *Invitation to Terror*, London, Continuum.
Jackson, R, Jarvis, L. Gunning, J. and Smyth, M. B. (2011) *Terrorism: A Critical Introduction*, Basingstoke, Palgrave Macmillan.
Jerard, J. A. and Mohamed, N. S. (2015) *Resilience and Resolve: Communities against Terrorism*, London, Imperial College Press.
Kennedy-Pipe, C., Clubb, G., Mabon, S. and Schmid, A. P. (eds) (2015) *Terrorism and Political Violence*, London, Sage.
Townshend, C. (2011) *Terrorism: A Very Short Introduction*, 2nd edn, Oxford, Oxford University Press.

Destruction of habitat

Fitzpatrick, T. (ed.) (2011) *Understanding the Environment and Social Policy*, Bristol, The Policy Press.

Klein, N. (2014) *This Changes Everything*, London, Penguin.
Mies, M. and Shiva, V. (2014) *Ecofeminism*, 2nd edn, London, Zed Books.
Roberts, J. (2004) *Environmental Policy*, London, Routledge.
Sessions, G. (ed.) (1995) *Deep Ecology for the Twenty-first Century*, Boston, Shambhala Publications.
Snell, C. and Haq, G. (2014) *The Short Guide to Environmental Policy*, Bristol, The Policy Press.

Useful websites

Adfam, Families, Drugs and Alcohol
adfam.org.uk
Age International
ageinternational.org.uk/policy-and-research/human-rights/
Amnesty International
www.amnesty.org.uk
Child Poverty Action Group
www.cpag.org.uk
Crisis
www.crisis.org.uk
Danny Dorling
www.dannydorling.org
Disability Rights UK
disabilityrightsuk.org
Equality and Human Rights Commission
equalityhumanrights.com
The Equality Trust
www.equalitytrust.org.uk
Hearing Voices Network
hearing-voices.org
hearingvoicesusa.org
humansolutions
www.humansolutions.org.uk
Fawcett Society
www.fawcettsociety.org.uk
Greenpeace International
www.greenpeace.org/international/en/
Innovation for Poverty Action
www.poverty-action.org
Joseph Rowntree Foundation
www.jrf.org.uk
MIND
www.mind.org.uk
NACRO
www.nacro.org.uk

National (UK) Unemployment Movement
http://unemploymentmovement.com/
NSPCC
www.nspcc.org.uk
Prison Reform Trust
www.prisonreformtrust.org.uk
Shelter
www.shelter.org.uk
Social Policy Research Centre, UNSW, Australia
sprc.unsw.au
Worldmapper
www.wroldmapper.org

Journals

Child Abuse and Neglect: The International Journal
www.journals.elsevier.com/child-abuse-and-neglect/
Critical Social Policy
csp.sagepub.com
Disability and Society
www.tandfonline.com/toc/cdso20/
Ecology and Society
www.ecologyandsociety.org/about/policies.php#focus
European Journal of Homelessness
http://feantsaresearch.org/spip.php?rubrique19
International Journal of Drug Policy
www.journals.elsevier.com/international-journal-of-drug-policy/
International Journal of Social Welfare
http://onlinelibrary.wiley.com/journal/10.1111/(ISSN)1468–2397
Journal of Adult Protection
www.emeraldinsight.com/doi/abs/10.1108/14668203200000006
Journal of Critical Psychology, Counselling and Psychotherapy
www.pccs-books.co.uk/products/personal-jcpcp-2014/#.Vwzg2M6cGM8
Journal of Human Rights Practice
http://jhrp.oxfordjournals.org/
Journal of Human Trafficking
www.tandfonline.com/loi/uhmt20#.Vwzefc6cGM8
Journal of Poverty and Social Justice
http://policypress.co.uk/journals/journal-of-poverty-and-social-justice
Journal of Social Distress and the Homeless
www.tandfonline.com/loi/ysdh20#.VwzcDc6cGM8
Journal of Social Welfare and Human Rights
http://jswhr.com/
Journal of Terrorism Research
http://jtr.st-andrews.ac.uk/articles/

Social Justice: A Journal of Crime, Conflict and World Order
socialjusticejournal.org
Social Justice Research
link.springer.com/journal/11211
Social Policy
www.socialpolicy.org
Social Problems
socpro.oxfordjournals.org
Work, Employment and Society
wes.sagepub.com

References

Adams, M., Bell, L. and Griffin, P. (eds) (1997) *Teaching for Diversity and Social Justice: A Sourcebook*, New York, Routledge.

Albee, G. W. and Joffe, J. M. (1977a) 'The Issues: An Overview of Primary Prevention' in Albee and Joffe (1977b).

Albee, G. W. and Joffe, J. M. (eds) (1977b) *The Issues: an Overview of Primary Prevention*, Hanover, NH, University Press of New England.

Alexander, B. K. (2008) *The Globalization of Addiction: A Study in the Poverty of Spirit*, NY, Oxford University Press.

Andrews, J. (2016) *The World in Conflict: Understanding the World's Troublespots*, London, Economist Books.

Arloc, S. (1997) *Poverty Matters: The Cost of Child Poverty in America*, Washington DC, Children's Defense Fund.

Atkinson, A. B. (2015) *Inequality: What Can Be Done?*, Cambridge, MA, Harvard University Press.

Ballat, J. and Campling, P. (2011) *Intelligent Kindness: Reforming the Culture of Healthcare*, London, The Royal College of Psychiatrists.

Barnshaw, J. (2013) 'Prophets in the Wilderness: Predicting Financial Collapse.' in Best and Harris (2013).

Barr, R., Taylor-Robinson, D., Stuckler, D., Loopstra, R., Reeves, A. and Whitehead, M. (2015) '"First Do No Harm": Are Disability Assessments Associated with Adverse Trends in Mental Health? A Longitudinal Ecological Study', *Journal of Epidemiology Community Health*, doi:10.1136/jech-2015–206209.

Barry, B. (2005) *Why Social Justice Matters*, Cambridge, Polity Press.

Bauman, Z. (2001) *The Individualized Society*, London, Polity Press.

Bauman, Z. and Donskis, L. (2016) *Liquid Evil*, Cambridge, Polity Press.

Beck, U. (2016) *The Metamorphosis of the World*, Cambridge, Polity

Beck, U. (2002) 'Beyond Status and Class?', in Beck and Beck-Gernsheim (2002).

Beck, U. and Beck-Gernsheim, E. (2002) *Individualization*, London, Sage,

Becker, J., Kugeler, M. and Rosemann, M. (eds) (2011) *Process Management: A Guide for the Design of Business Processes*, New York, Springer.

Bell, D. (2007) 'Was 9/11 Really That Bad?', *Los Angeles Times*, 28 January.

Bell, L. A. (1997) 'Theoretical Foundations for Social Justice Education', in Adams et al. (1997).

Bentall, R. (2004) *Madness Explained: Psychosis and Human Nature*, London, Penguin.

Bentall, R. (2010) *Doctoring the Mind: Why Psychiatric Treatments Fail*, London, Penguin.

Bentall, R., Corcoran, R., Howard, R., Blackwood, R. and Kinderman, P. (2001) 'Persecutory Delusions: A Review and Theoretical Integration', *Clinical Psychology Review* 21, pp. 1143–92.

Bernstein, W. J. (2013) *Masters of the Word*, New York, Grove Press.

Best, D. (2012) *Addiction Recovery: A Handbook: A Movement for Social Change and Personal Growth in the UK*, Brighton, Pavilion.

Best, J. and Harris, S. R. (eds) (2013) *Making Sense of Social Problems*, London, Lynne Rienner Publishers.

Birchwood, M., Meaden, A., Trower, P. Gilbert, P. and Plaistow, J. (2000) 'The Power and Omnipotence of Voices: Subordination and Entrapment by Voices and Significant Others', *Psychological Medicine* 30, pp. 337–44.

Blyth, M. (2013) *Austerity: The History of a Dangerous Idea*, Oxford, Oxford University Press.

Booth, W. (2002) '9/11 Trauma: Studies Find Resilience Worry', *Washington Post* 7 September.

Bordere, T. C. (2014) 'Adolescents and Homicide', in Doka et al. (2014).

Bordere, T. C. (2016) 'Social Justice Conceptualizations in Grief and Loss', in Harris and Bordere (2016).

Boswell, J. (2008) *The Life of Johnson*, London, Penguin.

Boyle, D. and Harris, M. (2009) *The Challenge of Co-production: How Equal Partnerships between Professionals and the Public are Crucial to Improving Public Services*, London, NEF/NESTA.

Bracken, P. (2002) *Trauma: Culture, Meaning and Philosophy*, London, Whurr.

Bracken, P. and Thomas, P. (2007) *Postpsychiatry: Mental Health in a Postmodern World*, Oxford, Oxford University Press.

Brynin, M. and Guveli, A. (2012) 'Understanding the Ethnic Pay Gap in Britain', *Work, Employment and Society*, 26(4).

Burney, E., (2009) *Making People Behave*, Cullompton, Willan Publishing.

Calhoun, L. G. and Tedeschi, R. G. (2006) *Handbook of Posttraumatic Growth*, New York, Routledge.

Chang, H-J. (2010) *23 Things They Don't Tell You About Capitalism*, London, Penguin.

Chomsky, N. (1999) *Profit Over People: Neoliberalism and the Global Order*, New York, Seven Stories Press.

Chomsky, N. (2003) *Power: The Indispensable Chomsky*, 2nd edn, New York, Vintage Books.

Chomsky, N. (2012) *Power Systems*, London, Penguin.

Christie, A., McLachlan H.V. and Swales, J. K. (2008) 'Scotland, Devolution and Justice', *Scottish Affairs*, 65 (Autumn).

Clewett, N. and Glover, J. (2009) *Supporting Prisoners' Families*, Ilford, Barnardo's.

Cockburn, P. (2015) *The Rise of Islamic State: ISIS and the New Sunni Revolution*, London, Verso.

Cohen, C. I. and Timimi, S. (eds) (2008) *Liberatory Psychiatry: Philosophy, Politics and Mental Health*, Cambridge, Cambridge University Press.

Cohen, S. (2011) *Folk Devils and Moral Panics*, London, Routledge.

Coleman, P. T. and Ferguson, R. (2014) *Making Conflict Work*, London, Piatkus.

Corby, B., Shemmings, D. and Wilkins, D. (2012) *Child Abuse: An Evidence Base for Confident Practice*, 4th edn, Maidenhead, Open University Press.

Corrigan, P. (1982) 'The Problem with Being Unemployed is that you Never Get a Day Off', paper presented at the Leisure Studies Association Conference on *Unemployment in the 1980s*, Polytechnic of North London.

Craig, G., Burchardt, T. and Gordon, D. (eds) (2008) *Social Justice and Public Policy*, Bristol, The Policy Press.

Croall, H. (2007) Social Class, Social Exclusion, Victims and Crime' in Davies et al. (2007).

Croall, H. (2012) 'Criminal Justice, Social Inequalities and Social Justice', in Mooney and Scott (2012b).

Cromby, J, Harper, D. and Reavey, P. (2013) *Psychology, Mental Health and Distress*, Basingstoke, Palgrave Macmillan.

Crossley, N. (2006) *Contesting Psychiatry: Social Movements in Mental Health*, London, Routledge.

Davidson, A. (2014) *Social Determinants of Health*, Oxford, Oxford University Press.

Davie, N. (2014) 'A Less than Polite People? Incivility, Ruffianism, and Anti-Social Behaviour in Urban England', in Pickard (2014).

Davies, J. (2012) *The Importance of Suffering: The Value and Meaning of Emotional Discontent*, London, Routledge.

Davies, P., Francis, P. and Greer, C. (eds) (2007) *Victims, Crime and Society*, London, Sage.

DeKeseredy, W. S., Alvi, S., Schwartz, M. D. and Tomaszewski, E. A. (2003) *Under Siege: Poverty and Crime in a Public Housing Community*, Lanham, MD, Lexington Books.

Dohrenwend, B. P. (2000) 'The Role of Adversity and Stress in Psychopathology: Some Evidence and its Implication for Theory and Research', *Journal of Health and Social Behaviour*, 41(1).

Doka, K. and Tucci, A. (eds) (2014) *Helping Adolescents Cope with Loss*, Washington DC, Hospice Foundation of America.

Dorling, D. (2011) *Injustice: Why Social Inequality Persists*, Bristol, The Policy Press.

Dorling, D. (2014) *Inequality and the 1%*, London, Verso.

Dorling, D. (2015) *All That Is Solid: How the Great Housing Disaster Defines Our Times, and What We Can Do About It*, London, Penguin.

Dorling, D. (2016) *A Better Politics: How Government Can Make Us Happy*, London: London Publishing Partnership.

Durkheim, E. (2006) *On Suicide*, London, Penguin.

Durkheim, E. (2014) *The Rules of Sociological Method*, New York, Free Press.

Fernando, S. (2010) *Race, Culture and Mental Health*, Basingstoke, Palgrave Macmillan.

Finney, N. and Harries, B. (2015) 'Which Ethnic Groups are Hardest Hit by the "Housing Crisis"?, in Jivraj and Simpson (2015).

Fitzpatrick, T. (ed.) (2011) *Understanding the Environment and Social Policy*, Bristol, The Policy Press.

Frenkel, E., Kugelmass, S., Nathan, M. and Ingraham, L. (1995) 'Locus of Control and Mental Health in Adolescence and Adulthood', *Schizophrenia Bulletin* 21, pp. 219–26.

Furedi, F. (2004) *Therapy Culture: Cultivating Vulnerability in an Uncertain Age*, London, Routledge.

Furedi, F. (2007) *Invitation to Terror*, London, Continuum.

Giddens, A. (1993) *New Rules of Sociological Method*, 2nd edn, Cambridge, Polity Press.

Gilbert, P. and Allen, S. (1998) 'The Role of Defeat and Entrapment (Arrested Flight) in Depression: An Exploration of an Evolutionary View', *Psychological Medicine* 28, pp. 585–98.

Gilliat-Ray, S. (2010) *Muslims in Britain: An Introduction*, Cambridge, Cambridge University Press.

Gilligan, J. (1996) *Violence: Our Deadly Epidemic and its Causes*, New York, G. P. Putnam.

Gilligan, J. (2001) *Preventing Violence*, New York, Thames and Hudson.

Goldacre, B. (2013) *Bad Pharma*, London, Fourth Estate.

Gorz, A. (1999) *Reclaiming Work: Beyond the Wage-based Society*, Cambridge, Polity Press.

Hari, J. (2015) *Chasing the Scream*, London, Bloomsbury.

Harris, D. and Bordere, T. (eds) (2016) *Handbook of Social Justice in Loss and Grief*, New York, Routledge.

Harris, S. R. (2013) 'Studying the Construction of Social Problems', in Best and Harris (2013).

Hattersley, R. and Hickson, K. (2012) 'In Praise of Social Democracy', *Political Quarterly*, 83, 5–12.

Haworth, J. and Hart, G. (eds) (2012) *Well-Being: Individual, Community and Social Perspectives*, Basingstoke, Palgrave Macmillan.

Heath, A. and Cheung, S. Y. (2006) *Ethnic Penalties in the Labour Market: Employers and Discrimination*, DWP Research Report 341, London, Department for Work and Pensions.

Hedges, C. (2009) *Empire of Illusion: The End of Literacy and the Triumph of Spectacle*, New York, Nation Books.

Heiner, R. (2006) *Social Problems*, Oxford, Oxford University Press.

Hertsgaard, M. (2000) *Earth Odyssey: Around the World in Search of our Environmental Future*, London, Abacus.

Hills, J. (2015) *Good Times, Bad Times: The Welfare State Myth of Them and Us*, Bristol, The Policy Press.

Hillyard P., Pantazis, C., Tombs, S. and Gordon, D. (eds) (2004) *Beyond Criminality: Taking Harm Seriously*, London Pluto Press.

Horne, M. and Shirley, T. (2009) *Co-production in Public Services: A New Partnership with Citizens*, London, Cabinet Office.

Illouz, E. (2008) *Saving the Modern Soul: Therapy, Emotions, and the Culture of Self-Help*, Berkeley, University of California Press.

Isaacs, S. (2015) 'Understanding and Defining Social Problems,' in Isaacs et al.

Isaacs, S. (2015) 'Poverty' in Isaacs et al. (2015).

Isaacs, S., Blundell, D., Foley, A., Ginsburg, B., McDonough, B., Silverstone, D. and Young, T. (2015) *Social Problems in the UK: An Introduction*, London, Routledge.

Jackson, R, Jarvis, L. Gunning, J. and Smyth, M. B. (2011) *Terrorism: A Critical Introduction*, Basingstoke, Palgrave Macmillan.

James, O. (2007) *Affluenza*, London, Vermillion.

James, O. (2008) *The Selfish Capitalist: Origins of Affluenza* London, Vermillion

Jansen, S. C. (2011) 'Introduction', in Jansen et al. (2011)

Jansen, S. C., Pooley, J. and Taub-Pervizpour, L. (eds) (2011) *Media and Social Justice*, Basingstoke, Palgrave Macmillan.

Jerard, J. A. and Mohamed, N. S. (2015) *Resilience and Resolve: Communities against Terrorism*, London, Imperial College Press.

Jivraj, S. and Simpson, L. (eds) (2015) *Ethnic Identity and Inequalities in Britain*, Bristol, The Policy Press.

Johnson, J. V. (2009) 'The Growing Imbalance: Class, Work, and Health in an Era of Increasing Inequality', in Schnall et al. (2009).

Jones, O. (2012) *Chavs: The Demonization of the Working Class*, London, Verso.

Jones, O. (2015) *The Establishment and How They Get Away with It*, London, Penguin.

Jones, R. (2014) *The Story of Baby P: Setting the Record Straight*, Bristol, The Policy Press.

Joseph Rowntree Foundation (2008) *What Are Today's Social Evils?*, www.socialevils.org.uk.

Kapadia, D., Nazroo, J. and Clark, K. (2015) 'Have Ethnic Inequalities in the Labour Market Persisted?', in Jivraj and Simpson (2015).

Kasser, T. (2002) *The High Price of Materialism*, Cambridge, MA, The MIT Press.

Kennedy-Pipe, C., Clubb, G., Mabon, S. and Schmid, A. P. (eds) (2015) *Terrorism and Political Violence*, London, Sage.

Keyes, C. L. M. (2006) *Women and Depression: A Handbook for the Social, Behavioral, and Biomedical Sciences*, Cambridge, Cambridge University Press.

Kirk, S. A., Gomory, T. and Cohen, D. (2015) *Mad Science: Psychiatric Coercion, Diagnosis and Drugs*, New Brunswick, NJ, Transaction Publishers.

Kleiman, M. A. R, Caulkins, J. P, Hawken, A. (2011) *Drugs and Drug Policy.*, New York, Oxford University Press.

Klein, N. (2007) *The Shock Doctrine*, London, Penguin.

Klein, N. (2014) *This Changes Everything*, London, Penguin.

Lister, R. and Lawson, N. (2015) 'Foreword', in Orton (2015).

McDonough, B, (2015) 'Work and Unemployment', in Isaacs et al. (2015).

McKittrick, D. and McVea, D. (2012) *Making Sense of the Troubles: A History of the Northern Ireland Conflict*, London, Penguin.

McLaughlin, E. and Baker, J. (2007) 'Equality, Social Justice and Social Welfare: A Road Map to the New Egalitarianisms', *Social Policy and Society*, 6(1).

Macleod, P., Page, L., Kinver, A., Iliasov, A. and Littlewood, M. and Williams, R. (2009) *2008/2009 Scottish Justice Survey: First Findings*, Edinburgh, Scottish Government.

Maguire, M. (2007) 'Crime Data and Statistics' in Maguire et al. (2007).

Maguire, M., Morgan, R. and Reiner, R. (eds) (2007) *The Oxford Handbook of Criminology*, 4th edn, Oxford, Clarendon Press.

Mandelstam, M. (2013) *Safeguarding Adults and the Law*, 2nd edn, London, Jessica Kingsley.

Marris, P. (1996) *The Politics of Uncertainty: Attachment in Private and Public Life*, London, Routledge.

Marshall, D. (2012) *Effective Investigation of Child Homicide and Suspicious Deaths*, Oxford, Oxford University Press.

May, V. (ed.) (2011) *Sociology of Personal Life*, Basingstoke, Palgrave Macmillan.

Mendoza, K-A. (2015) *Austerity: The Demolition of the Welfare State and the Rise of the Zombie Economy*, London, New Internationalist.

Merton, R. K. (1996) *On Social Structure and Science*, Chicago, University of Chicago Press.

Mies, M. and Shiva, V. (2014) *Ecofeminism*, 2nd edn, London, Zed Books.

Mills, C. W. (1959) *The Sociological Imagination*, Oxford, Oxford University Press

Mitchell. P. R. and Schoeffel. J. (eds) (2002) *Understanding Power: The Indispensable Chomsky*, London, Vintage.

Moghaddam, F. M. (2005) 'The Staircase to Terrorism: A Psychological Exploration', *American Psychologist*, 60, pp. 161–9.

Moloney, P. (2013) *The Therapy Industry*, London, Pluto Press.

Monahan, B. A and Maratea, R. J. (2013) 'Breaking News on Nancy Grace: Violent Crime in the Media', in Best and Harris (2013).

Mooney, G. and Scott, G. (eds) (2012b) *Social Justice and Social Policy in Scotland*, Bristol, The Policy Press.

Mooney, G. and Scott, G. (2012a) 'Devolution, Social Justice and Social Policy: The Scottish Context', in Mooney and Scott (2012b).

Morelli, C. and Seaman, P. (2012) 'Income and Wealth Inequalities in Scotland Since 1997', in Mooney and Scott (2012).

Moss, B. (2005) *Religion and Spirituality*, Lyme Regis, Russell House Publishing.

Moss, B. (2007) *Values*, Lyme Regis, Russell House Publishing.

Nobles, M. R. Ward, J. T. and Tillyer R. (2016) 'The Impact of Neighborhood Context on Spatiotemporal Patterns of Burglary', *Journal of Research in Crime and Delinquency*, 53(5).

Orton, M. (2015) *Secure and Free: 10 Foundations for a Flourishing Nation*, Compass (http://bit.ly/1JE7ByA).

Pfohl, S. (1977) 'The Discovery of Child Abuse', *Social Problems*, 24.

Pickering, J. (2012) 'Is Well-Being Local or Global? A Perspective from Ecopsychology', in Haworth and Hart (2012).

Munro, E. (2008) *Effective Child Protection*, London, Sage.

Newman, J. and Yeates, N. (eds) (2008) *Social Justice: Welfare Crime and Society*, Maidenhead, Open University Press.

Nietzsche, F. (2003) *Beyond Good and Evil*, London, Penguin.

Nutt, D. (2012) *Drugs Without the Hot Air*, Cambridge, UIT Cambridge.

Oliver, M. and Barnes, C. (2012) *The New Politics of Disablement*, 2nd edn, Basingstoke, Palgrave Macmillan.

Paris, J. W. (2011) *The End of Sexual Identity: Why Sex Is Too Important to Define Who We Are*, Downers Grove, IL, InterVarsity Press.

Parton, N. (2014) *The Politics of Child Protection: Contemporary Developments and Future Directions*, London, Palgrave Macmillan.

Pascall, G. (1997) *Social Policy: A New Feminist Analysis*, London, Routledge.

Pearson, G. (1983) *Hooligan: A History of Respectable Fears*, London, Macmillan.

Penketh, L. (2000) *Tackling Institutional Racism: Anti-racist Policies and Social Work Education and Training*, Bristol, The Policy Press.

Pickard, S. (ed.) (2014) *Anti-social Behaviour in Britain: Victorian and Contemporary Perspectives*, Basingstoke, Palgrave Macmillan

Pilgrim, D. and McCranie, A. (2013) *Recovery and Mental Health*, Basingstoke, Palgrave Macmillan.

Prilleltensky, I. and Prilleltensky, O. (2012) 'Webs of Well-Being: The Interdependence of Personal, Relational, Organizational and Communal Well-Being', in Haworth and Hart (2012).

Rice, J. S. (1996) *A Disease of One's Own: Psychotherapy, Addiction, and the Emergence of Co-Dependency*, New Brunswick, NJ, Transaction.

Road Safety Analysis Group (2010) *Child Casualties 2010: A Study into Resident Risk of Children on Roads in Great Britain 2004–08*, Gloucestershire Road Safety Analysis.

Rodger, J. J. (2013) *Criminalising Social Policy*, 2nd edn, London, Routledge.

Roeder, R, Eisen, L-B. and Bowling, J. (2015) *What Caused the Crime Decline?*, New York, Brennan Centre for Justice.

Rogers, A. and Pilgrim, A. (2014) *A Sociology of Mental Health and Illness*, 5th edn, Maidenhead, Open University Press.

Ryan, W. (1973) *Blaming the Victim*, 2nd edn, New York, Vintage Books.

Rymaszewska, J. and Philpot, T. (2006) *Reaching the Vulnerable Child: Therapy with Traumatized Children*, London, Jessica Kingsley Publishers.

Sartre, J-P. (1989) *No Exit, And Three Other Plays*, New York, Vintage.

Sayer, A. (2015) *Why We Can't Afford the Rich*, Bristol, The Policy Press.

Scandrett, E. (2012) 'Environmental Justice: A Question of Social Justice?', in Mooney and Scott (2012b).

Schnall, P. L., Dobson, M. and Rosskam, E. (eds) (2009) *Unhealthy Work: Causes, Consequences, Cures*, Amityville, NY, Baywood.

Schweingruber, D. and Horstmeier, M. (2013) 'The Evolution of Internet Addiction', in Best and Harris (2013).

Scott, S., Craig, G. and Geddes, S. (2012) *Experiences of Forced Labour in the UK Food Industry*, York, Joseph Rowntree Foundation.

Scraton, P. (2002a) 'Introduction', in Scraton (2002b).

Scraton, P. (ed.) (2002b) *Beyond September 11: An Anthology of Dissent*, London, Pluto Press.

Seabrook, J. (1985) *Landscapes of Poverty*, Oxford, Blackwell.

Selten, J-P. and Cantor-Graae, E. (2007) 'Hypothesis: Social Defeat as a Risk Factor for Schizophrenia', *British Journal of Psychiatry*, 191(suppl. 51): S9–12.

Sen, A. (1992) *Inequality Reexamined*, New York, Oxford University Press.

Sessions, G. (ed.) (1995) *Deep Ecology for the Twenty-first Century*, Boston, Shambhala Publications.

Sharvit, K. and Kruglanski, A. W. (2013) 'The Social Psychology of Terrorism: Individual, Group and Organizational Processes', in Zavala and Cichocka (2013).

Shore, T. H., Tashchian, A. and Jourdan, L. (2006) 'Effects of Internal and External Pay Comparisons on Work Attitudes', *Journal of Applied Social Psychology*, 36, pp. 2578–98.

Silvers, A. (2014) *Abuse OF Men BY Women*, Gig Harbor, WA, Silvers Publishing.

Singh, G. (2009) 'Racism', in Thompson and Bates (2009).

Southerton, D. (2011) 'Consumer Culture and Personal Life', in May (2011).

Spinoza, B. (1996) *Ethics*, London, Penguin.

Sprintzen, D. (2009) *Critique of Western Philosophy and Social Theory*, New York, Palgrave Macmillan.

Staddon, P. (ed.) (2015) *Women and Alcohol: Social Perspectives*, Bristol, The Policy Press.

Stepney, P. and Popple, K. (2008) *Social Work and the Community: A Critical Context for Practice*, Basingstoke, Palgrave Macmillan.

Stepney, P. and Popple, K. (2012) 'Community Social Work', in Stepney and Ford (2012).

Stepney, P. and Ford, D. (eds) (2012) *Social Work Models, Methods and Theories: A Framework for Practice*, 2nd edn, Lyme Regis, Russell House Publishing.

Stepney, P. (2012) 'An Overview of the Wider Policy Context', in Stepney and Ford (2012).

Stepney, P. (2014) 'Prevention in Social Work: The Final Frontier?, *Critical and Radical Social Work*, 2(3).

Stiglitz, J. (2016) *The Great Divide*, London, Penguin.

Summerskill, B. and Mahtani, D. (2002) 'Homelessness in Drugs Epidemic', *Observer*, 14 July.

Sutton, R. M, Cichocka, A, and Toorn, J. V. D. (2013) 'The Corrupting Power of Social Inequality: Social–Psychological Consequences, Causes and Solutions', in Zavala and Cichocka (2013).

Szasz, T. (2010) *The Myth of Mental Illness*, 2nd edn, London, Harper Perennial.

Taleb, N. N. (2010) *The Black Swan: The Impact of the Highly Improbable*, 2nd edn, London, Penguin.

Tew, J. (2011) *Social Approaches to Mental Distress*, Basingstoke, Palgrave Macmillan.

Thompson, M. (2009) *Mad or Bad?: Race, Class, Gender, and Mental Disorder in the Criminal Justice System*, El Paso, Texas, LFB Scholarly Publishing.

Thompson, N. (2007) *Power and Empowerment*, Lyme Regis, Russell House Publishing.

Thompson, N. (2010) *Theorizing Social Work Practice*, Basingstoke, Palgrave Macmillan.

Thompson, N. (2011a) *Promoting Equality: Working with Diversity and Difference*, 3rd edn, Basingstoke, Palgrave Macmillan.

Thompson, N. (2011b) *Effective Communication*, 2nd edn, Basingstoke, Palgrave Macmillan.

Thompson, N. (2012a) *The People Solutions Sourcebook*, 2nd edn, Basingstoke, Palgrave Macmillan.

Thompson, N. (2012b) *Grief and its Challenges*, Basingstoke, Palgrave Macmillan.

Thompson, N. (2016a) *Anti-Discriminatory Practice*, 6th edn, London, Palgrave Macmillan.

Thompson, N. (2016b) *The Professional Social Worker*, 2nd edn, London, Palgrave Macmillan

Thompson, N. (2016c) *The Authentic Leader*, London, Palgrave Macmillan.

Thompson, N. and Bates, J. (eds) (2009) *Promoting Workplace Well-being*, Basingstoke, Palgrave Macmillan.

Thompson, N., Cox, G. R. and Stevenson, R. G. (eds) (2017) *Handbook of Traumatic Loss*, New York, Routledge.

Thompson, S. and Thompson, N. (2008) *The Critically Reflective Practitioner*, Basingstoke, Palgrave Macmillan.

Thornicroft, G. (2006) *Shunned: Discrimination Against People with Mental Illness*, Oxford, Oxford University Press.

Tombs, S. (2004) 'Workplace Injury and Death: Social Harm and the Illusions of Law', in Hillyard et al. (2004).

Tomlinson, P. and Philpot, T. (2008) *A Child's Journey to Recovery: Assessment and Planning with Traumatized Children*, London, Jessica Kingsley Publishers.

Townshend, C. (2011) *Terrorism: A Very Short Introduction*, 2nd edn, Oxford, Oxford University Press.

Toynbee, P. (2003) *Hard Work Life in Low-pay Britain*, London, Bloomsbury.

Tummey, R. and Turner, T. (eds) (2008) *Critical Issues in Mental Health*, Basingstoke, Palgrave Macmillan.

Wilkinson, R. G. (2005) *The Impact of Inequality*, London, Routledge.

Wilkinson, R. G. and Pickett, K. (2009) *The Spirit Level: Why More Equal Societies Almost Always Do Better*, London, Allen Lane.

Wilson, J. P. (2006a) 'The Posttraumatic Self', in Wilson (2006b).

Wilson, J. P. (ed.) (2006b) *The Posttraumatic Self: Restoring Meaning and Wholeness to Personality*, London, Routledge.

Witcher, S. (2015) *Inclusive Equality*, Bristol, The Policy Press.

Zavala, A. G. D and Cichocka, A. (eds) (2013) *Social Psychology of Social Problems*, Basingstoke, Palgrave Macmillan.

Index

Other Books by Neil Thompson

Theorizing Practice, 2nd edition

The new updated edition of this popular text challenges the conventional notion of 'applying theory and practice', arguing that it oversimplifies and misrepresents the relationship between theory and practice. Instead of trying to fit the square peg of theory into the round hole of practice, Thompson convincingly argues the case for 'theorizing practice' – that is, beginning with real-life practice and drawing on theoretical understandings to make sense of it.

People Skills, 4th edition

A very popular text now in its 4th edition, this book is a firm favourite with a wide range of students, practitioners and managers whose work involves dealing with people and their problems. Divided into three sections, covering self-managements skills, interaction skills and intervention skills, it provides a sound foundation of understanding to inform practice.